Human Service Organizations and the Question of Impact

This volume offers empirically based insights and findings on the question of how human service organizations are reacting to the increasing need for greater impact, effectiveness, and performance.

As demand for increased impact outstrips our knowledge of how best to achieve these goals, the book's contributors discuss the innovative strategies being used to ensure that multiplex goals are being met and the degree to which client and staff concerns are being sacrificed for the organizational bottom line. Taken together, these discussions demonstrate that specific management strategies and collaboration based on trust and consideration of mission may help improve the quality of some services; however, many of the pressures which organizations and managers experience are resulting in lower staff morale, compromised missions, and inefficiencies.

This book will be of interest to those researching human service agencies, as well as those with a broader concern for how organizations react to doing more with less.

This book was originally published as a special issue of *Human Service Organizations: Management, Leadership & Governance*.

Jennifer E. Mosley is Associate Professor in the School of Social Service Administration at the University of Chicago, USA. She researches the role of nonprofit organizations as political actors, specifically the role human service organizations, community-based nonprofits, and philanthropic foundations play in advocating for underrepresented populations.

Steven Rathgeb Smith is the Executive Director of the American Political Science Association and Adjunct Professor at Georgetown University, USA. His research interests include nonprofit organizations, nonprofit and public management, philanthropy, and social services.

Human Service Organizations and the Question of Impact

Edited by
Jennifer E. Mosley and Steven Rathgeb Smith

LONDON AND NEW YORK

First published 2019
by Routledge
2 Park Square, Milton Park, Abingdon, Oxon, OX14 4RN

and by Routledge
52 Vanderbilt Avenue, New York, NY 10017

Routledge is an imprint of the Taylor & Francis Group, an informa business

British Library Cataloguing in Publication Data
A catalogue record for this book is available from the British Library

ISBN 13: 978-0-367-23578-9

Typeset in Minion Pro
by RefineCatch Limited, Bungay, Suffolk

Publisher's Note
The publisher accepts responsibility for any inconsistencies that may have arisen during the conversion of this book from journal articles to book chapters, namely the inclusion of journal terminology.

Disclaimer
Every effort has been made to contact copyright holders for their permission to reprint material in this book. The publishers would be grateful to hear from any copyright holder who is not here acknowledged and will undertake to rectify any errors or omissions in future editions of this book.

Contents

Citation Information

The chapters in this book were originally published in *Human Service Organizations: Management, Leadership & Governance*, volume 42, issue 2 (April 2018). When citing this material, please use the original page numbering for each article, as follows:

Chapter 1
Human service agencies and the question of impact: Lessons for theory, policy, and practice
Jennifer E. Mosley and Steven Rathgeb Smith
Human Service Organizations: Management, Leadership & Governance, volume 42, issue 2
(April 2018), pp. 113–122

Chapter 2
Remaking "Community" Mental Health: Contested Institutional Logics and Organizational Change
Matthew C. Spitzmueller
Human Service Organizations: Management, Leadership & Governance, volume 42, issue 2
(April 2018), pp. 123–145

Chapter 3
Marketization strategies and the influence of business on the management of child welfare agencies
Robbie Waters Robichau and Lili Wang
Human Service Organizations: Management, Leadership & Governance, volume 42, issue 2
(April 2018), pp. 146–165

Chapter 4
Frontline managers' contribution to mission achievement: A study of how people management affects thoughtful care
Eva Knies, Peter Leisink, and Sascha Kraus-Hoogeveen
Human Service Organizations: Management, Leadership & Governance, volume 42, issue 2
(April 2018), pp. 166–184

Chapter 5
Policy fields, data systems, and the performance of nonprofit human service organizations
Lehn M. Benjamin, Amy Voida, and Chris Bopp
Human Service Organizations: Management, Leadership & Governance, volume 42, issue 2
(April 2018), pp. 185–204

Chapter 6

What counts? Quantification, worker judgment, and divergence in child welfare decision making
Emily Adlin Bosk
Human Service Organizations: Management, Leadership & Governance, volume 42, issue 2
(April 2018), pp. 205–224

Chapter 7

Levels and consequences of embeddedness among private human service organizations: National survey evidence from child welfare
Alicia C. Bunger, Bowen McBeath, Crystal Collins-Camargo, Emmeline Chuang, and
Monica Perez-Jolles
Human Service Organizations: Management, Leadership & Governance, volume 42, issue 2
(April 2018), pp. 225–244

For any permission-related enquiries please visit:
http://www.tandfonline.com/page/help/permissions

Notes on Contributors

Lehn M. Benjamin is Associate Professor of Philanthropic Studies at IUPUI, Indianapolis, USA. Her research looks at how nonprofit organizations challenge and reinforce the marginalization of poor communities and the consequences for democratic citizenship.

Chris Bopp is a PhD student at the Atlas Institute, University of Colorado Boulder, USA. He studies how social service organizations use data and information systems to evaluate and improve their programs.

Emily Adlin Bosk is Assistant Professor of Social Work at Rutgers University, USA. Her research uses social science methods to theorize how organizations and individuals understand and intervene with vulnerable children and families, and to trace out the policy and practice implications of these approaches.

Alicia C. Bunger is Associate Professor in the College of Social Work at Ohio State University, USA. Her research asks how human service organizations and professionals can work together to improve service access, quality, and outcomes for the communities they serve.

Emmeline Chuang is Associate Professor in the Department of Health Policy and Management at the University of California Los Angeles, USA. Her research focuses on how the organization and management of health and human services affects service access and quality of care, particularly for underserved populations.

Crystal Collins-Camargo is Professor and Associate Dean for Research in the School of Social Work at the University of Louisville, USA. Her research focuses primarily on organizational interventions to promote outcome achievement in child welfare.

Eva Knies is Professor of Strategic Human Resource Management at the University of Utrecht, The Netherlands. Her work focuses on strategic HR management, particularly in the public sector; the role of managers in HR policy implementation; and sustainable employability.

Sascha Kraus-Hoogeveen is a PhD student in the Institute for Management Research at Radboud University Nijmegen, The Netherlands. Her research interests include HR management, performance, work stress, workplace enthusiasm, and sustainable employability.

Peter Leisink is Professor in the School of Governance at the University of Utrecht, The Netherlands. His research interests include the management and organization of service organizations, the contribution of strategic HR management to service performance, leadership and motivation in (public) organizations, and industrial relations governance in Europe.

Bowen McBeath is Professor in the School of Social Work at Portland State University, USA. His research interests include community-based practice, organizational and management practice, policy analysis, and human service model development.

Jennifer E. Mosley is Associate Professor in the School of Social Service Administration at the University of Chicago, USA. She researches the role of nonprofit organizations as political actors, specifically the role human service organizations, community-based nonprofits, and philanthropic foundations play in advocating for underrepresented populations.

Monica Perez-Jolles is Assistant Professor of Social Work at the University of Southern California, USA. Her research examines access to and implementation of innovative health delivery arrangements designed to address health disparities.

Robbie Waters Robichau is Assistant Professor in the Department of Public Service and Administration at Texas A&M University, USA. Her research examines issues of nonprofit management and values, marketization practices, civic health, and meaningfulness in public service work.

Steven Rathgeb Smith is the Executive Director of the American Political Science Association and Adjunct Professor at Georgetown University, USA. His research interests include nonprofit organizations, nonprofit and public management, philanthropy, and social services.

Matthew C. Spitzmueller is Assistant Professor in the School of Social Work at Syracuse University, USA. He specializes in clinical social work practice, community mental health policies, Medicaid reform, and street-level organizations.

Amy Voida is Assistant Professor of Information Science at the University of Colorado Boulder, USA. She conducts empirical and design research in philanthropic informatics, exploring the role of information and communication technology in supporting initiatives for the public good.

Lili Wang is Associate Professor of Nonprofit Leadership and Management at Arizona State University, USA. Her research focuses on individual philanthropy (charitable giving and volunteering), institutional philanthropy, collaborative governance, and international NGOs.

Human service agencies and the question of impact: Lessons for theory, policy, and practice

Jennifer E. Mosley ⓘ and Steven Rathgeb Smith

ABSTRACT

Human service agencies are facing an environment in which demands for impact, effectiveness, and performance are rising faster than our knowledge about how to best to achieve those goals. Organizations are increasingly pressured to do "more" with little guidance about what service-related changes might mean for the long-term well-being of their organizations, the consumers of their services, and the communities in which they are embedded. This article introduces a special issue on the effect of the pursuit of "impact" on staff, managers, and organizational processes by tracing the history of how human service organizations became targets for greater demands of efficiency and impact, some of the field level changes that are taking place as a result, and the managerial dilemmas that have arisen under this new regime.

Human service agencies are facing an increasingly uncertain and turbulent environment in the United States and abroad. Questions of impact, effectiveness, and performance are rising at the same time as competition and demand are increasing. Consequently, human service managers face complicated dilemmas, real and imagined: embrace evidence-based practice or coproduction of services? View fellow human service agencies as competitors or as collaborators? Embrace market principles or an ethic of care? Organizations are increasingly pressured to do it all with little guidance about what these changes might mean for the long-term well-being of their organizations, the consumers of their services, and their local communities.

This conceptual article focuses on the transformation of human services at the street level in response to new regimes of performance assessment and data-driven governance—all stemming from the drive for "impact." Although a wealth of literature exists documenting these changes, the demand for "impact" is rising faster than our knowledge about how best to achieve it. Although managers must respond in real time, the scholarly literature largely suffers from a "two-world" problem. The literature in nonprofit journals often condemns this shift but with little systematic evidence. It worries that client concerns may be sacrificed for the bottom line, missions will be compromised, and advocacy will decline, but relies more on normative arguments than empirical evidence (Eikenberry & Kluver, 2004). Meanwhile, the policy, public health, and social work literatures generally embrace these new technologies but with little critique. In those literatures, the drive for impact is seen as a solution to longstanding effectiveness and legitimacy concerns. This literature tends to assume a direct link between tracking and raising performance and is less concerned about implications for management and staff (Klassen et al., 2009).

Despite (or perhaps because of) this rhetorical division, we know little about how organizations have responded, or how these changes are being interpreted, adopted, and resisted on the ground.

This special issue brings together six articles that offer empirically based insights and findings on the question of how organizations are coping, what innovative strategies are being used to ensure that multiplex goals are being met, and the degree to which client and staff concerns are being sacrificed for the organizational bottom line. This introductory article traces the history of how human service organizations became targets for greater demands of efficiency and impact, some of the managerial dilemmas that arise in this new regime, and field-level changes that are taking place as a result.

A brief history of the drive for impact

Demands for performance currently drive every aspect of human services. This emphasis is quite a shift from longstanding practices in human services where impact, broadly defined, was not an explicit priority of government or service providers. To be sure, in the last half of the 20th-century human service nonprofits were expected to be accountable to their funders, but the emphasis tended to be more on compliance with the process of service delivery such as meeting service units, allocation of staff time, and compliance with budget expectations. Prior to our digitized era, public and private funders also faced inherent constraints on their ability to demand information from service providers. Thus, the accountability of public and nonprofit service providers depended substantially on professional norms and, in the case of nonprofits, on the oversight of boards of directors.

The structure of funding and the relative lack of attention to performance and program outcomes tended to encourage stability (or stagnation, depending on your point of view). Many executive directors were promoted from within ranks, competition for most government grants and contracts was nominal, and the role of for-profit organizations in social services was generally limited. This relative stability also led to a lack of substantial innovation in services from within the service system itself. In general, major innovations such as reforms in child welfare or deinstitutionalization in the fields of mental health and services for the disabled were driven by dedicated advocates and civil-rights activists who often used the courts to push for change to the status quo—and that change was sometimes resisted by existing providers.

This model of service delivery was significantly rethought with the advent of new public management (NPM) in the 1980s and 1990s. NPM has origins in the United Kingdom and elsewhere where scholars and policy makers were striving to improve public services by tapping more market-based incentives (Hood, 1991). Although NPM was building on at least a century of administrative reforms, NPM was seen by many as a shift away from "business as usual" (Page, 2005). NPM also made more explicit the objective of improving public services through increased accountability and performance, in accordance with the rise of neoliberalism worldwide. Although promoted as a way to enhance the responsiveness and flexibility of public services, NPM also reflects a set of larger cultural beliefs that were in ascendance at the time and are still dominant. These are that (1) promoting market-based competition will cause all providers to work harder, innovate more, and ultimately produce a system in which the 'best' will rise to the top and (2) that to maximize that competition, private providers—either nonprofit or for-profit—should be preferred in the delivery of public services. Of course it also assumes a level playing field for all competitors and that metrics for what "best" is can be reliably produced and agreed upon—neither of which are accurate.

NPM led to an increase in formal contracting between human service and government agencies. Initially, however, the focus on performance was mostly seen in incremental adjustments to traditional contracts—for example, more regulation, reporting, and information requests. These incremental changes were followed, however, by the creation of new high-stakes contracting mechanisms and increased competition for those contracts (Smith & Phillips, 2016). Many human service organizations that had historically received public subsidies through long-term relationships with local government were suddenly in a much more precarious environment.[1]

---

[1]Of course, the level of competition varies according to field and locale. There is less competition in rural areas than in urban areas, especially in specialized fields such as addiction services or child welfare.

Perhaps the most commonly recognized of these is performance-based contracting, which typically involves contracts that tie government reimbursement to the attainment of specific outcomes (Desai, Garabedian, & Snyder, 2012; Smith, 2012; Fraser & Whitehill, 2014; Freundlich & McCullough, 2012; Smith & Grinker, 2004). For example, a nonprofit job training program might only be reimbursed for services if it placed a disadvantaged person in permanent employment. Some jurisdictions use the term *results-based contracting* to refer to contracting with a specific focus on results (Office of the Mayor, 2017). Other government agencies have instituted what are known as "pay-for-success" models whereupon the government funder ties reimbursement for services to the attainment of specific performance targets (Corporation for National and Community Service, 2015; In the Public Interest, 2015; Roman, Walsh, Bieler, & Taxy, 2014). Supporters of pay-for-success models hope that nonprofit capital will be more efficiently allocated so high-performing nonprofits will be rewarded and poor performers will lose funding.

The same philosophy that increased contract competition will improve performance is also linked to cultural beliefs that bringing the market to bear on social issues can lead to social innovation and more positive outcomes. In other words, market discipline is an antidote to complacency and produces cognitive shifts on the part of staff and managers. Some research has shown that managers are able to use performance data to make better decisions (LeRoux & Wright, 2010). There remains controversy over what type of data is most useful, however. Although data on outcomes and impact is often desired, the level of abstraction required for many human service outcomes can sometimes point managers in the wrong direction (Dias & Maynard-Moody, 2006; Perrin, 1998). Some research has suggested that traditional accountability measures (e.g., output and process indicators) should continue to play an important role in determining performance (Heinrich, 2002).

In the last 15 years, the emphasis on impact, performance, and contract competition has become more widespread and rigorously measured, due in part to budget scarcity and the rapid growth of human service agencies in response to privatization of government services. But the drive for impact comes from directions other than just policy makers as well—which is part of what makes this shift in human services so pervasive. In this section we detail the role played by other groups, namely the professions, private philanthropy, and service users.

The professions

Broad support for evidence-based decision making has meant that policy makers and public and private funders are now creating expectations that human services should be evaluated according to classic principles of social science research including experimental designs with control groups, rigorous data gathering, and robust outcome evaluations. This trend reflects changing professional standards and expectations as key professions, including social work and psychology, emphasize evidence-based practice in their training. In addition, more individuals with MBAs or other professional management degrees are leading human service organizations; as a result, these leaders are often ill equipped to evaluate services beyond its economic value. Interestingly, some have argued that increased homogeneity in what is considered legitimate management approaches may lead to standardization, rather than experimentation, in the human services—a loss for those concerned about social innovation (Hwang & Powell, 2009)

Private funders

Private funders have also led the charge for accountability and outcome measurement, as a way of increasing the impact of their funds, which are often quite modest relative to need (or compared with public funding). For example, national foundations like Edna McConnell Clark, Kellogg, Kresge, Skoll, and Arnold have supported the implementation for various performance management and pay-for-success regimes. This effort is also part of a broader shift to an "impact investing" approach to grant making whereupon foundations and individual wealthy philanthropists regard themselves as investors looking for results and in some cases a return on their investment. Of course, foundations certainly have been interested in the results of their grant funding in earlier periods, but impact investing has encouraged foundations to focus on leverage and maximum impact including on programs with measurable results (Katz, 2005).

Users

In general, service users have emerged as a factor in the push for impact somewhat indirectly. Although users often face many logistical and informational obstacles to direct engagement in services, the shift to user-based subsidies has empowered clients, either directly or indirectly, to expect improved performance and quality among agencies. Nonetheless, this client role remains very unevenly distributed. Many clients face multiple health and social problems that make it virtually impossible for them to be involved in the evaluation or choice of their services, even when there are mechanisms for them to do so. Even in instances where clients are full partners with staff in service operation (such as the clubhouse model in the field of mental health) professionals generally play a key role in the management and evaluation of services (Alford, 2009; Bovaird, 2007).

Field-level changes as a result of the drive for impact

This push for performance has brought about multiple field level shifts with larger implications for the social service landscape than just management concerns. In this section, we discuss three particularly important developments: services integration and collaboration, mechanisms to increase user choice (e.g., vouchers), and social enterprise.

Service integration and collaboration

Concern with performance, in the current era of fiscal scarcity, is bringing forth new interest in services integration and collaboration among agencies.[2] Services integration is a policy priority with a long history in the public services. However, it has achieved new salience as a strategy to improve the performance of human services (Human Services Summit, 2010; Kresge Foundation, 2015; Loya, Boguslaw, Erickson-Warfield, 2015; New Zealand Productivity Commission, 2015; Organization for Economic Co-operation & Development, 2015; Timmins & Ham, 2013). Service integration requires collaboration across sectors, which is increasingly important given the reliance of many governments on contracting agencies. Part of this cross-sectoral collaboration represents an effort to achieve efficiencies, given the overlap among various public and private community organizations. However, this shift also represents an effort to improve the performance of local human service systems. Notably, contemporary service integration initiatives tend to be outcome-focused with an emphasis on using data to measure predetermined client outcomes.

The popular notion of "collective impact" is an exemplar of this kind of thinking. This strategy, as proposed by Kania and Kramer (2011), calls attention to the potential of thinking about community-wide impacts (e.g., on poverty or education) rather than individual program effects. They argue that traditional human service organizations have "isolated" impacts and only by working together can they create synergy and more profound impact on the local community. Among the preconditions for collective impact are sustained collaboration among local service agencies and shared measurement systems. The idea of collective impact has been embraced in a wide variety of public-private partnerships and collaborative initiatives.[3]

---

[2]Examples abound. In Canterbury, New Zealand, services integration for health and social services has entailed the implementation of an Electronic Shared Care Record View (Timmins & Ham, 2013). Meanwhile, policy makers are pushing the idea that the data should be posted on the web and public and private human services agencies should be as transparent as possible with their services. In Portugal, government has implemented a national network of integrated care that uses an online web-based data management system. In Scotland, a program to improve community care for older adults relies upon multi-agency assessment data collected and reported at the national level (Organization for Economic Co-operation & Development, 2015, p. 175).

[3]For instance, Kania and Kramer (2011) cite the example of Shape Up Somerville (a small city in Massachusetts) that is a city-wide public–private partnership focused on a comprehensive and successful effort to reduce childhood obesity.

This is possible because advances in data collection and program measurement mean that policy makers are in a much better position to collect relevant data and impose shared measurement systems on a local service system. Indeed, shared measurement is regarded as essential if service integration and collective impact schemes are to be effective in addressing the target social problem. Moreover, the trend toward "big data" is fueling the effort to create more integrated systems since government administrators now have much more data available to them to analyze system outcomes.

Mechanisms to increase user choice

Competition is also reinforced by encouraging more choice on the part of users. In the United Kingdom, personal budgets have been created that give individual users at least some control over the use of public funds for their services. Thus, a senior citizen might have a specific allocation of public funds that she can use to purchase home care and transportation (see Cunningham & Nickson, 2010; Center for Medicare and Medicaid Services, 2016). In the United States, vouchers, including for child care or housing, have tended to be the most prevalent user choice mechanism. Increased client choice is intended to increase the incentive of agencies for good performance, resulting in better outcomes. Whether client subsidies work this way in practice depends upon many factors including the number of agencies in local markets, the ability of funders to regulate and oversee these agencies, and the ability of clients to make performance-based decisions (as opposed to decision making on some other indicator, such as location or availability of services). Although client-based funding alters the power dynamic between providers and users in ways that can be positive, it also puts agencies in a more vulnerable and precarious financial situation, potentially alters the incentives to serve particular types of clients (e.g., creaming), and may affect the capacity of the agency to provide quality services if cash flow is unpredictable. These mechanisms, by encouraging consumers to "shop around" for services, lead to greater uncertainty in the funding streams for affected nonprofit agencies.

Social enterprise and social impact bonds

A final example of a field-level trend that can be tracked back to the demand for performance is the support among private funders for social enterprise. This term generally refers to organizations that have a social mission but also incorporate for-profit elements such as market income (Dees, 1998; Reiser, 2013; Skelcher & Smith, 2015). For example, Roberts Enterprise Development Fund (REDF), a nonprofit based in San Francisco offers multiple programs that creatively mix public, philanthropic, and earned income to support employment and job training for the disabled and disadvantaged, combining the traditional social mission of a nonprofit with market-based activity (Thornley, Anderson, & Dixon, 2015). Many social enterprises, like REDF, also have performance contracts and specific outcome measures.

The interest in mixed nonprofit/for-profit service models is also reflected in the widespread interest in social impact bonds (SIBs). Originally developed in the United Kingdom, SIBs are complicated initiatives that depend upon private investors assuming at least partial risk of social programs, with the government paying off those investments if and when the outcome goals are met. Private investors loan money to an intermediary that then subcontracts with service providers who then deliver services with specific performance targets. The project is evaluated by independent researchers and the government sponsor repays the loan, with interest, if the performance targets are met. Overall, the adoption of SIBs by state and local government has been slow, partly due to the relatively high transaction costs. However, enthusiasm about their use is high and their adoption will be important to watch.

Managerial dilemmas

In the popular and scholarly literature, *impact* is variously defined as innovation, effectiveness, or accountability. The vagueness of the term is perhaps part of its charm—it allows for funders to call on organizations to "do better" without giving clear guidance on what that really means. The ambiguity of the term is important to note because the nature of human service work is also indefinite and indeterminate at its core (Hasenfeld, 1983). As a result, the emphasis on impact has a new set of contradictions for agency leaders.

First, nonprofit leaders face demands to collaborate more and compete more. In other words, they find themselves navigating an increasingly competitive funding environment while facing pressure from funders and their own organizational circumstances to collaborate with many of the same agencies with which they are competing. A term—*coopetition*—has emerged to capture this phenomenon (Walley, 2007). This largely stems from the fact that impact is being pursued from two directions: (1) through increased competition embedded in contract mechanisms and (2) the belief that impact can be multiplied when agencies work to together to solve problems (resulting in greater services integration at the local level and many funders requiring agencies to collaborate, especially agencies with overlapping missions). This has led to a growth in mergers among similar service agencies—so as to neutralize both of those pressures. These demands lead to myriad management dilemmas because it is likely that services integration will remain a priority, but incentives for integration are elusive and difficult to sustain. Collaboration is often difficult because even agencies with similar service offerings—such as early childhood education—may have different missions, histories, or cultures (Sandfort, 1999). Further, the search for innovative solutions to social problems often fosters new start-ups, including social enterprises, that may directly compete with existing organizations and undermine collaborative efforts at the local level.

Second, managers face a set of dilemmas around the tension between client-centered practice—in which the user is engaged in decision making around their own care—professionalization, and evidence-based practice. Consumer engagement is often voiced as a high priority by public and private funders and agency leaders. Efforts to advance this in organization is sometimes known as the practice of coproduction and can refer to a wide variety of service initiatives that engage consumers directly—including having them work collaboratively with volunteers and professionals to develop responsive and effective service plans (Boviard 2007). Yet user engagement can conflict with the drive for evidence-based practice that tends to foster professionalization and may actually reduce the role of volunteers and users in service delivery. Moreover, more rigorous evaluation typically requires a professionalized infrastructure to gather and evaluate data and relevant information. Professionalization in governance can also create obstacles to user participation.

Direct conflict may also occur between the traditional emphasis in the human services on client-centered care and evidence-based practice. For example, funders increasingly require agencies to adopt manualized services with little flexibility and limit the types of services that are reimbursable. Consequently, there is often scant room for clients to provide input about their care. Not only does this sometimes create conflict in the staff–client relationship, many worthwhile services have not been rigorously evaluated. Thus a service preferred by the client and/or staff may be discarded for a service that neither prefers, simply because the evidence-based service is a better fit in an accountability chain lacking significant influence by clients and street-level staff.

Articles in this issue

The articles found in this special issue look at the question of impact from a variety of perspectives and shed vital empirical light on the questions raised above. Together, they demonstrate that specific management strategies and collaboration based on trust and consideration of mission may help improve the quality of some services (Bunger et al., this issue; Knies et al. this issue), but many of the pressures organizations and managers experience are resulting in lower staff morale, compromised missions, and inefficiencies (Spitzmueller, Robichau & Wang, Benjamin et al, and Bosk).

First, Matthew Spitzmueller tackles the question of how fee-for-service contracting is affecting street-level practice. In his ethnographic account of a community mental health service provider, he shows that due to contracting practices intended to increase accountability, Quality Assurance staff are increasingly focused not on "quality" per se, but on compliance with contract metrics, particularly "billable" services. Consequently, services that are not billable—like a milieu program highly valued by clients and believed by staff to promote belongingness and stability—are marginalized and diminished. Furthermore, because staff–client interactions needed to be codified and monitored, staff felt discredited and alienated from the parts of their work they felt to be most meaningful. The implications here are clear—the pursuit of "quality" can sometimes mean diminished quality if services and consumers are not looked at holistically and as individuals with complicated relational needs.

If fee-for-service contracting can have a wide ranging effect on internal organizational operations, including in ways that are contrary to what staff or clients would prefer, two other articles in this issue ask the logical next questions, "How are managers—at all levels—responding to these changing incentives in the environment? Do their activities actually contribute to improved organizational performance? How might that vary for organizations with different missions?"

In addressing these questions, Robbie Robichau and Lili Wang point out that the isomorphic demands of the market may homogenize human services, leaving some missions or populations vulnerable. They use survey data to show how nonprofit child welfare agencies are changing in the face of significant external demands to become more business like. They conclude that agencies with stronger ties to the business world are indeed more likely to lead by managers that believe that agencies should be "run more like a business." These managers, in turn, are more likely to charge fees for their services. Agencies that engaged in advocacy, however, were less likely to adopt these business practices, potentially helping insulate and support the mission of the organization.

Eva Knies, Peter Leisink, and Sasha Kraus-Hoogeveen focus on the activities of frontline managers, as opposed to top managers and provide evidence from the field of elderly care that the people management behavior of these managers can make a significant difference when it comes to mission achievement. A major contribution of their article, however, is their compact measure of mission achievement, which they argue must be context specific given the diversity of missions. This measure is an example of how we might measure organizational effectiveness as something other than just meeting particular contract metrics. In this field, it was determined that "thoughtful care" was a key employee behavior that would help to achieve mission, and line managers were found to contribute to organizational effectiveness by supporting employee behavior related to providing such thoughtful care.

Of course, to show performance, data must be carefully collected and tracked—and increasingly that data is being used to make decisions with major consequences. Two articles in this issue take on the topic of data use inside organizations but from very different starting points and in very different human service fields. First, Lehn Benjamin, Amy Voida, and Chris Bopp present a careful analysis of where the demand for data originates, how staff experience different data systems, and the degree to which those systems are in alignment with practice. Looking at the fields of HIV/AIDS and homeless services, they show that data systems are tied not just to funders' demands, but also to the larger policy field in which an organization is embedded. Given that data collection (to demonstrate effectiveness) now consumes an enormous amount of staff time and energy in human service organizations, this article provides important insights about how to think more carefully and specifically about how organizations collect, maintain, and use data. This article also provides important documentation regarding the fragmented data environments for human services agencies and the resultant inefficiencies for staff, including constraints on the usability of data.

Next, Emily Bosk highlights the deep tension in the human services field between evidence-based practice and practice wisdom by using qualitative data to show how algorithms and computer-assisted decision making—commonly used in child welfare agencies to minimize decision making errors—undermines staff knowledge and leads to lower job satisfaction. Her study also demonstrates that staff experience significant tension when their professional judgment is not in alignment with what the actuarial-based risk assessment tools indicate and points to ways in which the algorithm could be more nuanced. One key issue is that because these tools are meant to reduce "false negatives" and thus err on the side of removal, staff are limited in their ability to override removal orders, potentially leading to costly overtreatment and needless disruption for families and children. She tracks the use of these tools back to the chronic resource constraints, information uncertainty, and accountability pressures faced by child welfare agencies—pressures felt in other fields as well, even if such risk assessment tools are not yet in use.

Finally, Alicia Bunger and her colleagues Bowen McBeath, Crystal Collins-Camargo, Emmeline Chuang, and Monica Perez-Jolles, point out that the relationships nonprofit child welfare agencies have with their public counterparts is often much closer than the dispassionate "arms-length" relationship sometimes imagined by those calling for greater accountability and reliance on performance metrics. The difficulty of quantifying ambiguous outcomes and the limited market mean that public and nonprofit agencies often work together closely over time and develop mutual trust. In this article, Bunger and colleagues investigate the effect of the increasing embeddedness many human service agencies experience with government agencies. They use survey data to first assess the degree of fiscal and relational embeddedness experienced by different organizations and then assess the relationship between the level of embeddedness and nonprofits' finances, service programming, staffing, and performance. Encouragingly, they find that embeddedness has a positive effect on operations, and that nonprofits with stronger relational embeddedness with public agencies (not just fiscal embeddedness) report better organizational functioning in the areas of programming and performance. These findings have important implications in that they remind managers not to overlook the social dimensions of the contracting relationship, even in an era of quantification.

Conclusion

In sum, we believe that the field of human services needs to move beyond narrow performance targets and expectations, which lead to significant managerial dilemmas that are not well recognized or addressed by funders. The articles in this issue provide compelling evidence that meeting performance demands does not always fall into alignment with what staff consider to be high-quality services. It could be, in fact, that so much tracking and counting of particular indicators and metrics is actually leading to questionable decision making and lower job satisfaction. This does not mean that we should eliminate performance tracking completely, rather that performance regimes need to be rethought and made more nuanced and responsive to complexity. This sort of contingency approach may help address concerns about equity and context (Moynihan et al., 2011).

Importantly, one issue often overlooked by policy makers is that the pursuit of greater impact by public and private funders frequently means that organizations with greater scale are advantaged in the system (Alexander, Nank, & Stivers, 1999). Unless we are willing to move to a system where human services are provided predominantly by large, multiservice organizations with little connection to their immediate community, we need to consider carefully how to support smaller community-based agencies. We also need to think more carefully about how to integrate user voice with performance demands—when the client outcome is predetermined by the funder, where is the role of client self-determination?

It should be noted that the cyclical legitimacy crises many have noted in the human services make it prime target for those who wish to call into question the value of relational work in an outcomes-oriented society or challenge the notion that marginalized populations can make meaningful contributions to society. Calls for impact are tied, then, to larger cultural tropes about wastefulness in the human services and emphasis on economic value over moral value. These changes mean that we must understand much more fully the answer to two key questions. First, in terms of people, we need to know more about how impact demands affect four specific and distinct constituencies: service users, the larger marginalized communities in which they are embedded, the increasingly precarious human service workforce, and leaders of human service agencies. Second, we need to increase our knowledge of how the push for impact affects structural conditions that drive inequality and need.

The future of human services is really about the future of the social safety net and social policy more generally. As we have shifted from cash benefits to direct services, the organizational health and sustainability of human service organizations is essential to effective government safety net programs. We are challenged to find a way to provide human services in a way that provides a recognizable return on investment for funders, but also treats clients as individuals, instead of widgets. The articles in this issue provide a clear-eyed perspective on what the challenges are, as well as how staff, clients, and managers are responding.

ORCID

Jennifer E. Mosley http://orcid.org/0000-0002-9292-6710

References

Alexander, J., Nank, R., & Stivers, C. (1999). Implications of welfare reform: Do nonprofit survival strategies threaten civil society? *Nonprofit and Voluntary Sector Quarterly, 28*(4), 452–475.

Alford, J. (2009). *Engaging public sector clients: From service delivery to co-production.* London,England: Palgrave Macmillan.

Bovaird, T. (2007). Beyond engagement and participation: User and community coproduction of public services. *Public Administration Review, 67*(5), 846–860.

Center for Medicare and Medicaid Services. (2016). *Self directed services.* Washington, DC: Author. Retrieved from https://www.medicaid.gov/Medicaid-CHIP-Program-Information/By-Topics/Delivery-Systems/Self-Directed-Services.html

Corporation for National and Community Service, Office of Research and Evaluation. (2015). *State of the pay for success field: Opportunities, trends, and recommendations.* Washington, DC: Author.

Cunningham, I., & Nickson, D. (2010). *Personalisation and its implications for work and employment in the voluntary sector.* Glasgow, Scotland: University of Strathclyde. Retrieved from http://strathprints.strath.ac.uk/30955/1/Personalisation_20Report_20Final_2015th_20November.pdf

Dees, J. G. (1998). Enterprising nonprofits. *Harvard Business Review, 76*(1), 54–67.

Desai, S., Garabedian, L., & Snyder, K. (2012). *Performance based contracts in New York City: Lessons learned from welfare-to-work.* Albany, NY: Rockefeller Institute of Government. Retrieved from http://www.rockinst.org/pdf/workforce_welfare_and_social_services/2012-06-Performance-Based_Contracts.pdf

Dias, J. J., & Maynard-Moody, S. (2006). For-profit welfare: Contracts, conflicts, and the performance paradox. *Journal of Public Administration Research and Theory, 17*(2), 189–211.

Eikenberry, A. M., & Kluver, J. D. (2004). The marketization of the nonprofit sector: Civil society at risk?. *Public Administration Review, 64*(2), 132–140.

Fraser, J., & Whitehill, E. (2014). *Introducing performance-based contracts: A comparison of implementation models.* Pittsburgh, PA: Allegheny County Department of Human Services.

Freundlich, M., & Charlotte, M. (2012). *Privatization of child welfare services: A guide for state advocates.* Washington DC: First Focus. Retrieved from http://childwelfaresparc.org/wp-content/uploads/2014/07/17-Privatization-of-Child-Welfare-Services-A-Guide-for-State-Advocates.pdf

Hasenfeld, Y. (1983). *Human service organizations.* Englewood Cliffs, NJ: Prentice Hall.

Heinrich, C. J. (2002). Outcomes–based performance management in the public sector: Implications for government accountability and effectiveness. *Public Administration Review, 62*, 712–725.

Hood, C. (1991). A public management for all seasons? *Public Administration, 69*(1), 3–19.

Human Services Summit. (2010). *The next generation of human services: Realizing the vision.* Cambridge, MA: Harvard University Press. Retrieved from http://lnwprogram.org/sites/default/files/Realizing_the_Vision.pdf

Hwang, H., & Powell, W. W. (2009). The rationalization of charity: The influences of professionalism in the nonprofit sector. *Administrative Science Quarterly, 54*(2), 268–298.

In the Public Interest. (2015). *A guide to evaluating pay for success programs and social impact bonds*. Washington, DC: Author. Retrieved from http://www.inthepublicinterest.org/wp-content/uploads/ITPI-Pay-for-Success-Guide-Dec-2015.pdf

Kania, J., & Kramer, M. (2011), Winter. Collective impact. *Stanford Social Innovation Review*. Winter 2011, 36–41. Retrieved from http://ssir.org/articles/entry/collective_impact

Katz, S. N. (2005). What does it mean to say that philanthropy is "effective"? The philanthropists' new clothes. *Proceedings of the American Philosophical Society, 149*(2), 123–131.

Klassen, A., Miller, A., Anderson, N., Shen, J., Schiariti, V., & Maureen, O'Donnell. (2009). Performance measurement and improvement frameworks in health, education and social services systems: A systematic review. *International Journal for Quality in Health Care, 22*(1), 44–69.

Kresge Foundation. (2015). *A call for action: Strengthening the human services sector*. Troy, MI: Author. Retrieved from http://kresge.org/sites/default/files/Strengthening-the-Human-Services-Sector.pdf

LeRoux, K., & Wright, N. S. (2010). Does performance measurement improve strategic decision making? Findings from a national survey of nonprofit social service agencies. *Nonprofit and Voluntary Sector Quarterly, 39*(4), 571–587.

Loya, R., Boguslaw, J., & Erickson-Warfield, M. (2015). *Empowering prosperity: Strengthening human services impacts through asset integration*. Waltham, MA: Brandeis University, The Heller School, Institute on Assets and Social Policy.

Moynihan, D. P., Fernandez, S., Kim, S., LeRoux, K. M., Piotrowski, S. J., Wright, B. E., & Yang, K. (2011). Performance regimes amidst governance complexity. *Journal of Public Administration Research and Theory, 21*(1), 141–155.

New Zealand Productivity Commission. (2015). *More effective social services*. Wellington, NZ: New Zealand Productivity Commission. Retrieved from http://www.productivity.govt.nz/sites/default/files/social-services-final-report-main.pdf

Organization for Economic Co-operation & Development. (2015). *Integrating social services for vulnerable groups: Bridging sectors for better service delivery*. Paris, France: Author.

Office of Mayor. (2017). Mayor burgess advances results-based contracting legislation. Seattle, WA. Retrieved from http://mayorburgess.seattle.gov/2017/10/mayor-burgess-advances-results-based-contracting-legislation/#sthash.qo0yVvHy.dpbs

Page, S. (2005). What's new about the new public management? Administrative change in the human services. *Public Administration Review, 65*, 713–727.

Perrin, B. (1998). Effective use and misuse of performance measurement. *The American Journal of Evaluation, 19*(3), 367–379.

Reiser, D. B. (2013). Theorizing forms of social enterprise. *Emory Law Journal, 62*, 681–739.

Roman, J. K., Walsh, K. A., Bieler, S., & Taxy, S. (2014). *Pay for success and social impact bonds: Funding the infrastructure for evidence-based change*. Washington, DC: Urban Institute. Retrieved from http://www.urban.org/sites/default/files/alfresco/publication-pdfs/413150-Pay-for-Success-and-Social-Impact-Bonds-Funding-the-Infrastructure-for-Evidence-Based.PDF

Sandfort, J. (1999). The structural impediments to human service collaboration: Examining welfare reform at the front lines. *Social Service Review, 73*(3), 314–339.

Skelcher, C., & Smith, S. R. (2015). Theorizing hybridity: Institutional logics, complex organizations, and actor identities: The case of nonprofits. *Public Administration, 93*, 433–448.

Smith, D. C., & Grinker, W. J. (2004). *The promise and pitfalls of performance based contracting*. New York, NY: Seedco.

Smith, S. R. (2012). Government-Voluntary Sector Compacts Reconsidered. In Nonprofit Policy Forum. (Vol. 3, No. 2).

Smith, S. R., & Phillips, S. D. (2016). The changing and challenging environment of nonprofit human services: Implications for governance and program implementation. *Nonprofit Policy Forum, 7*(1), 63–76.

Thornley, B., Anderson, J., & Dixon, L. (2015). *Impact to last: Lessons from the front lines of social enterprise*. San Francisco, CA : REDF. Retrieved from https://redfworkshop.org/wp-content/uploads/2015/09/Impact-to-Last.pdf

Timmins, N., & Ham, C. (2013). *The quest for integrated health and social care: A case study in canterbury, New Zealand*. London, England: The King's Fund. Retrieved from http://www.kingsfund.org.uk/sites/files/kf/field/field_publication_file/quest-integrated-care-new-zealand-timmins-ham-sept13.pdf

Walley, K. (2007). Coopetition: An introduction to the subject and an agenda for research. *International Studies of Management & Organization, 37*(2), 11–31.

Remaking "Community" Mental Health: Contested Institutional Logics and Organizational Change

Matthew C. Spitzmueller

ABSTRACT
Neo-institutional studies of institutional entrepreneurship identify the important role that individuals play as drivers of institutional change. Institutional entrepreneurs leverage resources to create new institutions or to transform existing ones. Recent scholarship complicates the depiction of institutional entrepreneurship as merely creative, examining its disruptive effects on established logics and practices. This article uses ethnographic methods to investigate how institutional entrepreneurship functioned in one community mental health organization, and extends neo-institutional theory by demonstrating how street-level workers contested its advancement. It theorizes the entrepreneurial nature of Quality Assurance (QA) staff, who promoted the managerial logic and developed performance measures to recouple frontline practice to public demands for efficiency, standardization, and accountability. Street-level workers used the community logic of the clubhouse to order their therapeutic identities, strategies, and goals. When these competing logics came into contact, multiplicity produced deep contradiction, epistemic distress, and ongoing struggle. This article finds that new managerialism forced a reworking of the community logic, and weighs the implications of this transformation for human services rooted in the community logic.

Researchers contend that Quality Assurance (QA) workers play a pivotal role in shaping how mental health organizations manage public demands for enhanced effectiveness and accountability (Hermann, 2007). As a condition of accreditation, mental health agencies are increasingly required to implement managerial systems that monitor quality and promote ongoing improvement (Commission on Accreditation of Rehabilitation Facilities [CARF], 2013). Ganju (2006) argues that a quality and accountability framework is critical for obtaining better mental health outcomes from the implementation of evidence-based practices. The mental health literature broadly supports client collaboration in QA processes (Farkas, Gagne, Anthony, & Chamberlin, 2005), the use of evidence-based standards as a means of improving quality (Goldman et al., 2001), and benchmarks of service processes and outcomes (McMillen et al., 2005).

Scholars have documented a range of barriers to quality improvement in mental health organizations. There is a lack of uniformity in performance measurement (Ganju, 2006). Training may have a limited impact on practice (Torrey & Gorman, 2005). Resource limitations may constrain organizations' ability to invest in administrative support and information technologies (Zayas, McMillen, Lee, & Books, 2013). And, frontline workers may not buy-in when charged with implementing new standards and may view the QA role as antagonistic. Given these challenges, when undesirable outcomes occur, it may be difficult for QA staff to determine whether they reflect ineffective interventions, poorly implemented systems, inadequately trained workers, or insufficient funding (Panzano et al., 2005).

McMillen, Zayas, Books, and Lee (2008) conducted interviews with mental health QA professionals, asking them to describe their perceived roles, targets, and contributions. They found that the QA work role mostly involved monitoring the compliance of workers' everyday routines with external funding requirements. Occasionally, QA staff identified targets that were germane to quality improvement, such as evaluating consumer and staff experiences. However, most commonly, its activities bore no direct relationship to quality improvement. When asked to describe the incentives by which its own performance was measured, QA staff almost never reported that it was evaluated based on changing results for clients, and often struggled to produce a single concrete example of how its contribution made a difference to client outcomes. The authors observed, "it appears that some agencies were monitoring just to be able to report that they were monitoring" (p. 464). Although an emerging literature points to a disjuncture between everyday organizational practice and the ideal of the QA role (Hermann, 2007), scholars have not analyzed the dimensions of organizational structure and process that produce this misalignment, nor have they examined systematically its effect on street-level behavior.

This article uses ethnographic methods to investigate how QA staff in a community mental health organization that was in Chicago, Illinois, responded to reforms in governance and financing. Fieldwork was conducted during a time of marked public policy reform in Illinois, as the state transitioned from a block grant to Medicaid fee-for-service (FFS) system. Medicaid is a federal insurance program that provides health coverage to millions of low-income Americans. This article asks three related questions. How did QA staff respond to the managerial logic of FFS reforms? How did QA staff endeavor to link the managerial logic to everyday practice? And how did this shift interact with the community logic that guided workers' identities and practices at the street level? Findings from this study are relevant to scholarship on QA in mental health settings. They also contribute to the theoretical development of neo-institutionalism, demonstrating how institutional logics take hold in organizations, how institutional entrepreneurship produces turmoil and contestation at the site of logic incompatibility, and what these effects mean for human services rooted in the community logic.

Background and significance

Neo-institutionalism

Neo-institutionalism examines how organizations relate to the broader fields of which they are a part, investigating how extrinsic belief and rule systems influence organizational behavior (Powell & DiMaggio, 1991). It has evolved into a macrocultural theory, investigating how organizations mold to their environments through processes such as isomorphism, diffusion, and field transformation (DiMaggio & Powell, 1983; Schneiberg, 2013; Scott, Ruef, Mendel, & Caronna, 2000). The organizational field includes the producers, consumers, and regulatory agencies that constitute a recognized area of institutional life and produce a common meaning system (Wooten & Hoffman, 2008). Mental health organizations, for instance, are nested within multiple institutional orders that comprise the field, such as the state, which governs through rules and regulations, the profession, which governs through licensing standards and practice norms, and society, which governs through shared attitudes and dispositions. A subset of neo-institutional theory, the institutional logics perspective contends that each institution is defined by a central logic that "constitutes its organizing principals" (Friedland & Alford, 1991, p. 248). Institutional logics provide situated actors with vocabularies of identity that shape their pursuit of goals, determine what they value, and govern how values are indexed within specific historical contexts.

More recently, scholars of neo-institutionalism have endeavored to "inhabit" institutionalism by analyzing how institutional logics take hold in everyday organizational life (Binder, 2007; Hallett, 2010). This literature seeks to bring work "back in" to the study of institutions (Barley & Kunda, 2001, p. 76). Because organizations are nested within multiple institutional orders, the institutional logics perspective takes heterogeneity to be a constitutive feature of organizational life (Thornton, Ocasio, & Lounsbury, 2012). Scholarship demonstrates that multiplicity may produce a range of outcomes depending upon organizational context, including logic migration (Jain & Sharma, 2013) and the replacement of one logic by another (Booher-Jennings, 2005; Thornton, 2002). Besharov and Smith (2014) examine how dimensions of pluralism interact within organizations to produce distinct outcomes. They contend that two properties of heterogeneity shape how workers negotiate pluralism. *Low compatibility* describes the degree to which logic instantiations imply inconsistent and opposing actions. *High centrality* describes the degree to which multiple institutional demands permeate work activities that are essential to organizational functioning. In a highly contested organization, low compatibility and high centrality combine to produce ongoing conflict among actors over the chief meanings, identities, and operations of organizational life. Although the fact of logic multiplicity is a defining characteristic of human service organizations, the practical products of heterogeneity are not predetermined, but rather emerge path dependently as organizations negotiate internal and external conditions of work (Pierson, 2004; Skelcher & Smith, 2014).

The analytic concept of legitimacy is particularly relevant to the study of how institutional logics take shape in organizations. Neo-institutionalism defines *legitimacy* as a relational construct that is reflected in the alignment of an organization with the regulatory, normative, and cognitive rules that prevail in the wider organizational field and social environment (Scott, 2014). In their seminal analysis, Meyer and Rowan (1977) contend that there are two axes along which organizations vie for survival. The first depends on the efficient coordination and control of productive activities. The second depends on their ability to become isomorphic with the institutional environment and thus to secure legitimacy. The authors argue that organizations have a structural incentive to decouple coordination and control functions from everyday practices, because inconsistencies between them can lead to loss of legitimacy, and therefore to loss of resources. The authors state, "decoupling enables organizations to maintain standardized, legitimating, formal structures while their activities vary in response to practical considerations" (p. 357). Decoupling encourages internal managers and external auditors to perform "myths" of ceremonial inspection (p. 359), whereby managers minimize the force of evaluation to reduce conflicts, curtail evidence of contradiction, and secure legitimacy.

Recent scholarship suggests that new public management, which stresses market solutions to public problems, may unsettle decoupling as an organizational survival strategy (Bromley & Powell, 2012; Sauder & Espeland, 2009). In his investigation of an urban elementary school, Hallet (2010) finds that field transformations placed pressures on administrators to develop accountability measures that held teachers responsible for producing common standards. He argues that administrative technologies, such as performance measurement, outcome benchmarks, and curriculum standards, reversed the classic model of loose couplings and recoupled ceremonial myth with teachers' everyday practices. By tying organizational resources, rewards, and punishments to compliance and performance, school administrators made myths "incarnate" in practice, giving "tangible flesh" to public demands for accountability (p. 52). Rather than producing efficiency, achieving better outcomes, and reducing ambiguity, recoupling created "turmoil" on the ground, expressed through teachers' epistemic distress and redrawn battle lines (p. 63). As surveillance took hold, teachers faced fundamental threats to their autonomy and professionalism, which accelerated the experience of chaos in their daily routines and eroded their sense of security.

Binder's (2007) work on inhabited institutions suggests that field transformations may produce variegated responses at different levels of organizational operation. In other words, within a single organization, administrators and line staff may negotiate heterogeneity differently depending upon their unique identities and aims. This article builds on previous scholarship of inhabited institutions. It identifies the properties of new managerialism that reverse couplings from loose to tight, and demonstrates how differently situated actors draw on formal and informal resources to mobilize and contest institutional change.

Institutional entrepreneurship

Analysis of the microsociological foundation of institutionalism invites inquiry into who prompts organizational change, how it is advanced, and what it produces in practice. Relatively mature fields may be prone to sudden, acute pressures that create "disruptive uncertainty," requiring workers to reformulate novel solutions and rework core logics (Hoffman, 1999, p. 353). Changing field structures may dislodge dominant logics and create openings for workers to assume new roles and experiment with new technologies (Scott et al., 2000). *Technologies* include the knowledge, skills, and operations that workers use to anchor institutional logics to organizational practice, and play a central role in the process of organizational adaptation (p. 19).

The institutional logics perspective has generated critical inquiry into the role that "institutional entrepreneurs" play as agents and products of field transformation (DiMaggio, 1988, p. 14). The analytic construct of the institutional entrepreneur is particularly germane to this investigation of QA staff, which I will argue acted as a translator of field transformations within the mental health organization I studied. Maguire, Hardy, and Lawrence (2004) define *institutional entrepreneurship* as the "activities of actors who have an interest in particular institutional arrangements and who leverage resources to create new institutions or to transform existing ones" (p. 657). Actor-centered models theorize the individual traits that distinguish institutional entrepreneurs from others in the field, citing their knack for "initiating, creating, and leading organizations" (Dew, 2006, p. 16). Process-centered accounts push back against the tendency of actor-centered models to reify and valorize individual efficacy, theorizing how institutional entrepreneurship is shaped by an individual's structural position relative to the field. "Precipitating jolts," for instance, produced by regulatory change, may disturb the contingently aligned field, creating openings for institutional entrepreneurs equipped with new motives to ascend (Greenwood, Suddaby, & Hinings, 2002, p. 60). Although much of the literature examines the generative potential of institutional entrepreneurs to initiate new logics and operations, these actors have an equal capacity to disrupt and unmoor traditional logics and practices (Hardy & Maguire, 2008).

Research on institutional entrepreneurship examines the dialectical tension between agency and structure, theorizing what Battilana and D'aunno (2009) describe as "the paradox of embedded agency" (p. 32). Institutional entrepreneurs are equipped with material resources (Lawrence & Suddaby, 2006), discursive resources (Hensmans, 2003), and political, financial, and organizational resources (Greenwood & Suddaby, 2006) for anchoring organizational meanings and practice to field transformations. Although institutional entrepreneurs summon these resources to "create, reproduce, and change institutions" (Zilber, 2002, p. 236), their means and ends are determined by field resources that structure their mobility. Institutional entrepreneurs do not possess power in the colloquial sense but occupy subject positions that construct them as agentive within the bounds of specific and historically contingent fields (Bourdieu, 1977). The analytic goal of the study of institutional entrepreneurship is to examine how the field enables a certain kind of creative subject to emerge and behave in artful ways.

Competing institutional logics

This study uses the methods of organizational ethnography to analyze how QA staff interfaced with street-level workers at a clubhouse program, named "Community Club," located in Chicago, Illinois. I have altered all identifying information to protect the confidentiality of my research participants. The community logic of the clubhouse emphasizes membership, social connection, collaboration, and self-determination. The managerial logic of FFS reforms emphasizes cost-efficiency, standardization, and accountability.

The community logic of the clubhouse

Community Club was founded in the 1960s as a community mental health clubhouse, one of the earliest community-based treatment models to respond to the deinstitutionalization crisis in the

United States (Fountain House, 1999). The clubhouse has demonstrated effectiveness in reducing psychiatric hospitalization (Masso, Avi-Itzhak, & Obler, 2001), promoting health and wellness (McKay & Pelletier, 2007), improving quality of life (Rosenfield & Neese-Todd, 1993; Warner, Huxley, & Berg, 1999), and reintegrating people with serious mental illness into the competitive workforce (Fountain House, 1999; McKay, 2006).

The clubhouse model advances the community logic to operationalize a set of practices that destigmatize the identity of program participants, promote informality and flexibility, and maximize participation (Spitzmueller, 2016). Practitioners of the clubhouse model eschew the label of *mental health patient*, instead referring to participants as "members." Clubhouse proponents emphasize experiential approaches to learning and socialization within an intentionally designed therapeutic milieu. They describe the therapeutic milieu as a holistic treatment environment that can be mobilized as a therapeutic agent, providing a relational context for modeling and practicing desired behaviors (Smith & Spitzmueller, 2016). Clubhouse proponents assert that members should not "regard themselves as undergoing a formal rehabilitation process, in which something is being done to them" (Beard, Propst, & Malamud, 1982, p. 49) but should play a collaborative role in shaping program goals and activities. The model holds that, when members work side-by-side with staff to fulfill the everyday responsibilities of maintaining the clubhouse, they derive value and purpose from knowing that their contribution is needed and makes a difference (Propst, 1992). The clubhouse also functions as an informal social club, providing a context of acceptance and belongingness as a foundation for psychiatric rehabilitation and recovery (Dincin, 1975).

During fieldwork for this study, an average of 108 members attended Community Club daily. To be eligible for services, members were required to have a qualifying diagnosis of serious mental illness. Community Club is administered and managed by New Frontiers, a nationally recognized, multiprogrammatic community mental health agency that offers a range of evidence-based services.

The managerial logic of FFS reforms

Beginning in the 1980s, Illinois funded community mental health services using block grants, which advanced quarterly sums for services and placed few regulatory demands on mental health agencies. As a condition of receiving grants-in-aid, the Illinois Division of Mental Health (DMH), the state authority charged with overseeing planning and coordination of public mental health services, required agencies to submit biannual reports for each client, along with daily census records. Beyond these general indices of therapeutic inputs, agencies were not responsible for any additional reporting to the state. In 2004, DMH began a state-wide Systems Restructuring Initiative, with the aim of converting all community mental health payments from block grants to Medicaid FFS. Then Governor Rod Blagojevich (2004) announced the goal of using the Medicaid federal match to recuperate $60 million for state general funds. By "demanding accountability" from providers, he averred, FFS payments would promote the aims of efficiency and effectiveness, "doing more with the resources available to us" (p. 17). The Systems Restructuring Initiative lasted 5 years, producing a billing regimen that directly attached reimbursement to documentation.

FFS reforms transformed the organizational field and activated the managerial logic. They introduced new payment and monitoring technologies that centralized regulatory authority and redefined the scale and mode of community mental health service delivery. FFS reforms overhauled program-level grants, financing services in 15-minute units. To monetize payment and delivery systems, DMH overhauled its services taxonomy, referred to as "Rule 132" (59 Ill. Adm. Code 132), developing rigorous eligibility and practice standards for discrete interventions. As a condition of payment, Rule 132 required organizations to provide case note documentation of each service. A valid case note included a service code and location, along with the narrative elements of client presentation, clinical intervention, client response, and plan for future intervention or termination. Under the Systems Restructuring Initiative, the state would audit organizational records annually, monitoring case notes for fidelity to standards and procedural requirements. In October 2007, the state entered an ongoing contract with ValueOptions, Inc. to administer its FFS system. Through its partnership with ValueOptions, named "the Collaborative," the state contracted out administrative functions required to oversee FFS billing, including eligibility determination, service authorization, claims processing, and post-payment audits.

Fieldwork for this study was conducted between November 2009 and October 2010, during a time of profound dislocation in the organizational field. In July 2009, then Governor Pat Quinn passed what was widely called the doomsday budget (McKenna, 2009), threatening human services with $9.2 billion in cuts. Three months later, most of these cuts were restored, but not before many agencies in the state implemented layoffs in anticipation of lost revenues. In February 2010, Illinois was a national leader in state debt, carrying a deficit of more than $13 billion. Facing high unemployment and diminishing tax revenues, Quinn (2010) declared Illinois to be in a state of financial crisis. Much as Blagojevich had in 2004, he argued that "new and rigorous performance metrics" were needed to improve the accountability and efficiency of community mental health services. On July 1, 2010, Quinn signed into law the Emergency Budget Act (S.B. 96–3660) and the Budget Implementation Act (S.B. 96–3662), requiring $45 million in direct cuts to community mental health programs. DMH realized these cuts by tightening definitions of medical necessity that determined eligibility for Medicaid services, eliminating all community mental health payments for non-Medicaid eligible persons and services, intensifying utilization review, and restricting the hours that providers could bill for group-based services.

New public management is not only an instrument for monitoring and coordinating human services, it also changes the implicit conditions of work by transforming organizational incentives, resources, and demands (Brodkin, 2011; Kettl, 2000). This article complements recent ethnographic work that investigates the impact of Medicaid reform on mental health services. Previous studies demonstrate that new managerial reforms generate unintended consequences in practice (Lamphere, 2005), produce informal patterns of practice at the street level that contradict the manifest aims of policy (Spitzmueller, 2014, 2016), and incite pushback as committed workers wrestle with their perceptions of "institutional bad faith" (Hopper, 2006, p. 218).

Method

Recruitment and data collection

This study was approved by the School of Social Service Administration Institutional Review Board at the University of Chicago. I used a verbal consent script to inform Community Club workers and members of my status as a researcher and posted a written description of my study at the center. This study combines direct observation with interviewing and analysis of organizational documents. Over a 12-month period, I observed the day-to-day routines of approximately 20 street-level workers at Community Club. I conducted more than 1300 hours of direct observation, examining workers' therapeutic interactions and attending weekly meetings. I used jottings to formulate brief notes within a field journal as I observed therapeutic activities and staff meetings in real time. I then composed field notes at the end of each day of observation, turning jottings into more extended, narrative texts (Emerson, Fretz, & Shaw, 2011).

Staff meetings at Community Club provided an especially rich data source for this analysis. The program director and four team leaders attended weekly managers' meetings, in which managers discussed staffing, program planning and events, and issues related to members' treatment. A substantial amount of time was dedicated in each meeting to reviewing administrative procedures and addressing ongoing dilemmas with FFS documentation. I also attended weekly team meetings, which consisted of one team leader and between four and seven frontline workers, for each of the three treatment teams at the center. Team meetings addressed emerging treatment challenges, paperwork responsibilities, and performance evaluation. During the year that I conducted fieldwork for this study, a QA liaison attended five managers' meetings and one team meeting. I audio recorded all meetings and time-stamped jottings to allow for efficient retrieval, transcription, and analysis of key interactions.

As a complement to direct observation, I conducted interviews with workers and managers to better understand the challenges they faced in doing their jobs and the strategies they employed for managing them. I conducted 73 informal interviews and 28 semistructured interviews with frontline workers, team leaders, and administrators, including interviews with the director of Quality and Evaluation at New Frontiers and the QA liaison to Community Club. Semistructured interviews involved a managed verbal exchange in which I began with structured questions, listened attentively, and prompted appropriately, encouraging participants to generate their own insights (Gillham, 2005). All informal and semistructured interviews were audio recorded to preserve the viewpoints of workers in their own words. I had extensive access to documents such as agency reports, instruction manuals, and disciplinary actions. These records were selected for review based on their relevance to emerging research themes.

In addition to studying practices at Community Club, I gathered data from multiple sources that allowed me to develop a layered understanding of how the organizational field changed over time. I interviewed three key informants at DMH who played a substantial role in steering FFS reforms. For one year, I attended regional DMH meetings, webinars, and teleconferences. I also conducted semistructured interviews with five executives at the trade level, who played a role in the FFS transformation. For 2 years, I attended monthly meetings at the largest community behavioral health trade association in Illinois. These interviews and observations provided context for this study of Community Club.

Data analysis

In an organizational ethnography, data collection and analysis are iterative and ongoing, as the researcher uses field methods to establish hypotheses and fact-check them though ongoing observation and interviewing (Ybema, Yanow, Wels, & Kamsteeg, 2009). I used NVivo 8 to code field notes, audio recordings, and organizational documents and to render and preserve thematic connections between related episodes over time. These sources allowed me to triangulate multiple data points and to analyze continuities and differences among them. No one data source was privileged in this analysis. My goal was to understand the complex processes by which the organization adapted core logics and operations to reforms in governance and financing. In this way, I analyzed the multidimensional unfolding of everyday dilemmas, as managers and workers negotiated the challenges of responding therapeutically to members while also fulfilling documentation responsibilities.

Findings

Findings from this study demonstrate that QA staff responded to field disruptions by adopting the managerial logic as an organizing principle and transforming its core operations. I use the analytic construct of institutional entrepreneurship to show how the QA liaison to Community Club engaged in a project that was both creative and destructive. As QA staff endeavored to recouple demands for accountability to street-level practices, its surveillance and disciplinary tactics incited turmoil at the street level. When the managerial logic of FFS reform encountered the community logic of the clubhouse, heterogeneity produced deep rifts in meaning and unsettled the techniques that workers used to order their practice. These conflicts reshaped the nature of services at Community Club, remaking what a center could be for those who counted on it as a place to find membership and connection.

Recoupling processes and the activation of the managerial logic

This section addresses the question, "How did QA workers respond to the managerial logic of FFS reforms?" Jeanne was the director of Quality and Evaluation at New Frontiers. She was also a former program manager of a clubhouse. In an interview, she recalled that prior to FFS reforms QA emphasized the primary targets of workforce development and program evaluation. She noted that QA staff spent the bulk of its time focusing on human resources, training and supervision, and practice competencies. QA staff provided instruction to frontline workers on clinical skills such as engagement and treatment planning. It also used an annual review process to evaluate programs such as Community Club, ensuring that they delivered effective services. As a component of annual review, QA staff met with program managers and team leaders to discuss ways to improve services and promote better outcomes. FFS reforms fundamentally restructured how the state financed and governed community mental health services. These reforms had marked effects on the guiding logic that QA staff used to rationalize its operations and targets.

Gary was the QA liaison to Community Club. Before becoming QA staff at New Frontiers, he managed a rehabilitation day program that he described as being like Community Club. In an interview, he noted that the transition from block grants to FFS "shifted tremendously" how the state financed and monitored New Frontiers. Under block grants, funding allocations were "guaranteed" if New Frontiers demonstrated adequate census rates and payments toward allowable expenses. Under FFS arrangements, in contrast, New Frontiers received money only when it documented and billed a "viable hour or unit of service." This transition, he observed, placed tremendous strain on case note production as a site of revenue generation and regulatory oversight. Not only did FFS rates fund the cost of delivering and documenting services, they also financed the information technologies and managerial staffing necessary to review and process case note receivables. Low reimbursement rates guaranteed that management operated at tight fiscal margins.

To ensure that all billed services were delivered in compliance with FFS standards as set forth in Rule 132 the Collaborative audited New Frontiers' clinical records annually. Jeanne explained that, when it identified billing errors, the Collaborative sanctioned New Frontiers in three ways. It upheld funding for certain low-level errors, denied some bills outright, and most often required New Frontiers to correct errors and reprocess them in exchange for credit. Jeanne observed that when records needed to be canceled, corrected, and resubmitted, New Frontiers no longer covered its operating costs. Therefore, its ability to efficiently procure case notes that reflected compliance with practice standards directly affected its bottom line. In this way, FFS reforms tied organizational resources, rewards, and punishments to accountability demands. QA staff responded to field transformations by shifting managerial processes from loose to tight coupling, placing renewed emphasis on case note compliance. Jeanne observed, "unfortunately, that's what the Quality department has been focused on is compliance in the last three years. And, we do some quality but really our role has been turned to compliance."

New Frontiers responded to field transformations by reconstructing incentives on the front lines. In the month that I began fieldwork for this study, QA staff implemented a new productivity metric to monitor the activities of street-level workers as a function of billing volume. The blended hourly rate established a monthly billing target for each worker. To point workers' efforts toward blended hourly rates QA staff rolled out numerous supporting technologies that targeted frontline efficiencies within the FFS system. Database ticklers reminded workers of pending deadlines, such as mental health assessment and care plan renewals. A dashboard tool, located on workers' desktop computers, allowed them to track their real-time progress toward monthly billing targets. Administrators constructed a chart that linked service codes to action verbs, encouraging workers to post these above their computer terminals and to use only compliant verbs when writing case notes. These adaptations recoupled managerial inspection to frontline practice and commodified workers' activities as a function of billing productivity, targeting conformity with external governance structures.

FFS reforms also restructured how New Frontiers evaluated and incentivized the performance of QA staff. Jeanne employed a parallel technology of performance measurement to track the productivity of her staff, establishing monthly metrics for each QA liaison. These measures standardized the targets of QA performance, focusing work incentives on those managerial tasks that were deemed necessary for operating efficiently in the FFS environment. She described how productivity measures redefined the role of QA liaisons, subjecting their routines to rigorous and ongoing performance review.

> I have given my staff productivity measures of x-amount of charts reviewed, x-amount of onsite visits, number of phone calls or services rendered, approved, and fixed. I've kinda designed metrics for my staff, but they're not income-based metrics. They're reducing-risk metrics, really. Because if we get less bills rejected or less services—I'm sorry, I just keep calling them "bills," but less services rejected—then we'll have less resources to —it costs less resources, really. And so our goal is to do that.

QA staff responded to FFS reforms by appropriating the managerial logic. As evidenced by Jeanne's remarks, FFS reforms blurred the distinction between "services" and "bills," tying revenues to case note production. QA responded to this shift by measuring performance at the street level as a function of income-based metrics. It used risk-reducing metrics to link its core tasks to the management of scarce revenues, recalibrating its own performance as a function of documentation review, service volume, and case note correction. These adaptations promoted accountability, holding workers to common standards and making incarnate the myth of ceremonial inspection.

The social construction of an institutional entrepreneur

This section addresses the question, "How did QA staff endeavor to link the managerial logic to everyday practice?" Neo-institutionalism demonstrates that field transformations have the effect of unsettling the core logics that organizational actors use to rationalize their work roles and objectives (Scott et al., 2000). In the case of New Frontiers, QA staff responded to market inducements and auditing threats by adopting the managerial logic. Here, I examine how Gary fulfilled his managerial charge as QA liaison to Community Club. I argue that he is best understood as an institutional entrepreneur whose job was to translate the managerial logic to street-level workers and secure its faithful reproduction in their everyday routines. Scholarship on institutional entrepreneurship indicates that institutional logics are not self-actualizing but require agents equipped with discursive and technological resources to link them to the habits of organizational life (Dew, 2006). When emergent logics are incompatible with traditional ones, entrepreneurs must find ways to manage contradiction so that new significations can take hold and develop (Lawrence & Suddaby, 2006). At the heart of Gary's entrepreneurial project was the goal of bringing Community Club workers' activities into compliance with billing standards and ensuring the accurate and efficient propagation of case notes, or bills. However the managerial logic he sought to impart clashed with the community logic of the clubhouse, which workers had long employed to order their therapeutic identities and objectives. Logic incompatibility shaped the destructive character of Gary's entrepreneurial project.

Community Club workers were committed to the therapeutic milieu as a mental health practice approach that aligned strongly with their professional obligations, as they understood them. Although workers provided a range of discrete services at the center, such as individual case management, supported employment, and psychosocial rehabilitation (PSR) groups, there were numerous practice sites where they endeavored to facilitate interactions that operationalized the community logic of the clubhouse. The community logic advanced the idea that mental health services were most effective when workers collaborated with members to secure a space for socialization that was flexible and that maximized participation and self-determination. Members ran a café on the first floor where they could mix informally. Members could initiate and request informal groups, such as men's group or spirituality group, that did not directly conform to the medical model, but filled important areas of need in their lives. Around a pool table in the lounge on the second floor, workers used unstructured group formats to facilitate casual discussions among members about topics such as affordable housing or drinking and drugging. Members and workers collaborated to run a meal program, which served food twice a day. In each of these spaces, workers operationalized the milieu.

When I spoke to members, they consistently described the flexible and easygoing nature of Community Club as the programming feature they valued most, noting that it provided a place where others took an active interest in their lives, and where they could work on their treatment objectives at their own pace. One member, Gina, reported, "when you don't have it anywhere else in your life, I can't tell you how important it is to have a door that's open to you. You don't have to prove yourself here, you can just walk in." Noting the stigma and social isolation that many members experienced in normative settings, she continued, "there's nowhere else you can just go to collect yourself." In the many contested exchanges that I observed among Gary and Community Club workers, no subject was more vehemently quarreled over than the milieu. Here, the managerial logic clashed sharply with the community logic of the clubhouse. In an interview, Gary explained what he believed FFS reforms meant for how services should be delivered at Community Club.

> We used to provide something that was called "milieu," which was we'd create a safe place and informal community to just socialize and "engage," I think, is a good word. And, milieu is not seen as a viable PSR or [community support] service in the current model. That creates a little bit of a grey and also creates a lot of frustration for staff. Members informally hanging out, playing pool with a staff present really isn't quote-unquote billable, although a strong rationale of why that can be helpful can be made.

Gary employed the managerial logic to highlight a disjuncture between the community logic of the clubhouse and the demands of Rule 132. The clubhouse aimed to produce what he described as an "all-inclusive safe place to heal, to grow, to have camaraderie, peer support." FFS reforms, in contrast emphasized standardization and compliance, and were "much more prescriptive." This distinction was visible in the framework that FFS guidelines established for onsite group services. Per Rule 132, PSR services should use evidence-based curriculums that objectified stages of intervention. PSR group services should have a discrete beginning and end, target specific skill deficits, and be time limited in nature. These prescriptions conflicted with the milieu, where members were free to come and go as they saw fit and where participation was not bounded by time constraints or medical necessity. Gary used the managerial logic to rationalize objectification and monitoring, operations that promoted compliance with Rule 132, made workers' practices more accountable, and stimulated efficiency.

For a group service to be "quote" billable, street-level workers were required to generate a separate case note for each member that participated in that group. PSR standards required workers to provide a narrative of the group process, including the topic of discussion and targeted skills, along with a billable action verb and supporting sentence for every 15 minutes of service. Compliance standards required case notes to reflect the progress a member made during the group interval, along with a plan for continued services. These elements comprised what providers referred to as the golden chain of medical necessity.

Contests over case note production emerged as a high-stakes proxy war in an uneven struggle to define the core logics and operations of community-based programming. Gary had two resources at his disposal for recoupling the ceremony of inspection to Community Club practices: case note review and the blended hourly rate. Each of these technologies derived its legitimacy from field transformations. Gary used case note review to cull workers' reports and monitor them for compliance with billing standards. With great frequency, Community Club workers received notices from Gary, indicating that their case notes had been rejected from the database and required correction. I reviewed many of these notices and observed that Gary commonly flagged errors because workers' case notes too closely reproduced the community logic of milieu programming. In one such group note, a worker named Brit wrote:

> Facilitated a group activity to encourage socialization as a means to practicing and acquiring skills. Encouraged members to engage and socialize. Used verbal and nonverbal cues to prompt members to practice and acquire skills in communication, interpersonal effectiveness, sportsmanship, and conflict resolution. Modeled and coached members in these skills. Reminded members to be respectful. Praised members when they used skills.

In this note, which described an informal group session conducted around the pool table in the lounge, Brit provided numerous elements that fulfilled accountability demands. Most notably, she used an action verb for every fifteen minutes of service. By using verbs like "facilitated," "encouraged," and "modeled," Brit aligned her report with external standards. Action verbs received special attention in the FFS system. Since they signified the fit between therapeutic activities and practice standards, the Collaborative monitored them with added scrutiny when it audited documentation. Brit's case note demonstrates how a worker could use stock verbs to diminish the likelihood that her note would be flagged and rejected by QA staff. In this sense, her note might be interpreted as a simulacrum not of her practice in the milieu, but of Rule 132 itself. Here, however, Gary rejected Brit's note because "milieu services are not billable.... reads like it was an unstructured games session." Presumably, phrases such as "encourage socialization" and "sportsmanship" did not jibe with fee-for-service standards and might raise red flags in an audit.

Gary's case note reviews became a source of constant strain for street-level workers, intensifying their daily hassles, ratcheting up the most tedious aspect of their job, and producing mounting uncertainty over the central meanings of center-based mental health practice. In one managers meeting, Katherine, the leader of the team that provided onsite group services, confronted Gary, declaring that workers who provided outreach case management services to members in offsite locations often wrote notes that were highly unstructured, yet they were not reviewed with the same level of scrutiny that Gary applied to onsite PSR group notes. She stated:

> You know, if I go out into the community and I do a [community support note], I don't get the same pressure as I do—I can write, I swear to god, I feel like I can write such a looser note, less intensity. And, I'm very confused by it.

Gary affirmed her perception of inequity, noting that Rule 132 privileged services delivered in offsite locations and applied a stricter standard to onsite group services, stating "it's a mixed message." Later, he professed, "my biggest concern—Paul's groups are starting to look a little too milieu, or talking too much about playing pool versus building skills." Katherine became exasperated, insisting that, if workers applied the standards that Gary expected from group notes to their practices, routinization would prevent them from responding to members' emergent needs or forming therapeutic relationships as a basis for intervention. Informality and flexibility, workers argued, rationally ordered their therapeutic approach and provided footing to engage members whose very condition was marked by inconsistency and disorganization. Evincing goal displacement, where documentation production becomes more central to organizational functioning than the quality of services (Lipsky, 1980, p. 45), Gary responded to Katherine by suggesting that workers could simply use templates to generate case notes, ensuring that their notes complied with billing standards. Katherine protested:

> Okay, great, they've got their frickin' long notes and we're measuring progress, but it's bull shit. I'm just gonna put it out there. That's crazy. That is crazy. I mean, so, here's Paul, bless his heart, he's telling an honest note about an honest member that's measuring honest progress, and I'm gonna go back and tell him, "here, put in your bull shit." I mean, that's crazy!

Elsewhere, scholars have demonstrated how state regulations produce a tension that plays out in case note writing between the perspectival knowledge workers generate about clients and demands for objective reporting (Floersch, 2000; Hardesty, 2015). I observed many instances where workers interacted with members in ways that would raise red flags if case notes reflected them accurately. In one example, a member with bipolar disorder and thought disorganization, named Maria, became lethargic for a few weeks after she began taking a new medication that greatly reduced her energy level and attention span. Maria came to the center many times per week for about 2 weeks, avoiding staff, sitting out groups, and sometimes sparking conflict with other members. Workers used team meetings to report their familiarity with this pattern and strategize ways to engage her tactfully for a time. They observed that when they pushed too hard she had a history of detaching from services, decompensating, and substituting hard drugs for her prescriptions. Although workers successfully kept Maria engaged with the center during this tenuous period, they had difficulty summoning verbs that obtained the active force of billing standards. I observed Community Club workers endeavor daily to cultivate a milieu that could flexibly engage hard-to-reach people who struggled to socialize, fit in, stay on track, or derive a sense of connectedness from their interactions (Ware, Hopper, Tugenberg, Dickey, & Fisher, 2007). When workers' reports of these exchanges failed to demonstrate objective progress, or seemed too unstructured or too extemporaneous—in a phrase, when they started to look "too milieu"—their documentation produced reprisal from QA staff. Gary used the technology of case note review not only to flag and reject notes in the billing system, but to sanction Community Club workers who used the community logic of the clubhouse. Enacting power through managerial discipline, he operated as an institutional entrepreneur, re-centering the managerial logic and clearing the ground of a contradictory logic.

Gary had a second resource at his disposal for advancing his entrepreneurial project. The blended hourly rate, the productivity metric that measured street-level workers' progress toward monthly billing targets, combined with case note review to place enormous pressure on workers' daily routines. If workers failed to meet productivity benchmarks for two consecutive months, they were issued a warning. After 3 months, they were placed on probation. And, after that, they could be fired for failing to make productivity. Productivity pressures were especially onerous for workers who provided onsite group services. Calculations assumed an average group size of between six to eight members. This meant that a worker providing a center-based group service had to generate about seven case notes to document an hour of service. By comparison, when case managers provided an hour of service to an individual, they wrote a single case note for it. When Ethan, the director of Community Club, raised the concern that center-based workers were responsible for substantially more notes than community support workers, and that QA had not accounted for this in their productivity metrics, he was told that blended hourly rates would not be rebalanced to account for note writing. This managerial omission reproduced a structural gap in FFS payments, which only reimbursed providers for time spent with a client, not for time spent documenting case notes.

Productivity pressures disproportionately penalized workers who used the community logic of the clubhouse to rationalize their activities and goals. Over a 10-month period, Ethan calculated productivity averages across the three treatment teams. The two community support teams that operated out of the center and provided case management services offsite averaged 102% and 99.5% of full productivity, almost always receiving monthly bonuses for meeting full targets. The center-based team that provided mostly onsite group services averaged 81% productivity in the same period. These productivity differentials dramatically contrasted with the teams' revenue generation over the same period. Workers on the two community support teams generated $5,416 and $5,101, per month, per staff, while the center-based team generated $5,405. Ethan fought vigorously with front office management to rebalance productivity requirements for the center-based group workers but was consistently thwarted. In the 3 months between June and August 2010, five of six center-based team workers failed to meet productivity requirements. In total, one half of the team was issued written warnings for their performance in this period. In every instance that I observed, when sanctions were applied, they were levied against workers for failing to meet blended hourly rate targets, not for providing poor quality of service.

Street-level effects

This section addresses the question, "How did the managerial logic interact with the community logic of the clubhouse?" Research on institutional logics suggests that multiplicity combines with work conditions to produce variable outcomes at different levels of an organization (Binder, 2007). Because street-level workers experience the conditions of work differently than managers, and pursue competing aims in their daily activities, we would expect them to metabolize transformations in the organizational field differently, and for their logic reworkings to assume contrasting forms.

Lipsky (1980) describes *street-level practice* as "alienated work" (p. 79). Street-level workers do not control the raw materials, outcomes, or pace of their work and tend to work only on segments of the product of their work. Street-level workers also do not tend to control the means or metrics by which their performance is evaluated. These conditions of alienation combine with resource scarcity, pressing demands, and goal ambiguity to structure the particular tones of dissatisfaction and burnout workers experience as a course of doing their jobs, compelling them to adopt a range of coping strategies, such as excessive absenteeism, high turnover, disgruntlement, and work-arounds, all of which conspire to shape the informal composition of agency life, and ultimately the quality of care individuals receive from human service organizations. Here, I will show how Gary's entrepreneurial project combined with the conditions of work to disrupt and remake the community logic of the clubhouse.

From the perspective of street-level workers, new managerialism advanced a series of euphemisms that elided its punitive and destructive effects. Workers referred to the Collaborative ironically. Valued at more than $10 million annually, workers viewed its contract with the state as extractive and felt its effects on everyday practice were not collaborative at all, but punitive. Workers joked about ticklers, evocative of gentle and pleasurable touch, which filled their online accounts with a daily barrage of reminders, cueing a seemingly endless stream of deadlines with which they struggled to keep pace. New Frontiers named its database "Harmony," a moniker that workers chided. Harmony was well known for frequently crashing and randomly kicking workers off when they took hours of paperwork home each week on top of their 40 hours. Workers referred to the standardized tool they were required to administer at intake as "The Green Wall," comparing it to the famous Green Monster at Fenway Park, notorious as a formidable barrier to would-be hitters.

Through these tactics, workers engaged in a kind of low-level semiotic resistance, carving out meanings that subverted the managerial logic while remaining undetectable to QA. For a time, street-level workers' emergent logic wrested back some autonomy from management, if only in the form of gallows humor and innuendo. Workers' counterlogic creatively made visible what the managerial logic seemed to obscure, that is, the lived experience of frontline work, with its sundry hassles and rife contradictions. Sometimes workers experimented with trying on the negative. After a team meeting in which Paul reported that he had fallen behind his productivity targets a few months in a row, another worker, named Charlie, encouraged him to approach members in the milieu with his "billing cap on." However, mostly, workers recast the logic of practice as something they needed to smuggle in and keep hidden from management.

Workers viewed the community logic of the clubhouse as something that was unspeakable. A group worker, named Angelo, described the tactic he used to document onsite services. Riffing on the famous Las Vegas ad campaign, he noted, "what happens in the milieu stays in the milieu." While joking in a meeting about how he approached documentation, Charlie referenced the movie *Fight Club*, about an underground, quasi-criminal sect, noting, "the first rule of the milieu is: you don't talk about the milieu." Angelo's and Charlie's remarks attested to a strategy workers commonly deployed to escape QA's watchful gaze and the discipline it could levy against them. The technologies of case note review and productivity measurement could only sanction what workers wrote down. They were less able to monitor what workers actually did. As the tower of QA stretched upward to the regulatory field to secure legitimacy, workers retreated furtively into its long shadows, seeking to hide the milieu from view.

In the year that I conducted fieldwork, workers continued to cultivate the milieu, conducting center-wide pool tournaments, holding cookouts and corn hole competitions on the center's rooftop deck, designating Wednesday nights as Bingo Night, and working alongside members twice a day to maintain the member-led meal program, which provided a lifeline to many members who were homeless and food insecure. Workers used the community logic of the clubhouse to emphasize membership, social connection, collaboration, and self-determination. Meanwhile, they billed unstructured and informal group services under headings such as Conflict Negotiation, Community Integration, and Life Skills, using canned verb phrases in their notes and stressing concrete skill development. Workers shared among themselves strategies for gerrymandering documentation to produce what one worker dubbed a "Gary friendly" case note. Such a report over-emphasized objectification and minimized perspectival knowledge. I asked Ethan how he made sense of the gamesmanship paperwork demands seemed to require of workers. He noted:

> I still think it's the spirit of the law, but it's not the intent of the funding. I don't think it's wrong enough to question them on fraud. They really are providing the treatment, the skill-building that is necessary. But, it becomes very difficult to defend that under a hardcore—even with like Gary…. Because of the tremendous pressure that people are under and all the stuff that goes on here, it's not a clean process. It doesn't sit well with people who want things in nice neat boxes, and "you participate in this room for the next 45 minutes." I mean, our world just doesn't operate that way. So, that, I think, will be what really brings this place to a halt, is when somebody gets too afraid of the potential for failing an audit.

Ethan's comments highlight a contest that took place between QA staff and street-level workers in the struggle to define the core logics and operations of center-based group services. The managerial logic presumed "nice neat boxes," predictable routines, and "a clean process." The "world" workers inhabited "just doesn't operate that way." Street-level workers experienced a double onus. On the one hand, they were challenged to reach members who were difficult to serve and socially isolated. On the other, they were pressed to constantly document and reify their routines in the form of viable documentation. Instead of experiencing QA as an ally in this pursuit, that is, as an agent that could use its resources to decouple monitoring from practice, workers experienced recoupling as a kind of institutional bad faith that commodified their actions and unmoored the resources of informality and flexibility that stabilized and ordered their work. When the managerial and community logics came into contact, workers could not resolve multiplicity in practice. Ongoing antagonism between these logics produced incommensurability, corroding the foundation of clubhouse programming.

Turmoil became the dominant feature of life on the front lines. I observed street-level workers succumb to resource scarcity and competing demands, acting out many of the hallmarks of street-level behavior. Sensing profound burnout and frustration among center-based workers, Katherine routinely encouraged her team to take "mental health days." She viewed regular absenteeism as a survival strategy for workers to maintain a sound mind on the job. Although it provided a release valve for fatigue, frequent absenteeism compromised the tenability of the milieu and indirectly compounded workers' troubles. When workers had to cover for one another's absence, they borrowed against the time they were supposed to protect for completing paperwork each day. Per blended hourly rate calculations, workers were supposed to spend about 5 hours of an average workday providing direct services and use the remaining 3 hours for documentation. When workers covered for a coworker's absence by providing an extra hour of group service, they not only added that hour to their billing regimen, but lost it against their documentation time. Workers also struggled to keep their doors shut to members, often foregoing billing duties to respond to members unanticipated needs. When the multiplicity of the milieu failed to reproduce management's "neat boxes," workers bore the brunt of this contradiction. I observed workers routinely fall behind in their billing during the average workday, then report taking home about 10 hours of billing each week just to keep pace with their blended hourly rates. These challenges added up to a perverse outcome. Although failing to achieve their productivity targets, workers often left stacks of unprocessed group services on their desk at the end of the month, unremunerated by the state and unaccounted for in QA's measurements.

Daily turmoil on the front lines did not register on QA's radar unless low productivity metrics triggered warnings and sanctions. Meanwhile, informal patterns of practice affected the quality of services workers provided. The milieu was frequently understaffed and became chaotic when too few workers were on the floor to moderate interactions. In the year that I was in the field, the dilemmas of work produced high turnover. I was told in interviews how departing workers valued their interactions with members but couldn't justify the demands paperwork pressures placed on their health and personal time. Turnover compounded the problems associated with absenteeism, as vacant positions went unfulfilled for months at a time while New Frontiers struggled to manage the persistent threat of austerity cuts. Research demonstrates that community mental health workers commonly experience futility as core dimension of their jobs (Brodwin, 2010, 2012). However, where other studies have looked to the intractability of serious mental illness as a site of ethical conflict for workers who seek to promote treatment progress, my observations suggest that futility was most often mediated by the unyielding pressures of case note writing, in which workers were unable to resolve the contradictions they encountered between the managerial and community logics.

Postscript to community club: The future of center-based mental health services

Increasingly, interactions between Community Club workers and QA staff were marked by deep conflict and philosophical misalignment over the central logics and operations of community mental health services. These contests produced a sense of futility among street-level workers and a feeling that their autonomy to shape services to members' needs was radically curtailed by management's response to FFS reforms. Workers openly doubted whether Community Club itself was sustainable, further dampening morale and heightening their sense of fatalism about their work. In perhaps his most strident statement about the clubhouse milieu, Gary advanced the critique that centers themselves indirectly stigmatized members:

> In a way, going to a clubhouse is stigmatizing. In a way, it's going to the place where people with mental health [sic] get services. In a way, it's pulling people away from their true lives in the community amongst colleagues, peers, people that they would—the normal, average community. It's also a little bit skewed. There's a higher prevalence of odd behaviors in an area that's concentrated with people with mental illness, versus the learning that would occur if you're in a natural setting.... The need for community, I think, is something we all have, but to default to clubhouse, I believe, is a disservice.

In a setting characterized by heterogeneity, competing institutional logics necessarily interact. Because workers must adjust to internal tensions, which derive from the conflictive relationships among external institutions, they have partial "autonomy" to rework institutional logics as they negotiate local contexts of action (Friedland & Alford, 1991, p. 255). Here, we see evidence of logic drift and cooptation, as the managerial logic interpenetrated the community logic. To advance his entrepreneurial project Gary invoked an opposition between the "normal, average community" and that of the clubhouse, which was "skewed" because it is comprised predominantly people with serious mental illness. Gary's refashioned community logic functioned as a wedge against that of the clubhouse. Where normative community was reconstructed as "true," the community logic of the clubhouse was taken to be "stigmatizing," even counterfeit. Gary's entrepreneurial reconstruction of the community logic syncopated with field conditions as outlined in Rule 132. Both emphasized treatment in so-called natural settings, that is, "a setting where an individual who has not been diagnosed with a mental illness typically spends time" (59 Ill. Adm. Code 132). Per Rule 132, group services include only those activities that "facilitate independent living and adaptation, problem solving and coping skills development." Gary used the standards of treatment in natural settings and promotion of independence to discredit the community logic of the clubhouse, arguing that it was not a viable service, but precisely the opposite, a "disservice."

Community Club workers disputed the idea that they were "pulling people away" away from community, arguing that members who came to the center for programing relied on it as a resource to combat the social isolation they faced because of stigma in the broader society. Ethan described how he believed the therapeutic milieu instilled in members a sense that they mattered and belonged, creating a foundation they could draw from in their recovery:

> I certainly don't think that we've been disengaging people or giving them a false sense of community. I think that those individuals that come here have probably not had a strong sense of community. And what's attractive about this place is that it is here. And, yes, it's an instant community. Why shouldn't it be? Because that's how you learn what it's like. And even when people come here, it's not like they just walk in here and are friends with everyone. It's fringe. It's like any of us when we go into a strange environment. You pick and choose and then you learn the skills of how to build relationships, how to build community.

Under the combined pressures of field transformations and the conditions of work, the community logic of practice emerged as a site of division between QA staff and street-level workers. Despite informal opportunities for pushback, workers increasingly lost ground in the battle for legitimacy. In an interview, Jeanne forecasted what she took to be the future of center-based community mental health services:

> I think we're going to see center-based [services] less funded. They're going to devalue the center-based programs over time. You can already see; they've made that move. They've tried to make PSR a very specific reason why someone's there. I think they'll continue to drill down on that and move that away. I don't think they'll ever get rid of center-based, because I think there's too many people out there that see the value of it. But, I think it will continue to be decreased.

When I began fieldwork for this study, Community Club was the last remaining program of its kind in Chicago. The many drop-in centers and social programs that once peppered the community mental health service landscape had either shut down or converted to PSR programs that provided structured group services and were time bounded, curriculum-based, and focused on concrete skills deficits. In 2016, New Frontiers closed the building in which Community Club had operated since the early 1970s. The center was moved to a new, modern location that did not have a kitchen, lounge, pool table, or rooftop deck. Today, like all other PSR programs in the city, Community Club members are only allowed in the building if they have structured groups to attend that day and are limited in the amount of time they can spend in the building when they are not in groups. This transition brought to completion a transformation of community-based services that began in 2004 when Illinois commenced the System Restructuring Initiative. In place of the therapeutic milieu, with its inherent messiness, unpredictability, and sociality the center now operates, one might imagine, as a more orderly, compliant, efficient, and productive program.

Discussion

Recent organizational theory builds on Meyer and Rowan's (1977) model of decoupled organizations to suggest that, under certain conditions, human service organizations can harbor multiple institutional logics, without engendering deep rifts, by compartmentalizing their business and therapeutic functions (Garrow & Hasenfeld, 2012). Decoupling provides heterogeneous organizations with a source of stability and insulates subunits from the spread of contradiction (Binder, 2007). If organizations have a structural incentive to decouple their monitoring and service operations, and if they can harness ceremonial inspection to isolate the pernicious effects of field disruption, findings from this study raise the question, "what happened in the relationship of New Frontiers to the organizational field to upset this outcome, such that surveillance obtained added force and contradiction became a core feature of organizational life?" Besharov and Smith (2014) provide an entry point into this analysis. *Low compatibility* describes the extent to which the managerial logic of QA and community logic of the clubhouse implied inconsistent and opposing actions. The managerial logic emphasized performance measurement, standardization, and accountability. The community logic of the clubhouse, in contrast, emphasized membership, social connection, collaboration, and self-determination. *High centrality* describes the extent to which competing institutional demands permeate work activities that are essential to organizational survival. I will argue that precipitating jolts in the field had the effect of recentering the managerial logic and decentering the community logic of the clubhouse. Besharov and Smith argue that a highly contested organization is defined by low compatibility and high centrality, where actors strenuously contend the core meanings, identities, and operations of organizational life.

The value of the institutional logics perspective for this analysis is twofold. First, it directs analytic attention to the organizational field, offering a set of tools for theorizing how changing field structures linked to everyday practice. The shift from grants-in-aid to FFS funding reconstituted the regulatory environment and therefore the conditions of legitimacy and the terms for securing organizational resources. QA's appropriation of the managerial logic was inseparable from the political and policy environment that targeted community mental health services for retrenchment, combining demands for accountability with deep austerity measures. Billing pressures required New Frontiers to procure a daunting sum of case notes that reflected conformity to external standards, and auditing innovations attached financial penalties to noncompliance. Second, the institutional logics perspective examines the relationship between the field and the technologies that organizations use to anchor meanings to practice. In response to FFS reforms, QA staff introduced income-based metrics to monitor workers' practices as a function of billing, and risk-reducing metrics to measure its own performance as a function of rote surveillance tasks. The blended hourly rate and case note review combined with ancillary technologies of database ticklers, dashboard tools, and verb charts to tightly couple organizational incentives to case note production. This article not only describes how QA staff recoupled the myth of ceremonial inspection to everyday practice (Hallet, 2010), it builds a framework for identifying the core properties of reform that produced the most notable effects. By tying public resources and sanctions to organizational compliance and performance, FFS reforms reconstructed case notes as bills and focused the full force of inspection on them.

Although this article has much to say about changing QA logics and operations, the QA role obtained its influence at the site of contact with street-level practice. I use the construct of institutional entrepreneurship to analyze the creative and destructive qualities of Gary's interactions with street-level workers. Actor-centered models of institutional entrepreneurship suggest that logics are not self-executing but require active agents to animate them in organizations and bring them to bear on everyday conduct. Process-centered models emphasize the structural location of institutional entrepreneurs, examining how precipitating jolts in the field reconstruct actors as agentive within specific historical limits. A structural analysis of institutional entrepreneurship seeks to understand how the managerial logic was activated within a context of competing rationalities. Findings suggest that institutional entrepreneurship is indivisible from the field conditions that enabled it to act upon contending logics. Power, in this sense, is not absolute or endemic to actors but is expressed through the forms of knowledge and techniques of action that institutions make possible (Foucault, 1982). Gary's power to shape street-level workers' conduct was circumscribed by his direct relationship to field transformations and articulated through the disciplinary techniques it afforded him to codify and monitor workers' everyday transactions with members. FFS reforms conversely weakened workers' relationship to the field. Previous studies have demonstrated the ascendance of new managerialism over traditional modes of professionalism as the dominant discursive-technological framework in human services (Dunn & Jones, 2010; Scott et al., 2000). Here, field transformation had the effect of unsettling workers' autonomy to determine the logic of practice and restructured their diminished, oftentimes futile, opportunities for resistance. When workers conjured professional tenets of member self-determination and collaborative programming in their efforts to legitimate the community logic of the clubhouse, their appeals to QA at best fell on deaf ears, at worst were discredited. Hallet's (2010) discussion of turmoil provides a framework for explaining how workers' loss of flexibility and autonomy translated into epistemic distress, undermining the rationality they use to order their work in the face of endemic uncertainty and unpredictability. Community Club workers experienced mounting insecurity and chaos as an enduring effect of new managerial reform.

Theorizing Gary as an institutional entrepreneur transforms the conventional image of QA staff. Rather than positing it as the checkpoint within a mental health organization whose job it is to ensure quality, QA staff is reinterpreted as a peddler of the managerial logic and a disciplinary instrument for reconfiguring an incompatible practice logic. Through Gary's translative and technical project, institutional entrepreneurialism acquired a double meaning, describing at once the enterprising nature of his work and its resonance with the market. The notion that markets act with increasing force on traditional sites of democratic participation and transform them in ways that redistribute voice and opportunity is not new (Brown, 2015). Anthropologists have theorized how workplaces and public institutions are increasingly shaped by accountability practices, or audit cultures, that may be detrimental to the people they are intended to serve (Strathern, 2000). A growing literature examines how new public management intersects with multiple human service sectors, such as public education, child welfare, and work programs, producing damaging consequences and redefining the relationship between citizens, government, and markets (Courtney, Needell, & Wulczyn, 2004; Price, 2003; Soss, Fording, & Schram, 2011). But, the idea of a hegemonic meta-narrative, is somewhat at odds with the heterogeneity and struggle that I observed at Community Club. In the case of Community Club, the managerial logic had to act upon the already established community logic of the clubhouse, which generated an unmooring of the community logic and its transformation.

To preserve the milieu Community Club workers engaged in tactics to hide it from Gary's view. This elision caused them to reflect on the legitimacy of their work, openly wondering, for example, whether low-level documentation gamesmanship, a standard practice of street-level workers (Fording, Schram, & Soss, 2006), was fraudulent or merely a way to rationalize dimensions of the milieu within the managerial logic of QA. Workers' inability to secure legitimacy seemed to impinge on their capacity to derive a sense of achievement from their work, or a feeling that their community logic resonated with the central goals of the agency. Gary's technical intercessions functioned as a kind of self-fulfilling prophecy. His constant surveillance and sanctioning of workers' case notes combined with the conditions of work to produce a workspace where the milieu appeared at times chaotic and unmanageable. Although the idea that such a place could be "stigmatizing" may have had face validity, Gary's argument ignored the obvious stigma that members encountered as a fact of life in the so-called "normal, average community" and denied their deep attachment to the center, expressed in one member's statement of "how important it is to have a door that's open to you." Members stated that they obtained a sense of belongingness at Community Club. This end, however, clashed with the community logic of Gary, who argued, "to default to clubhouse, I believe, is a disservice."

Gary's refashioned community logic reflected not only a trend toward instrumentality, which other scholars of the community logic have noted (Lounsbury, 2005), but indicated a reliance on technical strategies and programs for its advancement. Rose (1999) cautions against a nostalgic interpretation of lost community, which figures as a recurring trope of the community logic. Instead, he investigates how power shapes the conditions of possibility for generating certain kinds of knowledge and truth, conferring legitimacy on those who possess the means to calibrate and map it. Community, in this sense, is not a previous space of freedom that is colonized and controlled by regulatory actors, but constitutes an assemblage of discourses, knowledges, programs, and techniques that are instituted through historically specific processes as a sector for government. This zone of governance derives its efficacy, in part, from its ability to appear natural and self-evident on its face, while requiring its protagonists to constantly reinterpret and reconstruct it as pre- or nonpolitical. It is tempting to see the battle between Gary and Community Club workers as a contest over the presence or absence of community. Certainly, when I talked to workers and members, this was their interpretation of the struggle. The potential of losing the center, which loomed in the background of just about everything workers did, occurred to them as a fundamental loss of community itself. Although this experience is important to observe, I will argue that it is more accurate and analytically useful to say that the community logic was not lost or extinguished, but rather remade at its point of contact with the managerial logic. A critical genealogy of the community logic traces the vectors of change that enable new actors—in other words, entrepreneurs of community—to emerge, equipping them with novel techniques of power and legitimacy.

The struggle I observed was waged over a community logic that was first forged under the social, political, and economic conditions of the Great Society, which emphasized empowerment and local control (O'Connor, 2002). The clubhouse took as its point of departure the idea that many people with serious mental illness face social isolation as a fact of life (Beard et al., 1982). Community Club workers deployed the community logic to argue that a mental health center could function as an "instant community" for such individuals, where members would have access to resources with which to "build community." The idea that a center-based therapeutic community could be "fringe" was not lost on workers but rather informed their efforts to cultivate opportunities for members to practice healthy ways of connecting and negotiating conflicts in the milieu (Smith & Spitzmueller, 2016).

Gary's entrepreneurial project to redefine and re-operationalize the community logic shares a family resemblance with shifts in the community logic that scholars have observed in other social welfare sectors (Fairbanks, 2008; McDonald & Marston, 2002). Policy debates in the 1990s reconstructed community as a third sector, or third space, outside of markets and government (Oldenburg, 1989). Cafes, parks, and libraries—in other words, the locations targeted by community support outreach services—were theorized as productive sites of for civil society and civic engagement that reinforced bonds of affinity and a sense of place. Rose (1999) asserts that the logic of community advanced by third-way proponents involves a double movement that autonomizes and responsibilizes individuals in relation to others. Although somewhat awkwardly phrased, Rose's use of the verb form highlights the capacity of governance to "act upon action" (p. 4). We see evidence of this kind of agency in the community logic Gary employs, which autonomizes and responsibilizes individuals with serious mental illness with respect to community. Reinforced by transformations in the organizational field that syncopated with neoliberal political-economic shifts, members who once had a right to a center that offered them social connection and belonging were newly charged with exercising community in natural settings, where individuals who have not been diagnosed with a mental illness typically spend time, and where such people demonstrate independent living, adaptation, problem solving, and social skills. Rose claims "what is perhaps novel is the attention paid to citizens as autonomous individuals who must actively construct a life through practical choices they make about their conduct, and who must bear individual responsibility for the nature and consequences of those choices" (p. 190).

Although the community logic of the third way has important implications for all citizens of advanced liberal societies, it may have the greatest bearing on those who are most marginalized and for whom the responsibility that comes with autonomy is most difficult to shoulder alone. This article considers the consequences of this shift for people with serious mental illness, whose very condition is defined by their struggle to fit within the contours and norms of mainstream society, and for whom a center that recognizes and embraces their differences may be their only lifeline to feelings of belongingness and connection.

Limitations

This study has limitations that are important to consider. Because Medicaid plans differ by state, the specific pathways of reform pursued by Illinois may vary in other state contexts. This article examines how actors in one community mental health organization negotiated changes in the field. The QA strategies, logic reworkings, and street-level contestations that I observed do not generalize to a population in the way that a representative sample might. The goal of an ethnography is to generate theory about how organizations behave, making visible the links between the conditions and products of practice. To the extent that street-level workers face similar conditions in other settings, one might expect to find similar patterns of practice emerge. In a study of this kind, there is always the possibility of bias. I made every effort to limit bias by collecting data at multiple levels of practice and building theory iteratively, generating and checking my hypotheses through sustained fieldwork.

Implications

Against an evolving backdrop of perceived failures in the public mental health system, policy makers have long advanced the goal of improving service effectiveness (Morrissey & Goldman, 1984). Increasingly, they frame the project of improving quality as a problem that calls for administrative solutions (Ganju, 2006). Organizational studies provide important lessons for community mental health scholars, demonstrating that oftentimes the most important dimensions of practice are unaccounted for by performance measurement (Price, 2003; Van Slyke, 2003). As a new generation of managed care reforms overhauls FFS models with technologies of care coordination, health information systems, and value-based payments (Druss & Mauer, 2010; McDonald et al., 2007), a full account of the impact of these reforms will require scholars to investigate what happens to field transformations as they work their way through organizations and touch down at the street level. This study points to the value of examining community mental health practice not as an event that can be isolated and controlled, but as a real-time unfolding of complex interactions between the extrinsic conditions of public policy and the intrinsic conditions of work.

It is worth stating the obvious: the keyword "community" is at the heart of the community mental health movement. And, though modes of knowledge and technologies of care, not to mention methods of payment and administration, have changed over time, this keyword has remained stable. This article demonstrates that the community and managerial logics are intimately linked and co-productive in sites of organizational practice. It is my hope that this article invites scholars of human services to reopen the discussion of what is meant by community, where is it located, how it acts upon people, even governs them, and who has a right to define it. Without critical inquiry into these questions, certain forms of voice, action, and identity may be at risk of losing legitimacy without ever having had their day in court. For the members of Community Club who lost their center, or at least the communal aspects of it that they cherished most, and for those workers who struggled tirelessly to guard the milieu against a shelling of discursive and technological strikes, this inquiry is perhaps too late. But, if this article achieves its objective, I hope it describes well the battle lines over which this struggle was waged, invites other scholars to examine sites where the community logic is in play or in trouble, and generates fresh arguments about how we define community and strive for it on behalf of those who are most socially vulnerable.

References

Barley, S. R., & Kunda, G. (2001). Bringing work back in. *Organization Science, 12*(1), 76–95. doi:10.1287/orsc.12.1.76.10122

Battilana, J., & D'aunno, T. (2009). Institutional work and the paradox of embedded agency. In T. B. Lawrence, R. L. Suddaby, & L. Bernard (Eds.), *Institutional work: Actors and agency in institutional studies of organizations* (pp. 31–58). Cambridge, England: Cambridge University Press.

Beard, J. H., Propst, R. N., & Malamud, T. J. (1982). The fountain house model of psychiatric rehabilitation. *Psychosocial Rehabilitation Journal, 5*(1), 47–53.

Besharov, M. L., & Smith, W. K. (2014). Multiple institutional logics in organizations: Explaining their varied nature and implications. *Academy of Management Review, 39*(3), 364–381. doi:10.5465/amr.2011.0431

Binder, A. (2007). For love and money: organizations' creative responses to multiple environmental logics. *Theory and Society, 36*(6), 547–571.

Blagojevich, R. (2004). *Budget Address: 80th Legislative Day, February 18, 2004.* Springfield, IL: State of Illinois.

Booher-Jennings, J. (2005). Below the bubble: "Educational triage" and the Texas accountability system. *American Educational Research Journal, 42*(2), 231–268. doi:10.3102/00028312042002231

Bourdieu, P. (1977). *Outline of a theory of practice.* Cambridge, England: Cambridge University Press.

Brodkin, E. Z. (2011). Policy work: Street-level organizations under new managerialism. *Journal of Public Administration Research and Theory, 21*(2), i253–77. doi:10.1093/jopart/muq093

Brodwin, P. (2010). Futility in the practice of community psychiatry. *Medical Anthropology Quarterly, 25*(2), 189–208. doi:10.1111/j.1548-1387.2011.01149.x

Brodwin, P. (2012). *Everyday ethics: Voices from the front line of community psychiatry.* Berkeley, CA: University of California Press.

Bromley, P., & Powell, W. W. (2012). From smoke and mirrors to walking the talk: Decoupling in the contemporary world. *Academy of Management Annals*, 6(1), 483–530. doi:10.1080/19416520.2012.684462

Brown, W. (2015). *Undoing the demos: Neoliberalism's stealth revolution*. Cambridge, MA: MIT Press.

Commission on Accreditation of Rehabilitation Facilities. (2013). *Behavioral health standards manual*. Tucson, AZ: CARF International.

Courtney, M. E., Needell, B., & Wulczyn, F. (2004). Unintended consequences of the push for accountability: The case of national child welfare performance standards. *Children and Youth Services Review*, 26(12), 1141–1154. doi:10.1016/j.childyouth.2004.05.005

Dew, N. (2006). Institutional entrepreneurship: A coasian perspective. *The International Journal of Entrepreneurship and Innovation*, 7(1), 13–22. doi:10.5367/000000006775870442

DiMaggio, P. J. (1988). Interest and agency in institutional theory. In L. G. Zucker (Ed.), *Institutional patterns and organizations: Culture and environment* (pp. 3–22). Cambridge, MA: Bellinger Publishing Company.

DiMaggio, P. J., & Powell, W. W. (1983). The iron cage revisited: Institutional isomorphism and collective rationality in organizational fields. *American Sociological Review*, 48(2), 147–160. doi:10.2307/2095101

Dincin, J. (1975). Psychiatric rehabilitation. *Schizophrenia Bulletin*, 13, 131–147. doi:10.1093/schbul/1.13.131

Druss, B. G., & Mauer, B. J. (2010). Health care reform and care at the behavioral health—primary care interface. *Psychiatric Services*, 1087–1092. doi:10.1176/ps.2010.61.11.1087

Dunn, M. B., & Jones, C. (2010). Institutional logics and institutional pluralism: The contestation of care and science logics in medical education, 1967,äì2005. *Administrative Science Quarterly*, 55(1), 114–149. doi:10.2189/asqu.2010.55.1.114

Emerson, R. M., Fretz, R. I., & Shaw, L. L. (2011). *Writing ethnographic fieldnotes*. Chicago, IL: University of Chicago Press.

Fairbanks, R. P. (2008). The political-economic gradient and the organization of urban space. In R. A. Cnaan & C. Milosfsky (Eds.), *Handbook of community movements and local organizations* (pp. 102–117). New York, NY: Springer.

Farkas, M., Gagne, C., Anthony, W., & Chamberlin, J. (2005). Implementing recovery oriented evidence based programs: Identifying the critical dimensions. *Community Mental Health Journal*, 41(2), 141–158. doi:10.1007/s10597-005-2649-6

Floersch, J. (2000). Reading the case record: The oral and written narratives of social workers. *Social Service Review*, 74(2), 169–192. doi:10.1086/514475

Fording, R., Schram, S. F., & Soss, J. (2006). *The bottom-line, the business model and the bogey: Performance management, sanctions and the brave new world of welfare-to-work in Florida* (UK Center for Poverty Research Discussion Paper Series, DP2006-10).

Foucault, M. (1982). The subject and power. *Critical Inquiry*, 8(4), 777–795. doi:10.1086/448181

Friedland, R., & Alford, R. R. (1991). Bringing society back in: Symbols, practices and institutional contradictions. In W. W. Powell & P. J. Dimaggio (Eds.), *The new institutionalism in organizational analysis* (pp. 232–263). Chicago, IL: University of Chicago Press.

Ganju, V. (2006). Mental health quality and accountability: The role of evidence-based practices and performance measurement. *Administration and Policy in Mental Health and Mental Health Services Research*, 33(6), 659–665. doi:10.1007/s10488-006-0071-1

Garrow, E. E., & Hasenfeld, Y. (2012). Managing conflicting institutional logics: Social service versus market. In B. Gidron and Y. Hasenfeld (Eds.), *Social enterprises: An organizational perspective* (pp. 121–143). London, England: Palgrave Macmillan.

Gillham, B. (2005). *Research interviewing: The range of techniques: A practical guide*. New York, NY: McGraw-Hill International.

Goldman, H. H., Ganju, V., Drake, R. E., Gorman, P., Hogan, M., Hyde, P. S., & Morgan, O. (2001). Policy implications for implementing evidence-based practices. *Psychiatric Services*, 52(12), 1591–1597. doi:10.1176/appi.ps.52.12.1591

Greenwood, R., & Suddaby, R. (2006). Institutional entrepreneurship in mature fields: The big five accounting firms. *Academy of Management Journal*, 49(1), 27–48. doi:10.5465/AMJ.2006.20785498

Greenwood, R., Suddaby, R., & Hinings, C. R. (2002). Theorizing change: The role of professional associations in the transformation of institutionalized fields. *Academy of Management Journal*, 45(1), 58–80. doi:10.2307/3069285

Hallett, T. (2010). The myth incarnate recoupling processes, turmoil, and inhabited institutions in an urban elementary school. *American Sociological Review*, 75(1), 52–74. doi:10.1177/0003122409357044

Hallett, T., & Ventresca, M. J. (2006). Inhabited institutions: Social interactions and organizational forms in Gouldner's patterns of industrial bureaucracy. *Theory and Society*, 35(2), 213–236. doi:10.1007/s11186-006-9003-z

Hardesty, M. (2015). Epistemological binds and ethical dilemmas in frontline child welfare practice. *Social Service Review*, 89(3), 455–498. doi:10.1086/682880

Hardy, C., & Maguire, S. (2008). Institutional entrepreneurship. In R. Greenwood, C. Oliver, R. Suddaby, & K. Sahlin-Andersson (Eds.), *The Sage handbook of organizational institutionalism* (pp. 198–217). Thousand Oaks, CA: SAGE Publications Inc.

Hensmans, M. (2003). Social movement organizations: A metaphor for strategic actors in institutional fields. *Organization Studies*, 24(3), 355–381. doi:10.1177/0170840603024003908

Hermann, R. C. (2007). *Improving mental healthcare: A guide to measurement-based quality improvement*. Washington, DC: American Psychiatric Publishing.

Hoffman, A. J. (1999). Institutional evolution and change: Environmentalism and the US chemical industry. *Academy of Management Journal*, 42(4), 351–371. doi:10.2307/257008

Hopper, K. (2006). Redistribution and its discontents: On the prospects of committed work in public mental health and like settings. *Human Organization*, 65(2), 218–226. doi:10.17730/humo.65.2.cktn1g0c7jj8hj9w

House, F. (1999). Gold award: The wellspring of the clubhouse model for social and vocational adjustment of persons with serious mental illness. *Psychiatric Services*, 50(11), 1473–1476. doi:10.1176/ps.50.11.1473

Jain, S., & Sharma, D. (2013). Institutional logic migration and industry evolution in emerging economies: The case of telephony in India. *Strategic Entrepreneurship Journal*, 7(3), 252–271. doi:10.1002/sej.v7.3

Kettl, D. F. (2000). *The global public management revolution*. Washington, DC: Brookings Institution.

Lamphere, L. (2005). Providers and staff respond to medicaid managed care: the unintended consequences of reform in New Mexico. *Medical Anthropology Quarterly*, 19(1), 3–25. doi:10.1525/maq.2005.19.1.003

Lawrence, T. B., & Suddaby, R. (2006). Institutions and institutional work. In S. R. Clegg, C. Hardy, T. B. N. Lawrence, & R. Walter (Eds.), *The Sage handbook of organization studies* (2nd ed., pp. 215–254). London, England: Sage.

Lipsky, M. (1980). *Street-level bureaucracy: Dilemmas of the individual in public services*. New York, NY: Russell Sage Foundation.

Lounsbury, M. (2005). Institutional variation in the evolution of social movements. In G. F. Davis, D. McAdam, W. R. Scott, & M. N. Zald (Eds.), *Social movements and organizational theory* (pp. 73–95). Cambridge, England: Cambridge University Press.

Maguire, S., Hardy, C., & Lawrence, T. B. (2004). Institutional entrepreneurship in emerging fields: HIV/AIDS treatment advocacy in Canada. *Academy of Management Journal*, 47(5), 657–679. doi:10.2307/20159610

Masso, J. D., Avi-Itzhak, T., & Obler, D. R. (2001). The Clubhouse model: An outcome study on attendance, work attainment and status, and hospitalization recidivism. *Work*, 17(1), 23–30.

McDonald, C., & Marston, G. (2002). Patterns of governance: The curious case of non-profit community services in Australia. *Social Policy and Administration*, 36(1), 376–391. doi:10.1111/1467-9515.t01-1-00260

McDonald, K. M., Sundaram, V., Bravata, D. M., Lewis, R., Lin, N., Kraft, S. A., & Owens, D. K. (2007). *Closing the quality gap: A critical analysis of quality improvement strategies (Volume 7—Care Coordination)*. Rockville, MD: U.S. Department of Health and Human Services, Agency for Healthcare Research and Quality.

McKay, C. E. (2006). Employment transitions for Clubhouse members. *Work*, 26(1), 67–74.

McKay, C. E., & Pelletier, J. R. (2007). Health promotion in Clubhouse programs: Needs, barriers, and current and planned activities. *Psychiatric Rehabilitation Journal*, 31(2), 155–159. doi:10.2975/31.2.2007.155.159

McKenna, A. (2009). Illinois' doomsday budget crisis. *Socialist Worker*. Retrieved from http://socialistworker.org/2009/07/01/illinois-doomsday-budget-crisis

McMillen, J. C., Proctor, E. K., Megivern, D., Striley, C. W., Cabassa, L. J., Munson, M. R., Dickey, B. (2005). Quality of care in the social services: Research agenda and methods. *Social Work Research*, 29(3), 181–191. doi:10.1093/swr/29.3.181

McMillen, J. C., Zayas, L. E., Books, S., & Lee, M. (2008). Quality assurance and improvement practice in mental health agencies: Roles, activities, targets and contributions. *Administration and Policy in Mental Health and Mental Health Services Research*, 35(6), 458–467. doi:10.1007/s10488-008-0189-4

Meyer, J. W., & Rowan, B. (1977). Institutionalized organizations: Formal structure as myth and ceremony. *American Journal of Sociology*, 83(2), 340–363. doi:10.1086/226550

Morrissey, J. P., & Goldman, H. H. (1984). Cycles of reform in the care of the chronically mentally Ill. *Hospital and Community Psychiatry*, 35(8), 785–793.

O'Connor, A. (2002). *Poverty knowledge: Social science, social policy, and the poor in Twentieth-Century U.S. History*. Princeton, NJ: Princeton University Press.

Oldenburg, R. (1989). *The great good place*. New York, NY: Marlowe & Company.

Panzano, P. C., Roth, D., Massatti, R., Crane-Ross, D., Carstens, C. (2005). The Innovation Diffusion and Adoption Research Project (IDARP): Moving from the diffusion of research results to promoting the adoption of evidence-based innovations in the Ohio mental health system. *New Research in Mental Health*, 16, 78–89.

Pierson, P. (2004). *Politics in time: History, institutions, and social analysis*. Princeton, NJ: Princeton University Press.

Powell, W. W., & DiMaggio, P. J. (1991). Introduction. In W. W. Powell & P. J. DiMaggio (Eds.), *The new institutionalism in organizational analysis* (pp. 1–40). Chicago, IL: University of Chicago Press.

Price, D. H. (2003). Outcome-based tyranny: Teaching compliance while testing like a state. *Anthropological Quarterly*, 76(4), 715–730. doi:10.1353/anq.2003.0060

Propst, R. N. (1992). Standards for Clubhouse programs: Why and how they were developed. *Psychosocial Rehabilitation Journal*, 16(2), 25–31. doi:10.1037/h0095711

Quinn, P. (2010, March 10). *Fiscal year 2011 budget fighting for Illinois: Creating jobs, cutting costs, moving forward*. Springfield, IL: State of Illinois.

Rose, N. (1999). *Powers of freedom: Reframing political thought*. Cambridge, England: Cambridge University Press.

Rosenfield, S., & Neese-Todd, S. (1993). Elements of a psychosocial Clubhouse program associated with a satisfying quality of life. *Hospital and Community Psychiatry, 44*(1), 76–78.

Sauder, M., & Espeland, W. N. (2009). The discipline of rankings: Tight coupling and organizational change. *American Sociological Review, 74*(1), 63–82. doi:10.1177/000312240907400104

Schneiberg, M. (2013). Movements as political conditions for diffusion: anti-corporate movements and the spread of cooperative forms in American capitalism. *Organization Studies, 34*(5–6), 653–682. doi:10.1177/0170840613479226

Scott, W. R. (2014). *Institutions and organizations: Ideas, interests, and identities* (4th ed.). Thousand Oaks, CA: Sage Publications.

Scott, W. R., Ruef, M., Mendel, P., & Caronna, C. (2000). *Institutional change and healthcare organizations: From professional dominance to managed care*. Chicago, IL: University of Chicago Press.

Skelcher, C., & Smith, S. R. (2014). Theorizing hybridity: Institutional logics, complex organizations, and actor identities: The case of nonprofits. *Public Administration, 93*(2), 433–448. doi:10.1111/padm.12105

Smith, Y., & Spitzmueller, M. C. (2016). Worker perspectives on contemporary milieu therapy: A cross-site ethnographic study. *Social Work Research, 40*(2), 105–116. doi:10.1093/swr/svw003

Soss, J., Fording, R., & Schram, S. F. (2011). The organization of discipline: From performance management to perversity and punishment. *Journal of Public Administration Research and Theory, 21*(Suppl 2), i203–232. doi:10.1093/jopart/muq095

Spitzmueller, M. C. (2014). Shifting practices of recovery under community mental health reform: A street-level organizational ethnography. *Qualitative Social Work, 13*(1), 26–48. doi:10.1177/1473325013507472

Spitzmueller, M. C. (2016). Negotiating competing institutional logics at the street level: An ethnography of a community mental health organization. *Social Service Review, 90*(1), 35–82. doi:10.1086/686694

Strathern, M. (2000). Introduction: New accountabilities. In M. Strathern (Ed.), *Audit cultures: Anthropological studies in accountability, ethics and the academy* (pp. 1–19). New York, NY: Routledge.

Thornton, P. H. (2002). The rise of the corporation in a craft industry: Conflict and conformity in institutional logics. *Academy of Management Journal, 45*(1), 81–101. doi:10.2307/3069286

Thornton, P. H., Ocasio, W., & Lounsbury, M. (2012). *The institutional logics perspective*. New York, NY: Oxford University Press.

Torrey, W. C., & Gorman, P. G. (2005). Closing the gap between what services are and what they could be. In R. E. Drake, D. W. Lynde, & M. R. Merrens (Eds.), *Evidence-based mental health practice* (pp. 167–188). New York, NY: Norton and Co.

Van Slyke, D. M. (2003). The mythology of privatization in contracting for social services. *Public Administration Review, 63*(3), 296–315. doi:10.1111/puar.2003.63.issue-3

Ware, N. C., Hopper, K., Tugenberg, T., Dickey, B., Fisher, D. (2007). Connectedness and citizenship: Redefining social integration. *Psychiatric Services, 58*(4), 469–474. doi:10.1176/ps.2007.58.4.469

Warner, R., Huxley, P., & Berg, T. (1999). An evaluation of the impact of Clubhouse membership on quality of life and treatment utilization. *International Journal of Social Psychiatry, 45*(4), 310–321. doi:10.1177/002076409904500410

Wooten, M., & Hoffman, A. J. (2008). Organizational fields: Past, present and future. In R. Greenwood, C. Oliver, R. Suddaby, & K. Sahlin-Andersson (Eds.), *The Sage handbook of organizational institutionalism* (pp. 130–147). Thousand Oaks, CA: SAGE Publications Inc.

Ybema, S., Yanow, D., Wels, H., & Kamsteeg, F. (2009). Studying everyday organizational life. In S. Ybema, D. Yanow, H. Wels, & F. Kamsteeg (Eds.), *Organizational ethnography: Studying the complexities of everyday life* (pp. 1–20). Thousand Oaks, CA: SAGE Publications.

Zayas, L. E., McMillen, J. C., Lee, M. Y., & Books, S. J. (2013). Challenges to quality assurance and improvement efforts in behavioral health organizations: A qualitative assessment. *Administration and Policy in Mental Health and Mental Health Services Research, 40*(3), 190–198. doi:10.1007/s10488-011-0393-5

Zilber, T. B. (2002). Institutionalization as an interplay between actions, meanings, and actors: The case of a rape crisis center in Israel. *Academy of Management Journal, 45*(1), 234–254. doi:10.2307/3069294

Marketization strategies and the influence of business on the management of child welfare agencies

Robbie Waters Robichau and Lili Wang

ABSTRACT

Nonprofit organizations frequently face external pressures like marketization and governmentalization as well as internal pressures like normative and value expectations on how they should behavior. Using survey data from approximately 150 child welfare administrators, we explore how these pressures combine to influence the adoption of business management practices. Evidence shows that the influence of the business community is persuading managers to implement business strategies while government control and funding have less predictive power on management practices. Surprisingly, a nonprofit mindset has no effect on the likelihood of using business-like management strategies. We conclude with implications and make suggestions for further research.

Public governance today reflects a growing pluralistic state where multiple private and nonprofit actors are needed to cope with complex societal problems (Osborne, 2010). One outcome of this pluralistic state is government increasingly turning over service provision to nonstate actors (Van Slyke, 2007; Witesman & Fernandez, 2012), especially in human services (Salamon, 2002). Indeed, a sizable majority of states report publicly funding various private nonprofit child welfare agencies (U. S. DHHS & ACF, 2001) while placing various performance measurement expectations on their actions (Collins-Camargo, Chuang, McBeath, & Bunger, 2014). For their part, nonprofit organizations (hereafter NPOs) across the sector are under pressure to secure funding through contracts and to become more entrepreneurial in their efforts to generate revenue. These pressures come in the form of marketization or commercialization (Eikenberry, 2009a; Maier, Meyer, & Steinbereithner, 2016; Salamon, 1993; Weisbrod, 1998), vendorism, bureaucratization, or governmentalization (Choi, Cho, Wright, & Brudney, 2005; Salamon, 1995; Smith & Lipsky, 1993). Nonprofit agencies are urged to provide more and better services to a greater number of individuals while simultaneously being compelled to do so in a similar fashion to government and business entities.

Theory suggests that nonprofits are simultaneously impacted by both marketization and governmentalization (i.e., influences external to the organization) and by internal organizational factors imbued in the nonprofit sector. These environmental pressures play a pivotal role in shaping nonprofit organizations and their management. Institutionalist scholars argued that behaviors, especially in the context of organizational life, can be altered by regulations and rules, norms and belief systems, and finally, cultural-cognitive systems that combine shared understanding and taken-for-granted processes in social life that exist external to the organization (Scott & Davis, 2007). Organizations become institutionalized to norms of behaviors and practices of other agencies through a social process of replicating patterns of activities (Jepperson, 1991). When NPOs succumb to isomorphic forces and replicate norms and behaviors of other agencies in the public and for-profit private sectors, their practices may homogenize leaving them at risk of losing what made them unique in the first place. It is not surprising that scholars have been noticing the tendency of nonprofits to replicate the structures and practices of businesses and government for years (e.g., Abzug & Galaskiewicz, 2001; Cooney, 2006). Concerns have been raised about how NPO's response to these changes and pressures will impact the distinctive ethos or identity of the nonprofit sector – what can be called nonprofitness, in general, and the ability of nonprofit organizations, in particular, to advance their missions and serve their clients (Eikenberry & Kluver, 2004; Frumkin, 2005; Knutsen & Brock, 2014; Robichau, Fernandez, & Kraeger, 2015). Scholars note the important space NPOs hold in society acting as stewards for multiple stakeholders (Van Puyvelde, Caers, Du Bois, & Jegers, 2012), adopting multiple institutional logics for instrumental and expressive action (Knutsen, 2012), and upholding essential public values and roles (Moulton & Eckerd, 2012).

Nonprofits are being driven to meet a 'triple bottom line' where the emphasis on financial management as well business practices and performance are seen as significant as the social benefits NPOs offer to society (Slaper & Hall, 2011). Nonprofit organizations are expected to professionalize and ascribe to the rational, managerialism approaches to management adopted by their private sector collaborators (Suárez & Esparza, 2016; Suárez & Hwang, 2013). Yielding to the demands of the market and government could jeopardize, or at the very least challenge, the delicate and somewhat distinctive moral and functional balance NPOs try to maintain. This raises unanswered questions regarding how nonprofit managers cope with their institutional environments and what managerial practices, logics, and values they adopt to achieve their goals. Salamon (2005, p. 96) refers to this as the "growing identity crisis" of nonprofit America.

This paper explores the extent to which external and internal organizational forces are shaping the adoption of more business-like management strategies by nonprofit organizations, particularly child welfare agencies. We study this topic by first reviewing the external forces affecting nonprofit organizations such as marketization and governmental influences; and then, we examine what, if any, role, nonprofitness (i.e., identifying with a core set of internal nonprofit values and purposes) has on the adoption of business management strategies. Next, we provide a brief overview of the reasons why examining child welfare agencies offers a rich context for study. Following the literature review and research hypotheses, methods and data are presented along with statistical results from a national survey of child welfare agency managers. Three multinomial logistic regressions and one ordered logistic regression model are used to explore the business management practices of charging fees for services, engaging in cause-related marketing alliances with business, replacing volunteers with professionals, and running their agencies like a business. This paper contributes to the child welfare and nonprofit literatures by showing the business-like management practices child welfare agencies are adopting and demonstrating the external and internal forces shaping those practices. We address how using institutional theory and nonprofit logics informs the study of nonprofit management. Finally, the implications for human service organizations and, the nonprofit sector in general, are discussed.

The marketization of the nonprofit sector

One trend significantly influencing the operations of nonprofit organizations is commercialization or marketization. Marketization or "the penetration of essentially market-type relationships into the social welfare arena" (Salamon, 1993, p. 17) of the nonprofit sector gained tremendous momentum in the 1980s and has continued apace. The terms marketization, commercialization, and privateness will be used interchangeably in this paper to refer to the influence of business sector rhetoric and the adoption of business-like practices by nonprofit organizations. While the study of marketization of the nonprofit sector is growing (see Maier et al., 2016 for a review of literature on NPOs becoming business-like), the implications for how management practices are being shaped by these pressures has received limited empirical examination. Some examples of business-like management practices include the generation of commercial revenues such as using fees for services, selling products and services, engaging in business ventures, and ascribing to neoliberal subjectivities or managerial ideologies (Kreutzer & Jäger, 2011; Maier et al., 2016).

Charging fees for services is one of the more commonly practiced commercialized activities among NPOs. During the 1980s until the 2000s, fees for services have accounted for over 50% of revenue growth in the sector (Aspen Institute, 2001; Kerlin & Pollak, 2011), and for social service agencies in particular, fee income makes up 35% of their revenue growth (Salamon, 2003). Recently, McKeever (2015) reports that charging fees for services still represents approximately 48% of the total revenue for public charities. Child (2010, p. 155) noted that while in some nonprofit subfields the reliance on commercial revenues have become stagnate, human service organizations like residential care facilities (e.g., group homes) have experienced increases in reliance on commercial revenues. During this same time period, more businesses ventured into areas traditionally relegated to NPOs, especially in the area of human and social services (Frumkin, 2005). NPOs now regularly compete with for-profits, other nonprofits, and even government agencies for resources, clients, and publicly funded contracts.

Accordingly, nonprofit executives are encouraged to be social entrepreneurs, employ business-like strategies for success, and explore various revenue streams (Ashton, 2011; Frumkin and Keating, 2011). Workers in NPOs must now strike a balance between achieving their mission and serving clients while also being innovative, resourceful, and opportunistic (Dees, Emerson, & Economy, 2001). Additionally, the sector itself has undergone a professionalization of employees as a response to various commercialization pressures (Salamon, 2005). Studies show that hiring professional staff, particularly those with college education and business training, may increase nonprofit organization's adoption of business-like practices as these professional staff are more amenable to the use of for-profit management tools (Suárez & Hwang, 2013). Many who work in nonprofit organizations are proud of the professionalization of the sector and view it as an advancement of the field whereas others approach this change with a bit more caution (Frumkin, 2005). Excessive professionalization of NPOs raises concerns about the sector being a legitimate representative of the community's needs, questions the 'voluntary' nature of agencies who are composed of working professionals, and increases the costs of handling social problems (Salamon, 2003).

The expansion of nonprofit partnerships and alliances with businesses to market an image, product, or service for mutual benefit reflects further expansion of business-like approaches and values into the sector (Weisbrod, 1998). These cause-related marketing ventures help businesses achieve strategic purposes while allowing NPO's to promote goals and social causes. Although businesses have been an important financial contributor to NPOs for decades, there seems to be a shift on the part of private firms from "benign benevolence" (Young, 2002, p. 6) to partnering for strategic reasons that lead to corporate success and "reputational capital" (Salamon, 2003, p. 65). Eikenberry (2009b, p. 51) took the critique of cause related marketing further by arguing that consumption philanthropy comes at a cost of "individualizing solutions to collective problems... [and] hiding how markets create many social problems in the first place." The growth of nonprofit-business partnerships brings with it the increasing use of business language, business planning and management, and terminology (Dart, 2004). The very nature of the relationship between businesses and nonprofits seems to be shifting, including NPOs mimicking business values and practices, and this swing could lead to competition replacing the presumed benevolent spirit of NPOs (Bush, 1992). For example, Bunger, McBeath, Chuang, and Collins-Camargo (2017) found that a child welfare agency's level of collaboration or competition with similar agencies can be attributed to various market and mimetic pressures.

Even though there is agreement about the emergence of these trends in the nonprofit sector, the consequences are not so clear. One side maintains that tapping into market-solutions increases nonprofits survival and flourishing. Thus, nonprofits who act more business-like can achieve greater resource stability, efficiency and innovation, focus on serving clients, and possibly increase legitimacy and accountability to the public (Aspen Institute, 2001; Dees et al., 2001). While having a business mindset does clearly provide NPOs with many opportunities to improve, it does come at a cost. LeRoux (2009, p.165) found that business funding can lead to the "transmitting [of] capitalist values and business sector practices to nonprofits" which may ultimately pull a NPO's focus away from client services and toward fund development. Frumkin warned that in some nonprofits, "intense commercialization has eroded the moral high ground of these organization and transformed nonprofits into shadow businesses" (2005, p. 10). Furthermore, marketization might lure nonprofits away from advancing their mission, serving the poor and hardest-to-reach clients, using volunteers, promoting democracy and advocacy, maintaining valuable community networks, and placing more emphasis on accepted management techniques over delivering services (Alexander, Nank, & Stivers, 1999; Eikenberry & Kluver, 2004). With this in mind, we explore the influence of the business community on NPO's management and expect that pressures and funding from the private sector will encourage NPOs to adopt business management practices. The following propositions are tested:

Hypothesis 1: The influence of the business community will increase the adoption of business management strategies by nonprofit managers.

Hypothesis 2: Receiving funding from businesses will increase the adoption of business management strategies by nonprofit managers.

The governmentalization of the nonprofit sector

While "public service itself has undergone a business-like transformation" following the notion of market-driven and results-oriented modes of governance (Haque, 2001, p. 65), NPOs have been simultaneously confronting influences from marketization (or privateness) and governmentalization (or publicness). Governmentalization, bureaucratization, and publicness in general refer to the influence of government on an organization's practices. Bozeman and several colleagues have argued that all organizations have varying degrees of publicness which can be measured from a "dimensional" approach i.e., mechanisms of ownership, control, and funding (Coursey & Bozeman, 1990) further illustrating the complex environments NPOs currently face. The publicness concept is often used to compare organizational and managerial behaviors between public and for-profit agencies (Andrews, Boyne, & Walker, 2011; Boyne, 2002); however, NPOs are not included in these comparisons as frequently. The argument is made that organizations experience governmental influence through various avenues of regulation, taxation, public policies, and contracts; making the state an ever-present factor of organizational life. Recently, Bozeman and Moulton (2011) sought to further clarify the boundaries of organizations by opposing explanations of "publicness" to those of "privateness." They argue that while publicness is understood as "the degree of political authority constraints *and* endowments affecting organizations" privateness captures "the degree of *market* authority constraints and endowments affecting the institution" (p. i365). Thus, since all organizations are subjected to influences of publicness and privateness, they can be identified as "more private" or "more public" (p. i365). Nonprofits therefore have strong dimensions of publicness and privateness and the degree to which they are subjected to either of these forces may also be reflected in governmental control or funding.

Greater governmental control or funding is a double-edged sword. On one hand, higher levels of publicness can positively impact NPOs. Studies show that nonprofit survival and growth can be attributed to government contracts and grants (Gazley, 2008). In addition, government funding affords NPOs access to the political process and provides further opportunities for advocacy (Chavesc, Stephens, & Galaskiewicz, 2004). Increased professionalism of workers within the nonprofit sector is also a noted consequence of government funding (Suárez, 2011).

Too much funding or control by government can lead NPOs to become government vendors that may drift away from their mission, goals, and clients (Frumkin & Andre-Clark, 2000; Salamon, 1995). Government control can come in many forms such as state regulations and the degree to which government agencies and the legislature holds NPOs accountable. For example, McBeath and Meezan (2010) find that the introduction of performance-based (i.e., use of incentive payment structure), managed care contracts with nonprofit child welfare agencies in Michigan led organizations to be overly focused on efficiency rather than foster care child outcomes of family reunification which may be a more accurate measure of program success. In the end, NPOs can become more bureaucratic, less flexible, and less autonomous from government (Frumkin, 2005; Smith, 2004). Research also demonstrates that reliance on government funding decreases the likelihood that nonprofit boards will be more representational of their communities; therefore, organizations which depend less on government funding and more on volunteer labor will have stronger boards that are more representative of their localities (Guo, 2007).

The propositions below seek to capture the effects of publicness (i.e., control and funding) on nonprofit management. We hypothesize that more government control encourages nonprofit managers to adopt business practices in order to please their government principals and thereby appear better managed and, overall, more efficient. This reflects a similar trend to what has occurred in public administration with its emphasis on New Public Management principles (i.e., a market orientation that stresses outcomes and efficiency). Conversely, NPOs may be selected for funding because they are nonprofits and are expected to deliver quality services motivated by their charitable missions. Government funding may increase a NPO's financial stability while decreasing its need to use business strategies. Given the pivotal role government plays in nonprofit sector management, it is expected that:

Hypothesis 3: Greater government control will increase the adoption of business management strategies by nonprofit managers.

Hypothesis 4: Receiving government funding will decrease the adoption of business management strategies by nonprofit managers.

Striving for nonprofitness?

Sociological institutionalism would suggest other cultural-cognitive and normative scripts such as shared understanding and logics of action, social obligation, moral governance, or mimetic pressures (Scott & Davis, 2007), which are more internal to the sector's identity and value systems are at work as well. The identity and values of the sector may seem to be nebulous to some, but the literature suggests that normative dimensions of management are important and to approach nonprofit management "as if value and normative orientations would not matter" is problematic (Anheier, 2014, p. 329). Therefore, nonprofitness is used in this paper as a framework for exploring how identification with nonprofit norms and values may influence the adoption of business-like practices. Nonprofitness is based on the theories of integrative publicness and nonprofit institutional logics.

Bozeman and Moulton (2011) expanded the theory of publicness to "integrative publicness" which seeks to capture organizations being influenced by both dimensional publicness (i.e., ownership, control, and funding) and normative publicness (i.e., the incorporation of public values). Thus, they recognize that values and ideals matter in shaping management choices as well. If it can be argued that publicness and privateness describe the core characteristics of organizations, is there room to incorporate a role for an agency's level of nonprofitness, i.e., their identification with a nonprofit core? While considering the distinctive "nature" of nonprofits must be approached with caution given the diversity of organizations, there are ways of depicting NPOs that capture their distinctiveness from government and business entities (Ott & Dicke, 2012). And, there is an assumption by many of those in the field and academic community that a nonprofit mindset, to at least some degree, shapes organizational management and action (Anheier, 2014).

The nonprofit sector is imbued with particular values and ideals that deserve recognition. Frumkin (2005) offered a framework for describing the nonprofit sector in terms of its expressive and instrumental role. He noted four distinct purposes of the sector, namely to promote service delivery, social entrepreneurship, civic and political engagement, and values and faith, and argued that while all nonprofit agencies should perform each of these functions to some extent, the biggest challenge in the sector is finding the right "fit" and balance between these four objectives. Not only do these purposes explain what NPOs do, but they also speak to an inherent value construct of what being a nonprofit should mean. Combining Frumkin's explanation with the integrative publicness literature, Robichau et al. (2015) created a framework for exploring what nonprofitness means in practice. They argue that while NPOs are submitted to a certain degree of market and political authority, they also have to adhere to a degree of "moral authority" infused with nonprofit values and purposes.

The institutional logics framework offers similar insight into how the nonprofit sector serves a particular role in society. Knutsen (2012) discussed how internal, unique institutional logics of NPOs like family, democracy, and religion may compete with the external logics offered by the state and capitalism. Her argument culminates with the claim that NPOs have "adapted institutional logics" and may adopt any or all logics at any point in time. In essence, NPOs can adopt a number of practices, or even normative stances, based on their institutional environments. This ability to adapt, however, does not detract from the unique logics and theoretical explanations of the nonprofit sector's special roles in society as providing public goods and services, promoting democratic institutions, and expressing faith and values. NPOs create social capital (Putnam, 1995), social trust (Fukuyama, 1996), and social change while also filling in the gap between the sectors, or acting as an alternative to government and business (Ott & Dicke, 2012), especially on behalf of those who are poor and under-represented. In effect, NPOs should fulfill a social contract, bestowed on them by the public's trust, which promotes important values and ethics like accountability, service, and charity (Jeavons, 2010, p. 1114).

Combined, these universal purposes and principles of NPOs lay a theoretical ground work for exploring practices and values practitioners in the sector may identify with and hold in high regard, i.e., a nonprofitness identity. As Knutsen (2012, p. 1007) argued, when it comes to nonprofit theory building more attention is given to economic and political approaches with less attention on the nonprofit sector itself as emphasizing "caring... religious beliefs, and professionalism." Perhaps, NPOs managers, professionals, and volunteers take these values and understanding of what makes NPOs distinct from other types of organizations into account when making decisions for their agencies. Yet, knowing the extent to which these values and identity shape management and actions is difficult. One concern is that nonprofits still have an "unsettled relationship between the state and the market" (Frumkin, 2005, p. 163) and the extent to which organizations fall into the "study of the space in-between" the sectoral boundaries presents theoretical and practical challenges (Knutsen & Brock, 2014, p. 1114). If nonprofits succumb to pressures from business and government, then they risk losing the essence of what makes them distinctive and being further institutionalized to practices of the market and state. In this scenario, like Bromley and Meyer (2014, p. 16) propose, "they are all organizations" and differences between the sector matter less. Given this, is it possible for nonprofit organizations to maintain their distinctive purposes in a milieu pressuring them to make decisions based on market and governmental norms? To begin exploring this question, the following propositions are offered:

Hypothesis 5 : Higher levels of nonprofitness will decrease the adoption of business management strategies by nonprofit managers.

Hypothesis 6: Receiving funding from other nonprofits or foundations will decrease the adoption of business management strategies by nonprofit managers.

It is expected that managers with a greater identification with core nonprofit values and purposes are less likely to utilize business management strategies in their agencies. These administrators may have stronger beliefs concerning how their NPO should be managed; furthermore, they could see what they do as something distinctive from what administrators in business and government do. In addition, NPOs who receive funding from other nonprofits or foundations are expected to be less likely to adopt business management strategies. This might be attributed to other nonprofit agencies encouraging one another to adopt similar norms of behavior or funding from other NPOs may allow administrators to manage without pressures to conform to the practices of business and government.

Background of child welfare agencies

There are compelling reasons for studying the impact of marketization, governmentalization, and nonprofitness on the management practices of nonprofit child welfare agencies. Providing services for children's welfare originally began in the private, philanthropic sector (Embry, Buddenhagen, & Bolles, 2000), starting as early as the 1800s and has continued thus forth (Flaherty, Collins-Camargo, & Lee, 2008). Caring for abused, neglected, and dependent children is "always [been] a 'privatized' system, never an exclusively public one" (Mangold, 1999, p. 1295). However, in the current arrangements, the state maintains the ultimate responsibility for children and serves as a "parent by proxy" responsible for decisions made regarding these children's future. In fiscal year 2011, 646,000 children were served by the public foster care system (U.S. Children's Bureau & ACYF, 2012) and the cost of providing services to these children averages around $20 billion dollars a year (Scarcella, Bess, Zielewski, & Geen, 2006). The magnitude of children receiving services represents only a small portion of those actually affected by the public foster care system since government also affects the families of these children and youth.

The states rely upon nonprofit expertise in running various programs aimed at caring for at-risk children and families (Barillas, 2011), and to some degree, all states have a varying levels of public-private partnerships in the child welfare system (Collins-Camargo et al., 2014). Therefore, the actions NPOs employ to serve children and their families is controlled to varying degrees by public policy and legislation, public administrators, and other environmental conditions like the Great Recession (Wells, Jolles, Chuang, McBeath, & Collins-Camargo, 2014). For example, the passage of welfare reform in 1996, The Personal Responsibility and Work Opportunity Reconciliation Act (hereafter PRWORA), eliminated many of the entitlement programs such as Aid to Families with Dependent Children (AFDC) while giving greater authority to states for providing welfare services. Some of the outcomes of PRWORA included: states and local governments funding more child welfare services than in the past; inclusion of the "Charitable Choice" provision which urges states to contract with Faith Based Organizations; and, it amended the Social Security Act to include for-profits as a provider of foster care services (Mangold, 1999; Scarcella et al., 2006). The National Survey of Child and Adolescent Well Being showed that in 2009, 69–80% of foster care and adoptive services were being subcontracted with 21% of CPS investigations also being contracted out indicating increases across the board from 1999 (Wells et al., 2014).

Unlike in the past century, for-profits and nonprofits are now competing for public funds; and, with growing efforts to redesign the child welfare system and stronger mandates to prove outcome effectiveness, the organizations themselves need to be examined more closely (McBeath et al., 2014). Nonprofit child welfare agencies are providing a critical service for government but their ability to administer their programs as they see fit may be limited. Researchers are finding that the push for greater performance measurement by public agencies onto other private agencies "has the potential for promoting market-oriented governance in the child welfare system" (Collins-Camargo et al., 2014, p. 140). The long-term implications of this are unknown. Until the recent and first National Survey of Private Child and Family Serving Agencies (NSPCFSA) in 2011, research on the private and nonprofit agencies proving child welfare services had been lagging, but even now, there are many more organizational questions that need answering (McBeath et al., 2014). Given the tensions among agencies striving to meet the service needs of children and their families through a web of state-market-civil society interactions, studying the management of child welfare agencies offers a rich context for exploring broader trends of the nonprofit sector.

Data and methods

The effects of marketization, governmentalization, and nonprofitness on the adoption of business management practices are examined through the perspective of agency managers. Administrators of nonprofit child welfare agencies from across the country were surveyed. The list of agencies was obtained from the 2012 National Center for Charitable Statistics database. Organizations were selected only if they were classified as a human service foster care agency by the National Taxonomy of Exempt Entities Core Codes, or NTEE-CC, code P32. Many of these NPOs perform a variety of child welfare services (e.g., adoption, advocacy, and family preservation).

Upon creating a list of nonprofit foster care agencies, we conducted further research online and by telephone to find contact information of top administrators at each agency and to ensure the NPOs provided some form of child welfare or advocacy service. The design of the survey instrument is derived from a combination of literature reviews as well as the results of research conducted by the National Quality Improvement Center on the Privatization of Child Welfare Services. We piloted the survey questionnaire with 7 practitioners and 10 academics who were experts in the field and amended the initial survey based on their feedback. The final 51-item survey was conducted online between April 12, 2012 and June 27, 2012. A total of 426 managers were surveyed, and of that, 184 individuals participated in this research giving a response rate of 43%.[1] Respondents were asked to respond to questions regarding management, finances, relationships with other organizations, and other general agency and individual characteristics.[2] Observations come from NPOs in 38 different states. T-Tests were conducted to examine the nonresponse biases between respondents and non-respondents based on observable characteristics of these agencies such as total revenue, net income, liabilities, and assets (retrieved from the IRS Form 990 data). No statistically significant differences were found.

Dependent variables

Four dependent variables measure the adoption of business management strategies in nonprofit child welfare agencies. These dependent variables are *charging fees for services, engaging in marketing alliances with businesses, need to professionalize agency* by replacing volunteers, and *running my agency like a business*. The frequency of acquiring private fees-for-services (client-paid or insurance reimbursement) and using cause-related marketing alliances with businesses are measured on a three-point scale of never, occasionally, and frequently. Some examples of when a child welfare agency might charge a fee for services would be when they complete an adoption, provide family/ child therapy, or provide residential treatment. The third dependent variable is three-point scale based on whether managers agree, are neutral, or disagree with a statement that the agencies need to replace volunteers with professional staff. The last variable is four-point scale measuring whether managers perceive it not important at all, slightly important, moderately important, or extremely important to run their agency like a business on a day-to-day basis. Table 1 presents the descriptive statistics in detail.

---

[1]There were a totally of 177 different organizations represented in this survey. A few (*n*=7) large organizations with multiple program managers had more than one respondent.
[2]Dummy Variable Adjustment is used in the models to handle missing data in the independent variables and thereby prevents losing observations at the case level when a question is not answered (For review of the method see Cohen & Cohen, 1985).

Table 1. Descriptive statistics.

Dependent	Percentage				
Fees for services (*n*=151)	Never: 51.7%; Occasionally: 28.5%; Frequently: 19.9%				
Marketing alliances (*n*=149)	Never: 40.9%; Occasionally: 38.3%; Frequently: 20.8%				
Need to professionalize (*n*=163)	Disagree: 37.4%; Neither agree nor disagree: 28.8%; Agree: 33.7%				
Running agency like business(*n*=148)	Not important: 10.8%; Slightly important: 18.2%; Moderately important: 39.9%; Extremely important: 31.1%				
	Mean	SD	Min	Max	N
Independent					
Influence of the business*	0.00	1.00	−1.98	2.97	138
Receives funding from businesses	0.78	0.41	0.00	1.00	166
Government control*	0.00	1.00	−2.20	2.18	134
Receives funding from government	0.80	0.40	0.00	1.00	179
Nonprofitness*	0.00	1.00	−4.38	1.16	156
Receives funding from nonprofits	0.64	0.48	0.00	1.00	159
Controls					
Agency's operational budget	3.54	1.47	1.00	6.00	184
Range of services	5.11	3.07	0.00	14.00	184
Offers advocacy service	0.48	0.50	0.00	1.00	184
Board member from business	0.82	0.38	0.00	1.00	145
Board member from government	0.32	0.47	0.00	1.00	145
Provides services in rural area	0.31	0.46	0.00	1.00	167
Female	0.55	0.50	0.00	1.00	143
Education level	2.74	0.79	1.00	4.00	146
Business background and training	0.28	0.45	0.00	1.00	153

*Factor scores are standardized, with a mean of 0.00 and a standard deviation of 1.00.

Independent variables

The role marketization trends may play in the adoption of business management practices is examined through two variables. As the literature suggests, market influences on nonprofit organizations and management can come through a variety of mechanisms (Eikenberry & Kluver, 2004; Suárez & Esparza, 2016) and thus our first variable, *influence of the business community*, seeks to capture multiple facets of these influences. It is based on an exploratory factor score created from respondents' agreement and disagreement with the following five statements: 1) There is greater competition with businesses for government contracts and funding; 2) there is pressure to generate commercial revenues and fees-for-services; 3) businesses providing child welfare services presents a challenge to your agency's service provision; 4) competition with other agencies over funding presents a challenge to your agency's service provision; and 5) large donors or corporations influencing management or programs presents a challenge to your agency's service provision. Questions 1 and 2 were based on seven-point Likert scale and 3–5 were based on a five-point scale. The principal-factor method and orthogonal varimax rotation were used in the factor analysis, which is the same for all factor analyses in this study. These variables factor around one score (eigenvalue = 1.53) and the Cronbach's alpha's is .67, both of which indicate that the retained factor is capturing the underlying construct of what we have termed the influence of the business community. The factor score generated from the factor analysis was then standardized with a mean of 0 and a standard deviation of 1 to create the influence of the business community index.[3] A second, binary variable of whether a NPO *receives funding from business corporations* is used to further explore the effects of marketization.

The impact of publicness on the adoption of business management practices is measured with two variables. First, a *government control index* factor score is created from answers to six different survey questions that collectively seek to address the pressures child welfare managers may face in

---

[3]The eignevalues-greater-than-one rule or the *Kaiser criterion* is the "most widely used procedure for determining the number of factors" (Fabrignar & Wegener, 2012, p. 55).

areas such as government regulation, oversight, and other broad influences. These questions are: 1) If your agency stopped receiving government funds, how would this affect daily operations; 2) how involved are the public child welfare agencies and 3) state legislatures in holding your agency's operations accountable; 4) the level of influence of State Child and Family Services Review findings and your state's Program Improvement Plan on your agency's operations; 5) the level of influence of state regulations on agency operations; and 6) the extent to which strong governmental influence over agency operations presents a challenge to effectively providing services. Questions 1–3 were based on three-point scales and 4–6 and were based on a five-point scale. The retained one factor has an eigenvalue of 1.52 and the Cronbach alpha is .67. Another binary variable that helps explore the influence of publicness is whether or not a NPO *receives government funding* from either state legislatures or public child welfare agencies. Because nonprofit ownership is hard, if not impossible to measures, the ownership variable used in many studies on publicness is not employed in our models.

The final variables of interest address how managers identify with nonprofit purposes and values that NPOs serve in society – nonprofitness – and whether they are receiving funding from other nonprofits and foundations. Factor analysis is employed to demonstrate the extent to which managers strongly disagree to strongly agree on a seven-point Likert scale with the following seven statements about nonprofit organizations' role in society: 1) Act as an alternative to government by protecting and promoting individual and community values and interests; 2) experiment or be innovative in programs, processes, and service delivery; 3) drive social change; 4) serve poor, under-represented, or disadvantaged individuals; 5) promote causes and policies on behalf of clients and communities; 6) bring communities together and develop social trust; and 7) provide or supplement services government and business cannot or does not offer. Rather than viewing nonprofits' purposes independently, the real distinctive nature of NPOs may be in the combination and clustering of their roles (Salamon, Hems, & Chinnock, 2000). Explaining the identity and values of the nonprofit sector is comparable to what Moulton and Eckerd (2012) refer to as their "Nonprofit Sector Public Role Index." Similar to their findings, the managers in this sample identify with the particular purposes of the nonprofit sector. Combined, these measures have one retained factor with a high eigenvalue score of 4.31 and the Cronbach alpha is .91. The final binary variable that explores the influence of other nonprofits and foundations is whether NPOs *receives funding from other nonprofits and foundations*.

Control variables

Agency and individual level characteristics are controlled for in these models. There are six agency level controls. The first measure is of an a*gency's operating budget revenues* for fiscal year 2011 with 45% of managers reporting revenues under one million, 30% between $1 and $4.9 million, and 25% $5 million or more. *Range of services offered* captures the different number of child welfare services an agency provides with up to 14 different choices available (mean = 5.11 and standard deviation = 3.07). The most frequently reported types of services agencies provided were foster parent recruitment and support, foster care placement, case management, and advocacy for children and families.[4] Almost half of NPOs surveyed (48%) *offer advocacy services* for children and families. *Provides services in rural area* measures whether a nonprofit organization offers services in rural areas (31%). Two other agency level

---

[4]Respondents could choose from a range of services. Their options and percentage of agencies providing these types of services are listed: Foster care placement (57%), Adoption (34%), Family preservation & reunification (34%), Residential treatment or congregate care (27%), Case management (49%), Crisis or emergency care (30%), Counseling, therapy, or mental health services (38%), Foster parent recruitment & support (59%), Adoptive parent recruitment & support (40%), CPS investigation or assessment (5%), Advocacy for children & families (48%), Independent living (32%), Mentoring programs for children (31%), or other (28%).

controls are whether they have a *board member from business* (82%) and a *board member from government* (32%).[5]

At the individual level there are five control variables for managerial characteristics. These controls are important because they could have different effects on agency practices and their reported adoption of business management strategies and thus needed to be accounted for. *Females* account for 55% of respondents. *Education level* is a categorical variable on their level of education with 8% reporting less than a BA/BS degree, 23% reporting a BA/BS degree, 56% reporting a Master's degree, and 13% reporting a PhD/Doctorate degree. The *business background and training* variable measures whether they have a professional background or training in the area of business (11%). Table 2 presents the correlations between the independent variables.

Methods

All four models of business management practices are based on categorical dependent variables. Two dependent variables, *charging fees for services* and *engaging in marketing alliances with business*, are based on a frequency of occurrence from never to occasionally to usually. *Need to professionalize agency* ranges from agree, neither agree nor disagree, or disagree with this practice. We test all these relationships using a multinomial logistic model given that the dependent variables in these three models do not have a natural ordering to them. *Running my agency like a business* has a natural ordering based on a range of importance from one to four; hence, an ordered logistic model is employed. Odds ratios are reported for each model.[6]

Results

The results of the multivariate models of nonprofit adoption of business management strategies are presented in Table 3.

Fees for services

Three of the key independent variables (1) *influence of the business community index*, (2) *receiving funding from business*, and (3) *government control index* are significantly related to charging fees for services. First, a one point increase in the *influence of the business community index* is associated with increased odds of occasionally charging fees for services by 86% ($p < .10$), and usually charging fees for services by 151% ($p < .05$). Secondly, agencies *receiving funding from business* are about three times more likely to occasionally charge fees for services compared to those who never do ($p < .10$). And finally, a one point increase in the *government control index* decreases the likelihood of occasionally and usually charging fees for services by 50% and 67%, respectively. The other key variables of interest – *receiving funding from government, nonprofitness index*, and *receiving funding from nonprofits and foundations* – are not significant predictors of the frequency with which agencies charge fees for services.

By examining the model of charging fees for services, we find support for hypotheses 1 and 2 that increased influence of the business community and accepting funding from business corporations can lead to the adoption of business management practices by child welfare agencies. Businesses

---

[5]We tested agency age in the model but since it was not significant in our study and since other researchers (Gazley, 2010; Foster & Meinhard, 2002) have not found organizational age to be a consistent predictor of different organizational management practices such as collaboration, we choose not to keep this in our model.

[6]We did run the test of parallel lines assumption (i.e., proportional odds assumption) to see whether these variables did in fact have an ordinal relationship. The assumption is violated for charging fees for services (significance 0.0004), using cause-related marketing alliances with business (significance 0.0026), and professionalizing agency (significance 0.0917); therefore, the null hypothesis is rejected and dependent variables are determined not to be ordinal. The multinomial logistic model is preferred to using an improperly specified ordinal logit model (Liao, 1994, p. 50).

Table 2. Pearson's correlation.

	1	2	3	4	5	6	7	8	9	10	11	12	13	14
1. Influence of the business														
2. Receives funding from businesses	0.02													
3. Government control	0.37*	-0.12												
4. Receives funding from government	0.15*	0.03	0.40*											
5. Nonprofitness	0.21*	0.19*	0.08	-0.07										
6. Receives funding from nonprofits	-0.06	0.60*	-0.03	0.07	0.20*									
7. Agency's operational budget	0.08	0.21*	0.26*	0.43*	-0.03	0.15*								
8. Range of services	0.13	0.13	0.28*	0.36*	-0.01	0.09	0.64*							
9. Offers advocacy service	0.12	0.09	0.02	0.15*	0.05	0.05	0.00	0.36*						
10. Board member from business	0.01	0.27*	0.08	0.01	0.03	0.23*	0.19*	0.08	0.00					
11. Board member from government	-0.07	0.10	-0.03	-0.05	0.00	0.19*	0.07	-0.05	-0.05	0.37*				
12. Provides services in rural area	0.00	0.03	0.05	0.05	-0.07	-0.02	0.15*	0.03	-0.12	0.01	-0.03			
13. Female	0.12	0.05	0.05	-0.01	0.11	0.05	-0.16*	-0.12	0.16*	0.11	0.08	0.07		
14. Education level	0.02	0.13	0.06	0.13	0.10	0.10	0.26*	0.19*	-0.02	0.51*	0.18*	0.09	0.21*	
15. Business background and training	0.07	0.08	-0.06	-0.14*	0.08	0.10	-0.03	-0.07	-0.00	0.12	-0.01	0.13	-0.01	-0.01

* $p < .05$

Table 3. Multinomial and ordered logistic regression models.

Independent variables	Charging Fees for Services		Engaging in Marketing Alliances with Businesses		Professionalizing Agency		Running Agency Like a Business
	Occasionally versus Never	Usually versus Never	Occasionally versus Never	Usually versus Never	Neutral versus Disagree	Agree versus Disagree	Ordered Logit
	Odds Ratio/(SE)		Odds Ratio/(SE)		Odds Ratio/(SE)		Odds Ratio/(SE)
Influence of the business community index	1.863*	2.508**	1.262	2.448**	2.025*	4.402***	1.566*
	(0.695)	(0.971)	(0.419)	(0.937)	(0.794)	(1.683)	(0.384)
Receives funding from businesses	3.886*	1.041	0.506	1.832	0.449	0.672	0.627
	(2.824)	(0.853)	(0.321)	(1.478)	(0.298)	(0.445)	(0.294)
Government control index	0.498	0.325**	1.000	1.507	0.809	0.600	0.944
	(0.204)	(0.167)	(0.357)	(0.684)	(0.316)	(0.232)	(0.253)
Receives funding from government	1.373	0.526	0. 327*	0.301	5.536**	1.078	1.949
	(1.023)	(0.403)	(0.206)	(0.255)	(4.363)	(0.728)	(1.004)
Nonprofitness index	1.203	0.774	1.172	1.836	0.936	1.309	1.136
	(0. 373)	(0.240)	(0.299)	(0.689)	(0.234)	(0.359)	(0.236)
Receives funding from nonprofits	0.458	1.812	2. 407	0.836	1.057	1.143	0.889
	(0.270)	(1.276)	(1.365)	(0.558)	(0.616)	(0.643)	(0.368)
Agency's operating budget	1.650*	0.794	1. 623*	1.152	0.544**	0.616**	1.447**
	(0.468)	(0.246)	(0.403)	(0.364)	(0.146)	(0.161)	(0.271)
Range of services offered	1.347**	1.625***	0.865	1.126	1.234*	1. 256*	0.932
	(0.180)	(0.272)	(0.099)	(0.175)	(0.157)	(0.166)	(0.086)
Offers advocacy service	0.855	1.303	0.608	0.148**	0.396*	0.390*	0.386**
	(0.486)	(0.841)	(0.305)	(0.112)	(0.219)	(0.218)	(0.161)
Business board member	1.099	1.862	1.380	3.304	0.541	1.050	4.832***
	(0.789)	(1.606)	(0.868)	(2.766)	(0.336)	(0.657)	(0.853)
Government board member	1.343	0.976	0.506	0.717	1.377	0.914	2.392
	(0.694)	(0.612)	(0.247)	(0.442)	(0.719)	(0.474)	1.070
							(0.407)
Provides services in rural area	0.594	0.665	0.568	1.957	1.786	1.190	0. 492*
	(0.326)	(0.422)	(0.292)	(1.107)	(0.888)	(0.594)	(0.185)
Female	1.359	0.98	0.899	2.199	1. 491	1.715	2. 289**
	(0.715)	(0.609)	(0.424)	(1.279)	(0.738)	(0.8820)	(0.853)
Education level	0.318**	0.891	0.479*	1.500	0.345**	0.322***	3. 292***
	(0.144)	(0.456)	(0.187)	(0.726)	(0.147)	(0.134)	(1.064)
Business background and training	0.872	1.248	3.382	3.082	0.900	1.412	4. 430**
	(0. 692)	(1.118)	(2.947)	(3.341)	(0.792)	(1.058)	(2.620)
Constant	0.186	0.057*	9.269*	0.028*	35.147**	48.853***	
	(0.270)	(0.097)	(12.51)	(0.051)	(53.703)	(72.021)	
	*Reference category: Never; N = 151; χ2 = 87.30***; Log likelihood full model = -110.370*		*Reference category: Never; N = 149; χ² = 66. 92***; Log likelihood full model = -124.455*		*Reference category: Disagree; N = 163; χ2 = 64. 76***; Log likelihood full model = -145.778*		N = 148;χ² = 62.00***; Log likelihood full model = -158. 548; Pseudo R² = 0.164

Notes: * p < .10, ** p < .05, *** p < .01

commonly charge for their services and products, and in the context of these child welfare agencies, 48% of them reported charging fees for services at least on an occasional basis. Contrary to what was suspected, more government control does not lead to an increase in the likelihood of using fees for services. This could be attributed to the fact that if government is controlling an agency through state and federal regulations or accountability measures (e.g., specified in contracts), government may also discourage agencies from charging fees. It is also possible that government could have more control of one service area (e.g., foster care and adoption) and less control in another (e.g., advocacy or family support services). In addition, government funding may be sufficient to cover the costs associated with service provision making fee charges no longer necessary.

Alliances with businesses

The *influence of the business community index* and *receiving government funding* are significant predictors of NPOs engaging in cause-related marketing alliances with businesses to market an image, product, or service for mutual benefit. An increase in the *influence of the business community index* increases the odds of usually engaging in marketing alliances with business when compared to never, while *receiving funding from government* is associated with a decrease in the odds of occasionally creating business alliances. Respectively, a one point increase in the *influence of the business community index* increases the odds of usually versus never creating alliances with businesses by 145% ($p < .05$). Nonprofits that accept government funding are 67% less likely to occasionally use marketing alliances with businesses ($p < .10$). Creating marketing alliances with businesses was not found to be associated with *receiving business funding, government control index, nonprofitness index,* or *receiving funding from nonprofits and foundations*. The results do show that offering advocacy services decreases the odds of engaging in marketing alliances.

Thus, the findings support hypotheses 1 and 4. An increasing level of business community influence does increase the likelihood that a child welfare agency will engage in marketing alliances with businesses. NPOs may actively seek out alliances with businesses because they believe it will be financially beneficial and/or improve their agency's presence and recognition in the community. On the other hand, these agencies could feel pressured to seek out alliances with businesses out of necessity or due to the lack of other resources. Correspondingly, child welfare agencies who accept government funding may be less likely to financially need to engage with business marketing alliances.

Need to professionalize

The *influence of the business community index* (hypothesis 1) and *receiving government funding* (hypothesis 4) are related to the likelihood of nonprofit managers reporting a need to professionalize their agencies. A one point increase in the *influence of the business community index* is positively associated with managers agreeing that there is a need to professionalize their agency by 4.4 times ($p < .01$) and by almost 2 times ($p < .10$) for those who are neutral, compared to those in the disagree category. Additionally, nonprofits that take government funding are over four times ($p < .05$) more likely to be neutral regarding professionalizing their staff when compared to those who disagree with replacing volunteers. As in similar business management practices, *nonprofitness index,* and *receiving funding from nonprofits and foundations* are not significant predictors of perceived need of agency professionalism. Furthermore, the *government control index* is not significant while *receiving government funding* is only significant in the neutral category.

Among those child welfare agencies with managers who report needing to replace volunteers with professional staff members, evidence suggests they are being impacted by the business community. Not surprisingly, growing influence from the business community predicts the likelihood that managers will want to professionalize their agencies. Interestingly, the results show that managers working for child welfare agencies that offer advocacy services are less likely to perceive the need to professionalize the agency.

Running their agency like a business

The only key variable of interest that positively and significantly increases the likelihood of NPO managers choosing to run their agency like a business is the *influence of the business community index* (hypothesis 1). Managers are 60% more likely to consider it more important to run their agency like a business with a one point increase in the influence of the business community index (OR = 1.6, $p < .10$). In Table 3, two additional variables that further explain why managers run their agency like a business are included: having a *business board member* and receiving a *business background and training*. These variables are not significant in the other business management strategies models, but are reported here because they depict just how powerful the business community via business education and board member influence is on management strategies. NPOs with a *business board member* are 383% more likely to run their agency like a business ($p < .01$). Additionally, NPO managers with a *business background and training* are 343% more likely to report running their agency like a business ($p < .05$). However, managers of child welfare agencies that offer advocacy services are less likely to run their agency like a business. The other key variables of interest were not statistically significant predictors of manager's running their agencies like a business.

Similar to the other business management practices models, greater influence from the business community increases the odds that administrators will report that running their agency like a business is important to them. Some may find it surprising that these managers would identify with the statement of "running my agency like a business" when they work in the child welfare field. However, our finding gives further credence to the power of a business-minded approach and philosophy within nonprofit agencies (Dart, 2004). Interestingly, other factors like having a business board member and professional training also cause managers to identify with the value in running their agency like a business.

Discussion and conclusion

There are a few data limitations to address before discussing the results of this study. First, due to the cross-sectional nature of the data, the results suggest relationships between the variables rather than causation. Second, this study is based on a small number of respondents from agencies categorized as NTEE Code P32. The way the NTEE classification codes are designed can limit the number of possible survey respondents because some large human service agencies, who may provide child welfare services as well, are categorized differently and may not have been surveyed (e.g., Catholic Charities). As McBeath and colleagues (2014, p. 89) point out, however, research on child welfare agencies, their management, and service provisions is greatly needed and there is "considerable value in... small-N studies to inform... theory development" in an area where the universe of organizations providing these types of services is unclear. Additionally, human service agencies like these represent 35% of all public charities (McKeever, 2015) so understanding more about the child welfare environment may inform broader trends in social service nonprofits. Third, in addition to the factors examined in this study, nonprofit child welfare agencies' managerial practice could be influenced by other factors, such as the amount of funding from various sources, the length of government funding, and the number of volunteers the agencies have. Due to data limitation, these factors are not examined in this study. However, future studies should take these factors into consideration. With these limitations in mind, the contributions and implication are discussed.

This study examines whether nonprofit child welfare agencies are implementing business-like management strategies, and, the extent to which these agencies' practices are associated with influences of marketization, governmentalization, and nonprofitness. The results of the analysis empirically supports the theory that nonprofits are undergoing the marketization of some of their practices which may impact civil society values and views toward providing public and social goods (Maier et al., 2016; Ott & Dicke, 2012; Weisbrod, 1998). The paper contributes to the child welfare and nonprofit literatures in three specific areas.

First, responses from managers of child welfare nonprofits confirm that these nonprofits are adopting business-like practices and our analysis demonstrates the empirical connections between some of the external and internal pressures and the adoption of these practices. One key contribution of this paper is to show what business management practices child welfare agencies are adopting and why. Some of the results indicate that child welfare nonprofits are charging fees for services and the likelihood of usually imposing fees are positively associated with the influences of the business community and negatively associated with government control. The likelihood of managers usually engaging in cause-related marketing alliances with businesses increases with more business community influence. Child welfare managers who agree that their agency needs to professionalize its workforce are also being impacted by the business community's influence. And finally, administrators, who report "running their agency like a business" is important to them, can be attributed to pressures from the business community, having business board members, and having a background and training in business. Unlike the positive influences of the business community, offering advocacy services lowers the likelihood of employing business management strategies. It is interesting that managers whose organizations promote advocacy are less likely to report engaging in marketing alliances, professionalizing their agency, and finding the rhetoric of running one's agency like a business as important. Advocacy seems to change the orientation of these managers. In the nonprofit sector, advocacy is one of the important roles NPOs fulfill and aids in promoting democratic discourse (Eikenberry, 2009a; Moulton & Eckerd, 2012). Promoting advocacy may help keep managers focused on their client's needs rather than simply pursue agency revenues or lowing cost.

These findings add to the literature on how nonprofits are increasingly responding to governmental or market pressures by professionalizing and adhering to organizational management practices that dominate the business sector. The consequences of child welfare agencies embracing a market orientation will likely have significant impacts on children and their families. Scholars suggest that viewing clients and citizens as consumers, due in part from commercial and business pressures, can have negative effects on civil society, citizens, and other major institutions (Backman & Smith, 2000; Eikenberry & Kluver, 2004). On the positive side, business-like practices may encourage greater forms of accountability, organizational performance, and client satisfaction (Levine & Zahradnik, 2012; Shoham, Vigoda-Gadot, & Schwabsky, 2006). Conversely, it could have negative consequences for youth, or other nonprofit clients, if less emphasis is placed on the quality of services while the measurable outputs are stressed over outcomes. Ultimately, the effects of nonprofits becoming business-like and how this shapes organizational performance, advocacy, and the nonprofit sector's ability to fulfill their civic functions are mixed, and thus, warrants further studies (Maier et al., 2016).

Secondly, while our findings have specific implications on child welfare management, they are also applicable to human service organizations more broadly. This study builds upon the growing literature showing the increasing tendency of NPOs to subscribe to managerialism, professionalism, and rationality as general norms of operation (Barman & MacIndoe, 2012; Bromley & Meyer, 2014; Suárez & Esparza, 2016; Suárez & Hwang, 2013). This raises normative questions regarding what *should* be influencing the management of nonprofits organizations. One might expect that some sense of a nonprofit identity and values (i.e., nonprofitness) would impact a manager's decision to utilize business management practices i.e., decrease the likelihood that administrators would rely on these strategies in running their agency. However, evidence from this research suggests otherwise.

While the ramifications of these trends on day-to-day nonprofit management and ultimately how these practices will influences outcomes are unclear, administrators will still face tough choices on how best to manage for their mission and clients (Maier et al., 2016). Making these choices come with trade-offs. For example, will NPOs choose to adopt a professional, managerial identity versus a volunteer identity (Kreutzer & Jäger, 2011) or will they embrace a market-orientation versus adopting a democratic counterdiscourse where distinctive values like public good delivery and advocacy are emphasized through participatory means (Eikenberry, 2009a)? These trade-offs are especially troubling if they lead to a sole focus on instrumental rather than expressive purposes of the nonprofit sector. Part of the intrigue over what nonprofit management of human service organizations should look like lies in attempting to determine the tipping point for when NPOs become 'shadow businesses' (Frumkin, 2005) or 'for-profits in disguise' (Weisbrod, 1988).

Lastly, this paper argues for the importance of using the theoretical lens of institutionalism by contending that certain nonprofit institutional logics and values (referred to here as nonprofitness) are a critical mechanism for exploring managerial behaviors. And, when nonprofitness is not found to be a predictor of nonprofit organizations' management practices, scholars should seek to examine why and what other influences are shaping their behaviors. Institutional theory predicts organizations in similar fields embrace similar forms of operations through social processes (Jepperson, 1991). Bromley and Meyer (2014) take sociological institutionalism further by arguing that "organizations" should be a field of study because of the standardization and replication of structures and processes occurring among all organizations regardless of sector (Bromley & Meyer, 2014). Knusten proposed that when NPOs are striving for survival (i.e., their instrumental function), "most NPOs have to adapt to the institutional logic of the state and capitalism for resources from the government or the market" (p.1006) which could essentially crowd out more unique institutional logics and expressive values promoted through "democracy, family, professions, and religion" (p. 1009). Others echo Knutsen's concern about NPO's becoming too business or governmental-like suggesting, "When faced with large new opportunities for commercialism, many nonprofits seem quite willing to shed their altruistic cover and assume the values and behavior of for-profits" (James, 1998, p. 285). What can counteract these forces to conform to the dominant logics of the state or market?

We proposed that manager's who identified with higher level of nonprofitness (i.e., nonprofit values and norms for behaviors) would be less likely to adopt business management practices, the results did not support this. Interestingly, offering advocacy services seemed to lessen the adoption of business management practices. Measures of government control and funding did not reduce the adoption of business management strategies in most models either. The findings indicate that while publicness and nonprofitness may matter in some nonprofit management practices (e.g., Robichau & Fernandez, 2016), their influences on using business management practices did not discourage the adoption of business-like practices in this study. Eikenberry (2009a, p. 583) warned that the "colonization of everyday life by the market is problematic" and that nonprofits should offer a counter discourse to this by focusing on democratic participation. Thus, we suggest more research that contrasts the influences of government and business logics on nonprofit behavior with the more normative, expressive role and expectations of how NPOs should behave such as advocating for those who have no voice.

In conclusion, our response to Dekker's (2001) question of what happens "when nonprofitness makes no difference?" is that "they may adopt business management strategies and start running their nonprofit like a business." This study provides empirical evidence of the business community's influence on the management of child welfare agencies. It demonstrates how child welfare agencies take on management strategies similar to that of private, for-profits under isomorphic pressures from the market. The verdict is still out on whether becoming business-like helps or hinders nonprofit organizational legitimacy and outcomes; however, some theoretical concerns speak to a "legitimacy paradox, which in the long run erodes their [NPOs] special role in society" (Maier et al., 2016, p. 78). We conclude with a call for more studies that address the various nonprofit management strategies child welfare agencies, and other human service organizations, are employing to provide services and how the delivery of these services are being impacted by influences from the market, government, and nonprofit sector.

References

Abzug, R., & Galaskiewicz, J. (2001). Nonprofit boards: Crucibles of expertise or symbols of local identities? *Nonprofit and Voluntary Sector Quarterly, 30*(1), 51–73.

Alexander, J., Nank, R., & Stivers, C. (1999). Implications of welfare reform: Do nonprofit survival strategies threaten civil society? *Nonprofit and Voluntary Sector Quarterly, 28*(4), 452–475.

Andrews, R., Boyne, G. A., & Walker, R. M. (2011). Dimensions of publicness and organizational performance: A review of the evidence. *Journal of Public Administration Research and Theory, 21*(Supplement 3), i301–i319.

Anheier, H. (2014). *Nonprofit organizations: Theory, management, and policy* (2nd ed.). New York, NY, United States of America: Routledge.

Ashton, R. (2011). *How to be a social entrepreneur: Make money and change the world.* West Sussex, U.K.: Capstone Publishing.

Aspen Institute. (2001). *The nonprofit sector and the market: Opportunities and challenges.* Washington, DC: Author.

Backman, E. V., & Smith, S. R. (2000). Healthy organizations, unhealthy communities? *Nonprofit Management and Leadership, 10*(4), 355–373.

Barillas, K. H. (2011). State capacity: The missing piece in child welfare privatization. *Child Welfare, 90*(3), 111–127.

Barman, E. A., & MacIndoe, H. (2012). Institutional pressures and organizational capacity: The case of outcome measurement. *Sociological Forum, 27*(1), 70–93.

Boyne, G. A. (2002). Public and private management: What's the difference? *Journal of Management Studies, 39*(1), 97–122.

Bozeman, B., & Moulton, S. (2011). Integrative publicness: A framework for public management strategy and performance. *Journal of Public Administration Research and Theory, 21*(Supplement 3), i363–i380.

Bromley, P., & Meyer, J. W. (2014). They are all organizations: The cultural roots of blurring between the nonprofit, business, and government sectors. *Administration & Society, 46,* 1–28.

Bunger, A. C., McBeath, B., Chuang, E., & Collins-Camargo, C. (2017). Institutional and market pressures on interorganizational collaboration and competition amgong private human service organizations. *Human Service Organizations: Management, Leadership & Governance, 41*(1), 13–29.

Bush, R. (1992). Survival of the nonprofit spirit in a for-profit world. *Nonprofit and Voluntary Sector Quarterly, 21*(4), 391–410.

Chavesc, M., Stephens, L., & Galaskiewicz, J. (2004). Does government funding suppress nonprofits' political activity? *American Sociological Review, 69*(2), 292–316.

Child, C. (2010). Whither the turn? The ambiguous nature of nonprofits' commerical revenue. *Social Forces, 89*(1), 145–161.

Choi, Y.-S., Cho, C.-L., Wright, D. S., & Brudney, J. L. (2005). Dimensions of contracting for service delivery by American state administrative agencies: Exploring linkages between intergovernmental relations and intersectoral administration. *Public Performance & Management Review, 29*(1), 46–66.

Cohen, J., & Cohen, P. (1985). *Applied multiple regression and correlation analysis for the behavioral sciences* (2nd ed.). Hillsdale, NJ: Erlbaum.

Collins-Camargo, C., Chuang, E., McBeath, B., & Bunger, A. C. (2014). Private child welfare agency managers' perceptions of the effectiveness of different performance management strategies. *Children and Youth Services Review, 38,* 133–141.

Cooney, K. (2006). The institutional and technical structuring of nonprofit ventures: Case study of a US hybrid organization caught between two fields. *Voluntas: International Journal of Voluntary and Nonprofit Organizations, 17*(2), 137–155.

Coursey, D., & Bozeman, B. (1990). Decision making in the public and private organizations: A test of alternative concepts of "Publicness". *Public Administration Review, 50*(5), 525–534.

Dart, R. (2004). Being "business-like" in a nonprofit organization: A grounded and inductive typology. *Nonprofit and Voluntary Sector Quarterly, 33*(2), 290–310.

Dees, J. G., Emerson, J., & Economy, P. (2001). *Enterprising nonprofits: A toolkit for social entrepreneurs* (Vol. 159). New York, NY, United States of America: John Wiley & Sons.

Dekker, P. (2001). What crises, what challenges? When nonprofitness makes no difference. In: H. K. Anheier, & J. Kendall (Eds.), *Third sector policy at the crossroads: An international nonprofit analysis* (pp. 61–68). London, United Kingdom: Routledge.

Durnford, J. (2011, December 12). [Personal communication].

Eikenberry, A. M. (2009a). Refusing the market: A democratic discourse for voluntary and nonprofit organizations. *Nonprofit and Voluntary Sector Quarterly, 38*(4), 582–596.

Eikenberry, A. M. (2009b). The hidden costs of cause marekting. *Stanford Social Innovation Review, 7*(3), 51–55.

Eikenberry, A. M., & Kluver, J. D. (2004). The marketization of the nonprofit sector: Civil society at risk? *Public Administration Review, 64*(2), 132–140.

Embry, R. A., Buddenhagen, P., & Bolles, S. (2000). Managed care and child welfare: Challenges to implementation. *Children and Youth Services Review, 22*(2), 93–116.

Fabrignar, L. R., & Wegener, D. T. (2012). *Exploratory factor analysis: Understanding statistics.* Oxford, United Kingdom: Oxford University Press.

Flaherty, C., Collins-Camargo, C., & Lee, E. (2008). Privatization of child welfare services: Lessons learned from experienced states regarding site readiness assessment and planning. *Children and Youth Services Review, 30,* 809–820.

Foster, M. K., & Meinhard, A. G. (2002). A regression model explaining predisposition to collaborate. Nonprofit and Voluntary Sector Quarterly, *31*(4), 549–564.

Frumkin, P. (2005). *On being nonprofit: A conceptual and policy primer.* Cambridge, MA, United States of America: Harvard Univ Press.

Frumkin, P., & Andre-Clark, A. (2000). When missions, markets, and politics collide: Values and strategy in the nonprofit human services. *Nonprofit and Voluntary Sector Quarterly, 29*(supplemental 1), 141–163.

Frumkin, P., & Keating, E. K. (2011). Diversification reconsidered: The risks and rewards of revenue concentration. *Journal of Social Entrepreneurship, 2*(2), 151–164.

Fukuyama, F. (1996). *Trust: The social virtues and the creation of prosperity.* New York, NY, United States of America: Free Press.

Gazley, B. (2008). Beyond the contract: The scope and nature of informal government–nonprofit partnerships. *Public Administration Review, 68*(1), 141–154.

Gazley, B. (2010). Why not partner with local government? Nonprofit managerial perceptions of collaborative disadvantage. Nonprofit and Voluntary Sector Quarterly, *39*(1), 51–76.

Guo, C. (2007). When government becomes the principal philanthropist: The effects of public funding on patterns of nonprofit governance. *Public Administration Review, 67*(3), 458–473.

Haque, M. S. (2001). The diminishing publicness of public service under the current mode of governance. *Public Administration Review, 61*(1), 65–82.

James, E. (1998). Commercialism among nonprofits: Objectives, opportunities, and constraints. In: B. A. Weisbrod (Ed.), *To profit or not to profit: The commercial transformation of the nonprofit sector* (pp. 271–286). Cambridge, MA, United States of America: Cambride University Press.

Jeavons, T. H. (2010). Ethical nonprofit management: Core values and key practices. In: D. O. Renz & Associates (Eds.), *The Jossey-Bass handbook of nonprofit leadership and management* (3rd ed., pp. 178–205). San Francisco, CA, United States of America: Jossey-Bass.

Jepperson, R. L. (1991). Institutions, institutional effects and institutionalism. In: W. W. Powell, & P. J. DiMaggio (Eds.), *The new institutionalism in organizational analysis* (pp. 143–163). Chicago, IL, United States of America: University of Chicago Press.

Kerlin, J. A., & Pollak, T. H. (2011). Nonprofit commercial revenue: A replacement for declining government grants and private contributions? *The American Review of Public Administration, 41*(6), 686–704.

Knutsen, W. L. (2012). Adapted institutional logics of contemporary n tions. *Administration & Society, 44*(8), 985–1013.

Knutsen, W. L., & Brock, K. L. (2014). Introductory essay: From a closed system to an open system: A parallel critical review of the intellectual trajectories of publicness and nonprofitness. *Voluntas: International Journal of Voluntary and Nonprofit Organizations, 25,* 1113–1131.

Kreutzer, K., & Jäger, U. (2011). Volunteering versus managerialism: Conflict over organizational identity in voluntary associations. Nonprofit and Voluntary Sector Quarterly, *40*(4), 634–661.

LeRoux, K. (2009). Managing stakeholder demands. *Administration & Society, 41*(2), 158–184.

Levine, H., & Zahradnik, A. G. (2012). Online media, market orientation, and financial performance in nonprofits. *Journal of Nonprofit & Public Sector Marketing, 24*(1), 26–42.

Liao, T. F. (1994). *Interpreting probability models: Logit, probit, and other generalized linear models.* Thousand Oaks, CA: Sage Publications.

Maier, F., Meyer, M., & Steinbereithner, M. (2016). Nonprofit organizaitons becoming business-like: A systematic review. Nonprofit and Voluntary Sector Quarterly, *45*(1), 64–86.

Mangold, S. V. (1999). Protection, privatization, and profit in the foster care system. *Ohio St.LJ, 60,* 1295–1326.

McBeath, B., Collins-Camargo, C., Chuang, E., Wells, R., Bunger, A. C., & Jolles, M. P. (2014). New directions for research on the organizational and institutional context of child welfare agencies: Introduction to the symposium on "The Organizational and Managerial Context of Private Child Welfare Agencies". *Children and Youth Services Review, 38,* 83–92.

McBeath, B., & Meezan, W. (2010). Governance in motion: Service provision and child welfare outcomes in performance-based, managed care contracting environment. *Journal of Public Administration Research and Theory, 20*(Supplemental 1), i101–i123.

McKeever, B. S. (2015). *The nonprofit sector in brief 2015: Public charities, giving, and volunteering.* Washington, DC: Urban Institute.

Moulton, S., & Eckerd, A. (2012). Preserving the publicness of the nonprofit sector: Resources, roles, and public values. *Nonprofit and Voluntary Sector Quarterly, 41*(4), 656–685.

Osborne, S. P. (2010). The (new) public governance: A suitable case for treatment. In: S. P. Osborne (Ed.), *The new public governance? Emerging perspectives on the theory and practice of public governance* (pp. 1–16). London, United Kingdom: Routledge.

Ott, J. S., & Dicke, L. A. (Eds.). (2012). *The nature of the nonprofit sector* (2nd ed.). Boulder, CO: Westview Press.

Putnam, R. D. (1995). Bowling alone: America's declining social capital. *Journal of Democracy, 6*, 65–78.

Robichau, R. W., & Fernandez, K. (2016). Intersectoral experiences: Nonprofit managers and sector influences in child welfare agencies. *Human Service Organizations: Management, Leadership, & Governance.* doi:10.1080/23303131.2016.1193586

Robichau, R. W., Fernandez, K., & Kraeger, P. (2015). An integrated framework of intersectorality: Nonprofitness and its influence on society and public administration programs. *Journal of Public Affairs Education, 21*(3), 315–336.

Salamon, L. M. (1993). The marketization of welfare: Changing nonprofit and for-profit roles in the American welfare state. *The Social Service Review, 67*(1), 16–39.

Salamon, L. M. (1995). *Partners in public service: Government-nonprofit relations in the modern welfare state.* Baltimore, MD: Johns Hopkins University Press.

Salamon, L. M. (2002). *The tools of government: A guide to the new governance.* Oxford, United Kingdom: Oxford University Press.

Salamon, L. M. (2003). *The resilient sector: The state of nonprofit America.* Washington, D.C.: Brookings Institution Press.

Salamon, L. M. (2005). The changing context of American nonprofit management. In: R. D. Herman & Associates (Eds.), *The Jossey-Bass handook of nonprofit leadership and management* (2nd ed., pp. 81–101). San Francisco, CA, United States of America: Jossey-Bass.

Salamon, L. M., Hems, L. C., & Chinnock, K. (2000). The nonprofit sector: For what and for whom? (Working paper of The Johns Hopkins Comparative Nonprofit Sector Project). Baltimore, MD: The Johns Hopkins Center for Civil Society Studies.

Scarcella, C. A., Bess, R., Zielewski, E. H., & Geen, R. (2006). *The cost of protecting vulnerable children V: Understanding state variation in child welfare financing.* Washingon, D.C.: The Urban Institute.

Scott, W., & Davis, G. (2007). *Organizations and organizing: Rational, natural, and open systems perspectives.* Upper Sadle River, NJ: Prentice Hall.

Shoham, A., Vigoda-Gadot, E., & Schwabsky, N. (2006). Market orientations in the nonprofit and voluntary sector: A meta-analysis of their relationships with organizational performance. *Nonprofit and Voluntary Sector Quarterly, 35*(3), 453–476.

Slaper, T. F., & Hall, T. J. (2011). The triple bottomo line: What is it and how does it work. *Indiana Business Review, 86*(1), 4–8.

Smith, S. R. (2004). Government and nonprofits in the modern age: Is independence possible? In: P. Frumkin, & J. B. Imber (Eds.), *In search of the nonprofit sector* (pp. 3–18). Oxford, United Kingdom: Oxford University Press.

Smith, S. R., & Lipsky, M. (1993). *Nonprofits for hire: The welfare state in the age of contracting.* Cambridge, MA, United States of America: Harvard University Press.

Suárez, D. F. (2011). Collaboration and professionalization: The contours of public sector funding for nonprofit organizations. *Journal of Public Administration Research and Theory, 21*(2), 307–326.

Suárez, D. F., & Esparza, N. (2016). Institutional change and management of public-nonprofit partnerships. *American Review of Public Administration, 4*:, 379–501.

Suárez, D. F., & Hwang, H. (2013). Resource constraints or cultural conformity? Nonprofit relationships with businesses. *Voluntas: International Journal of Voluntary and Nonprofit Organizations, 24*(3), 581–605.

U.S. Children's Bureau, & ACYF. (2012). Trends in foster care and adoption - FY 2002-FY 2011. Retrieved July 26, 2012, from http://www.acf.hhs.gov/programs/cb/stats_research/afcars/trends_june2011.pdf

U.S. DHHS, & ACF. (2001). *National survey of child and adolescent well-being: State child welfare agency survey: Report.* Washington, D.C: United States Department of Health & Human Services and Administration for Children & Families.

Van Puyvelde, S., Caers, R., Du Bois, C., & Jegers, M. (2012). The governance of nonprofit organizations integrating agency theory with stakeholder and stewardship theories. *Nonprofit and Voluntary Sector Quarterly, 41*(3), 431–451.

Van Slyke, D. (2007). Agents or stewards: Using theory to understand the government-nonprofit social service contracting relationship. *Journal of Public Administration Research and Theory, 17*(2), 157–187.

Weisbrod, B. A. (1988). *The nonprofit economy.* Cambridge, MA, United States of America: Harvard University Press.

Weisbrod, B. A. (Ed.). (1998). *To profit or not to profit: The commercial transformation of the nonprofit sector.* Cambridge,UK: Cambridge University Press.

Wells, R., Jolles, M. P., Chuang, E., McBeath, B., & Collins-Camargo, C. (2014). Trends in local public child welfare agencies 1999–2009. *Children and Youth Services Review, 38*, 93–100.

Witesman, E. M., & Fernandez, S. (2012). Government contract with private organizations: Are there differences between nonprofits and for-profits? *Nonprofit and Voluntary Sector Quarterly, 42*(4), 689–715.

Young, D. R. (2002). The influence of business on nonprofit organizations and the complexity of nonprofit accountability. *The American Review of Public Administration, 32*(1), 3–19.

Frontline managers' contribution to mission achievement: A study of how people management affects thoughtful care

Eva Knies, Peter Leisink, and Sascha Kraus-Hoogeveen

ABSTRACT

This study addresses the question to what extent frontline managers' people management activities contribute to mission achievement through frontline workers' behaviors. Drawing on the case of elderly care, we contribute to the literature by: (1) providing a compact measure of mission achievement in elderly care and specifying the requisite employee behaviors; and (2) showing that frontline managers' people management activities impact on employees' behaviors, and ultimately on mission achievement. In doing so, we also contribute to more knowledge about elderly care, which is an under-researched sector, and about the role of line managers (instead of top managers) in HRM implementation.

Introduction

Performance continues to be one of the most studied topics in management research, both of business organizations (Richard, Devinney, Yip, & Johnson, 2009) and of nonprofit and public organizations (Andersen, Boesen, & Pedersen, 2016; Andrews, Boyne, & Walker, 2006). Business management research is predominantly interested in organizational performance with a focus on financial, market, and shareholder performance indicators (Richard et al., 2009, p. 722). Researchers of nonprofit and public organizations prefer the term organizational effectiveness (Sowa, Selden, & Sandfort, 2004) or use the terms organizational effectiveness and performance interchangeably (Rainey & Steinbauer, 1999) as they recognize that these organizations have different types of goals, which are often multiple.

Studies of nonprofit and public organizations use a multitude of performance indicators. This is illustrated by Andrews and Boyne's (2010) study of English local governments, which assesses organizational performance on the basis of 108 best value performance indicators. Although Andrews, Boyne and Walker (2006, p. 15) claim that 'clarity has been brought to the criteria of performance' by Boyne's (2002) proposal to distinguish between five conceptual categories, it is still hard to see the forest from the trees represented by tens and hundreds of performance indicators suggested by performance studies. Here, we argue that to address these measurement issues we need a compact singular measure of effectiveness that can be used across public and nonprofit human service organizations. One such compact measure would be a tailored measure of mission achievement: the extent to which an organization achieves its ultimate goals. The focus on mission achievement follows from Rainey and Steinbauer (1999) who define organizational effectiveness as follows: 'the agency performs well in discharging the administrative and operational functions pursuant to the mission' (p.13). We follow their view that 'evidence that the agencies' operations have contributed substantially to the achievement of these goals [included in the mission] provides evidence of agency effectiveness' (p. 13). The need for a measure of mission achievement is also felt in practice as human service organizations find it hard to define client outcomes that adequately capture the nature of the human service they provide (Carnochan, Samples, Myers, & Austin, 2014).

Studies of organizational performance or effectiveness as a rule are interested in the question how performance/effectiveness can be achieved (Lynn, Heinrich, & Hill, 2000). Typically, these studies focus on management's contribution to performance. More specifically, conceptual models (e.g. Rainey & Steinbauer, 1999; Sowa et al., 2004) as well as empirical studies (e.g. Andrews & Boyne, 2010; Meier, O'Toole, Boyne, & Walker, 2007; Moynihan & Pandey, 2005) tend to concentrate on the contribution of top managers, maybe as a result of their interest in the effect of management systems and strategies. In doing so, these studies tend to ignore the role of frontline managers, who are typically responsible for supervising frontline employees and can be expected to contribute to performance because they are close to the service delivery process (Guest, 2011). Since frontline employees are critical agents in the provision of human services, how these employees are managed is of great relevance (Wright & Nishii, 2013). Therefore, in this study we will focus on frontline managers' people management activities aimed at supporting the employees they supervise at work. Following the human resource management (HRM) literature and the work of Purcell and Hutchinson (2007) in particular, people management refers to line managers' implementation of HRM practices and their leadership behavior. In doing so, we add to the knowledge base on how management affects performance outcomes by looking at a particular set of management activities (i.e. people management by frontline managers), and by making clear decisions about how outcomes are specified (i.e. mission achievement). The question of frontline managers' contribution to performance or effectiveness is particularly relevant in the context of nonprofit or public human service organizations. It is often suggested that frontline managers in nonprofit or public organizations may have limited impact on performance because of constraints imposed by government directives, red tape, and detailed regulations which apply particularly to the area of personnel management (Brewer & Walker, 2012; Feeney & Rainey, 2010). This raises the question to what extent people management activities of frontline managers in nonprofit and public human service organizations are related to mission achievement through employees' behaviors (see also Riccucci, 2005).

Therefore, the research question which this article answers is: to what extent do frontline managers' people management activities contribute to mission achievement through front-line workers behaviors? Drawing on the case of elderly care, this article's contribution to the literature on performance and human service management is twofold. First, we contribute by providing a compact (i.e. a short and reliable) measure of mission achievement in elderly care and specifying the requisite employee behaviors, which represent respectively the product and process dimensions of service provision (Donabedian, 1980). Second, this article contributes by showing to what extent frontline managers' people management activities impact on employees' behaviors, and ultimately on mission achievement in elderly care. In doing so, we also contribute to more knowledge about elderly care, which is an under-researched sector, and about the role of line managers in implementation linked to quality of care, as called for by Cooke and Bartram (2015) in their introduction to a recent special issue of *Human Resource Management*, entitled 'Human Resource Management in health care and elderly care: current challenges and toward a research agenda'.

Theoretical framework

In this section, we substantiate the argument that frontline managers' people management activities are positively related to mission achievement through frontline workers' behaviors by combining insights from the public management and HRM bodies of literature.

Mission achievement

Nonprofit and public organizations researchers agree that performance is multidimensional and that the primary thing that researchers have to define is the stakeholders whose interests are taken into account when measuring performance (Andersen et al., 2016; Richard et al., 2009). Different stakeholders hold different views on good performance and different performance dimensions are of varying interest to them. This can be illustrated by the dimensions of public service performance of local authorities which are distinguished by Boyne (2002): outputs, efficiency, service outcomes, responsiveness, and democratic outcomes. For instance, responsiveness can be seen from the perspective of the direct service user, whose preferences as a recipient of social services are matched, or from the perspective of the wider community of local citizens who are interested as taxpayers. Efficiency also relates to taxpayers' interests while it is of less interest to the direct service user. Therefore, it is necessary to be explicit about the focal stakeholder(s) whose interests are the basis for constructing a measure of mission achievement.

According to Hasenfeld (2015, p. 1), the common mission of human service organizations is 'to meet the social welfare needs of vulnerable populations, reduce social inequality and advocate social rights'. From the perspective of society as a whole this description relates to the service and democratic outcomes dimensions in Boyne's concept of performance. From the perspective of individual service users this mission description relates to outputs (the quantity and quality of service), service outcomes (longer term effects), and responsiveness (user satisfaction). For the purpose of this article, we follow the view that a service user-based conception of quality can be regarded as closely aligned with the goals of human service organizations and that user outcomes are the bottom line (Cronley & Kim, 2014, p. 75, 86). This means that for a compact measure of mission achievement it is important to take into account three public service performance dimensions distinguished by Boyne (2002): outputs, service outcomes, and responsiveness, as these concern the primary service quality interests of the service user.

In terms of operationalizing mission achievement, we observe that studies of organizational performance have resulted in a multitude of performance indicators but do not provide a compact measure of mission achievement (e.g. Andrews & Boyne, 2010). Thus, it might seem attractive to fill this gap by constructing one or two questions asking service users to rate the service quality experienced directly. However, earlier discussions of measurement validity regarding organizational performance provide important warnings to take into account. Meier and O'Toole (2013) note that the bias in perceptual assessments is greater the more general a performance indicator is. They argue that the correlation between subjective assessment and objective performance information is greater in the case of more specific indicators (see also Richard et al., 2009, p. 735).

There is also a theoretical reason for concern about using general questions to gauge mission achievement. General questions do not tap into the mission of specific organizations, because they neglect that such a measure means something different in the case of elderly care than in the case of for instance secondary education. Making a similar observation about the difference between mental health programs and early childhood or welfare-to-work programs, Sowa et al. (2004, p. 717) argue that measures of what they call 'program effectiveness', which refers to the effectiveness of the specific service or interventions offered by nonprofit organizations, will generally vary depending on the nature of the programs operated. Measures should capture the degree to which the program achieves its purposes and should tap into the 'service technology underlying the program process in order to demonstrate whether these processes are effective' (Sowa et al., 2004, p. 720).

Applying these insights to the case of elderly care in the Netherlands and the mission to provide 'thoughtful care', our purpose is to create a compact measure gauging this mission in terms of questions tapping specific aspects of thoughtful care which reflect the interests of the client as the focal stakeholder. Thoughtful care is conceptualized as care aimed at supporting the autonomy, relatedness, and healthy life of elderly clients (for an elaborate discussion see Research Context). This interest in thoughtful care is not restricted to elderly care in the Netherlands. In their introduction to a special issue on the development of long-term care for older people in Europe, Deusdad, Pace, and Anttonen (2016) also address this topic. They observe a strategy pursued by governments to cope with the costs of welfare policies and the challenge of aging societies, which leads to deinstitutiona- lization and privatization of long-term care. Deusdad et al. also note a reappraisal of family care and traditional care values. Indeed, since the 2008 economic and state financial crisis the Dutch government has stepped up its policies to deinstitutionalize long-term care for older people and make them live at home as long as possible with the help of their social networks. However, older people with complex health problems who can no longer live at home will continue to depend on the medical and non-medical care provided by residential homes. The challenge for these organizations is to provide thoughtful care akin to the quality associated with family care.

Frontline managers' people management

Given that frontline employees are critical agents in the provision of human services, how these employees are managed is of great relevance. Therefore, we now turn to frontline managers' contribution to mission achievement, in particular their people management activities. The question how to achieve performance has been a core issue in HRM research (Guest, 2011; Paauwe, 2009) ever since Huselid's (1995) study which showed that HRM has a positive effect on organizational performance. There is an increasing interest in high performance work systems (HPWSs), representing the whole system or subsystems of HR practices, which are designed to enhance performance and improve employee outcomes. This interest has also led to studies of HPWSs in human services organizations (Boselie & Veld, 2012; Selden & Sowa, 2015). HR practices that are often included in studies of HPWSs are: training and development, participation and autonomy, performance appraisal and rewards, teamwork, work-life balance, recruitment and selection, and employment security (Boon, Den Hartog, Boselie, & Paauwe, 2011).

Unfortunately, these studies' interest in HR systems has not been complemented by an interest in their implementation by frontline managers. However, a study by Ang, Bartram, McNeil, Leggat, and Stanton (2013) shows that the intended effects of HPWSs is dependent on whether management's implementation of HPWSs is similar to the espoused policy. This finding supports current HRM-performance models (Purcell & Kinnie, 2007; Wright & Nishii, 2013) which distinguish between intended HR policy, implemented HR practices, and employees' perceptions of the HR implementation, which have an impact on employees' attitudes and behaviors, and hence on performance outcomes. The literature draws attention to several HR 'delivery channels', such as HR professionals, HR service centers, and line managers. In this article, we specifically focus on frontline managers as organizational agents because in many organizations frontline managers have an important responsibility for HRM (Brewster, Brookes, & Gollan, 2015).

According to Purcell and Hutchinson (2007), employees' perceptions are not only influenced by their line managers' HR implementation, but also by their leadership behavior. They state that: 'the twin aspects of FLMs' [frontline managers] people management activities, leadership behaviour and the application of HR practices, imply a symbiotic relationship between them. FLMs need well designed HR practices to use in their people management activities [...] The way FLMs enact these practices will be influenced by their leadership behaviour' (pp. 3–4). They coined the term people management to cover both aspects. Following Purcell and Hutchinson, people management is defined as line managers' implementation of HR practices and their leadership behavior in supporting the employees they supervise at work.

The first element of the people management concept, the implementation of HR policies, has its roots in the HR devolution literature. According to Larsen and Brewster (2003, p. 228), 'the notion of line management accepting greater responsibility for human resource management within employing organizations is now received wisdom'. When studying the impact of HRM on employees it is important to focus not only on the presence of specific HR practices but also on perceptions that employees have of the reasons why management adopts certain HR practices (so-called HR attributions). Nishii, Lepak, and Schneider (2008) show that practices that are perceived as commitment-focused (i.e. intended to enhance service quality and employee wellbeing) are positively related to employee attitudes, while practices that are perceived as control-focused (i.e. designed to reduce costs and exploit employees) are negatively associated with their attitudes. Therefore, when studying the implementation of HR practices by line managers it is important to determine to which extent employees feel supported or controlled by the implementation of these practices. Following Guest (2007), we distinguish two levels of HR implementation. On the one hand, line managers implement general practices, ones that apply to all employees in their team. On the other hand, line managers are increasingly expected to make tailor-made arrangements with individual employees. HR practices established at the organizational level outline the framework for such deals.

The relevance of the second element of the people management concept, leadership behavior, builds on theories of social exchange and perceived organizational support (POS). Based on social exchange theory, Eisenberger, Huntington, Hutchinson, and Sowa (1986) argue that employees who experience high levels of POS feel that they ought to reciprocate and engage in behaviors that support organizational goals. Organizational support theory holds that employees see supervisors as agents acting on behalf of the organization, and therefore regard the degree to which supervisors value their contributions and care about their wellbeing as an important indicator of the organization's support (Rhoades & Eisenberger, 2002). In this article, leadership behavior is understood as a manager demonstrating supportive behavior through specific acts that have the intention of helping one's employees. More specifically Greenhaus, Parasuraman, and Wormley (1990) describe supportive behavior by supervisors as including the provision of career guidance, performance feedback, and opportunities that promote employee development. Oldham and Cummings (1996) observe that supervisors are supportive when they show concern for their employees' feelings and needs, encourage them to voice their own concerns, provide feedback, and facilitate their development.

Employees' behavior: linking people management and mission achievement

Although managers are assumed to play an important role in managing performance, their contribution is indirect. Frontline employees play a pivotal role in service provision and it is through managing their employees' behavior that managers have an impact on performance. This is the assumption underlying HRM-performance models (Purcell & Kinnie, 2007; Wright & Nishii, 2013) which hypothesize that employees' perceptions of their line managers' people management impact on performance through employees' behaviors. This assumption is based on the resource-based view (RBV) of the firm, which holds that the viability and performance of an organization result from the effective interaction of scarce, inimitable, and non-substitutable human and non-human resources (Barney, 1991). One of the underlying assumptions of the RBV is that human resources can be managed in order to increase the value of their contribution.

The importance attributed to employees' behaviors resonates with Donabedian's (1980) framework for organizing quality of care. This involves that the behaviors of nursing staff in giving care are the link between the system that provides care, which includes such organizational characteristics as review practices and continuing education programs for nursing staff, and the outcome which refers for instance to improvements in clients' health. Generally for human service organizations 'employees are one of the most critical inputs required to deliver on mission and make a difference in the lives of people served' (Selden & Sowa, 2015, p. 197).

HRM studies (e.g. Aryee, Walumba, Seidu, & Otaye, 2011; Jiang, Lepak, Hu, & Baer, 2012; Knies & Leisink, 2014) provide theoretical explanations and empirical support for the assumption that employees' attitudes and behaviors partially mediate the relationship between HR practices/people management and performance. Jiang et al. (2012) distinguish two theoretical logics that explain the mechanisms linking people management and performance. The first one is a social exchange perspective, which suggests that HRM impacts on performance through employees' attitudes and behaviors. The second one is a resource-based perspective, which focuses on employees' competencies and their impact on employee behavior. Their meta-analysis provides evidence for both mechanisms (see also Combs, Liu, Hall, & Ketchen, 2006). This perspective is also supported by studies in care organizations, such as the one by Piening, Baluch, and Salge (2013) on the relation-ships between employees' perceptions of HR systems and organizational performance of public hospitals in England.

For human service organizations the importance of the role of line managers in the HRM-performance link has been demonstrated by Alfes, Truss, Soane, Rees, and Gatenby (2013). Their study draws both on the assumptions underlying HPWS—involving that systems of HR practices support employees' abilities, motivation, and opportunity to perform, and thereby their task perfor-mance—and on social exchange theory. Alfes et al. show that employees' perceptions of line manager behavior (regarding its effectiveness, equity, and integrity) and of HRM practices are linked with employee engagement which in turn is strongly linked to individual performance. Rowold, Borgmann, and Bormann (2014) report a comparative study of profit and nonprofit organizations regarding the leadership behavior component of line managers' people management impacting on employee attitudes and behavior. They find that different leadership constructs are related to employees' job satisfaction, commitment, and job performance.

The HRM-performance models and the related studies of line managers' people management, employee behaviors, and performance ground the hypothesis that is tested in this article: line managers' people management activities are positively related to thoughtful care in elderly care organizations through employees' behavior.

Research context and research design

Research context

This article focuses on elderly care organizations in the Netherlands providing medical and non-medical care for the elderly. Over the last decade, poor performance in elderly care has frequently attracted media attention, leading to debates in parliament, increased health inspectorate scrutiny, and specific policy interventions. One of the effects of public disapproval was that various stake-holders got together and developed a Quality Framework Responsible Care (2010). This framework was meant to help organizations deal with accountability requirements and the increasing pressure to demonstrate their effectiveness. The quality framework distinguishes between quality of life, quality of care providers, quality of care organizations, and quality of care and safety, supplying tens of indicators for each domain.

However, over recent years critique of this framework has grown. A central element in the critique by elderly care organizations themselves was that the quality framework did not concern what they regard as the essence of care, namely the support for elderly people to continue leading their life as much as they used to. The mounting critique of the framework led the association of elderly care organizations (ActiZ) to develop a vision of the care that elderly care organizations should provide to clients (ActiZ, 2010). The concept 'thoughtful care' was coined to indicate the mission of elderly care organizations to provide care aimed at supporting the autonomy, relatedness, and healthy life of elderly clients. Its continued relevance is illustrated by a recent government policy document which echoes ActiZ' call for thoughtful care under the heading 'Dignity and pride: Loving care for our elderly' (Van Rijn, 2015).

Elderly care in the Netherlands is largely publicly funded and provided by nonprofit organiza-tions. This study is conducted in a large foundation that provides medical and non-medical care for the elderly in 31 residential homes covering a wide region in the southern part of the Netherlands. In total, the organization employs about 4,000 workers. The foundation invited the authors to help them conceptualize thoughtful care and determine the factors that impact on the provision of thoughtful care, including their frontline managers' people management. This section focuses only on the variables relevant for answering this article's research question.

Exploratory study

The study reported here consists of a first phase aimed at exploring the concepts of thoughtful care and related employees' behaviors. This exploratory study was conducted in two elderly homes, which differ on several characteristics such as their quality care assessment scores. Several methods were used to collect data. First, several team meetings were attended. Second, 14 working shifts were observed, which involved following the work of individuals and teams of care workers. Third, 30 care workers and supervisors were interviewed. The reason to interview care workers and their supervisors instead of clients themselves is that the mental abilities of the psycho-geriatric clients living in these two homes do not permit them to be interviewed.

The topics for these interviews were distilled from the attended team meetings and the observations. Two open questions guided the interviews. The first question is: what is important from the perspective of a client to make them feel happy? The second question is: what do you need to do in your work to make a client happy? Interviews were recorded and transcribed. Data analysis was done by coding the transcripts using open codes suggested by terms that the interviewees used themselves. Next, labels indicating the variables and/or dimensions of the constructs were extracted by condensing and categorizing the codes.

Three types of specific behaviors needed to provide thoughtful care—paying attention to clients; showing respect for clients; treating each client as an individual person—and descriptions of clients' thoughtful care experiences were derived from the observations and interviews (see Results). We validated these conceptualizations in conversations about the results of the qualitative study with care workers' teams. The rich descriptions provided by the qualitative study were used to generate questionnaire items for a survey of care workers.

Quantitative study

The second phase of this study is a survey study aimed at validating the constructed scales and testing the hypothesized model. The quantitative data come from 693 employees from 69 teams, providing elderly care in 19 residential homes. Residential homes were free to decide on participation in the research, the foundation had no influence on which residential homes participated. The 19 out of 31 residential homes that participated in the study cover the diversity of types of services provided by the foundation, the urban and rural areas served, and the care inspectorate's assessments of the service quality provided by the residential homes.

The response rate as a percentage of all employees working in the homes that participated in the survey is 67.5%, with 23 men (3.5%) and 635 women (96.5%). The mean age of the respondents is 43.9 years (SD = 11.8 years). These averages are quite consistent with Dutch averages for this sector (92% female, mean age 41 years; ActiZ, 2012). The average job tenure is 10.3 years (SD = 9.3 years). The majority of respondents are care workers (67.1%); others work in housekeeping (16.6%), catering (3.8%), or other activities (12.6%). As is usual in elderly care, the majority of employees have taken secondary vocational education (62.4%); the educational levels of others varied between primary education (2.3%), general secondary education (19.5%), higher education (3.1%), and other/unknown (12.6%).

Measures

The variables outlined below are all measured using five-point Likert scales, with a score of 1 indicating very weak support for the item statement, and a 5 very strong support. The full list of the questionnaire items is included in the appendix.

Following Purcell and Hutchinson (2007), the concept of *people management activities* is divided into two main components: the application of HR practices and leadership behavior. All respective sub-scales were developed and validated by Knies, Leisink & Van de Schoot (2017).

Based on the suggestion by Guest (2007) that two levels of application of HR practices can be distinguished: 'general' practices, which apply to all employees, and tailor-made arrangements with individual employees, the sub-scales measuring line managers' application of HR practices were:

Supportive HR practices
This variable is based on seven items asking employees to indicate to what extent they felt supported by a range of HR practices being applied (aimed at, for example, training and development, or obtaining a good work-life balance).

Implementation of tailor-made arrangements
This variable is based on two items asking employees to indicate to what extent tailor-made employment arrangements were negotiated between them and their supervisors.

Leadership behavior is understood as a manager demonstrating supportive behavior and is defined as specific acts that have the intention of helping one's employees. This variable is similarly broken down into two sub-variables:

Support of employees' commitment
This variable is based on four items asking employees to indicate their support for statements about their supervisor's interest in how they are doing their job, and in their personal functioning.

Support of employees' career development
This variable is based on four items asking employees to indicate their support for statements about the extent to which their supervisor facilitates their participation in training and their use of career opportunities.

To determine the relationship between the observed variables (questionnaire items) and the latent variables (constructs), we conducted a confirmatory factor analysis (CFA). To assess the model fit, we examined the comparative fit index (CFI), the Tucker-Lewis index (TLI), and the root mean square error of approximation (RMSEA). Acceptable fit is evidenced by a CFI and TLI of .90 or higher, and an RMSEA of .08 or lower (Bentler, 1990). The results of this analysis confirm the existence of the factor structure described above with two modifications. First, the scale measuring 'supportive HR practices' consists of two dimensions: HR practices aimed at supporting employees' commitment (3 items) and HR practices aimed at supporting employees' personal development (2 items). These dimensions parallel the two sub-scales of leadership behavior. Second, based on the fit indices we deleted one of the items of the sub-scale 'support of employees' career development', resulting in a 3-item scale. The standardized coefficients all had values between .672 and .943. Additional information on the results of the CFA is provided in the appendix.

To verify whether these sub-scales are indeed dimensions of the underlying construct people management, we conducted third-order CFA. First, we loaded the two sub-dimensions of 'supportive HR practices' on the second-order construct. This second-order model was significant. Second, we loaded all four sub-scales (supportive HR practices, implementation of tailor-made arrangements, support of employees' commitment, and support of employees' career development) on the third-order construct. The results of these tests confirm the proposed structure. Factor loadings of the four sub-dimensions on the third-order construct vary between .728 and .911. Fit indices for this model are acceptable (CFI = .987; TLI = .966; RMSEA = .110). The Cronbach's alphas for reliability are good for all sub-scales as well as for the overall construct (>.70). Because the mediating variables measuring employees' behaviors and the dependent variable thoughtful care are developed for this study, these variables are discussed in the results section.

Developing a compact measure

One of the aims of this paper is to deliver a compact measure of mission achievement. Here, we elaborate on our understanding of a compact measure and deduce several features which characterize it. In the next section we apply these criteria to develop a measure of mission achievement in elderly care. DeVellis (2003, p. 97) states that generally shorter scales are preferred over longer ones because these place less of a burden on respondents. Schaufeli, Bakker, and Salanova (2006, p. 702–703) add that long questionnaires increase the likelihood of attrition. According to DeVellis, there exists an inherent trade-off between reliability and brevity. The challenge is to find the right balance between the two. That is, developing a measure that is short ánd reliable. Looking at examples of previously developed and validated scales which claim to be 'short', 'compact', or 'abridged' (e.g. public service motivation: Coursey & Pandey, 2007; work engagement: Schaufeli et al., 2006; leader-member exchange: Schriesheim, Neider, Scandura, & Tepper, 1992), we note that the length of the scale varies between 6 and 10 items, depending on the complexity and nature of the concept. This gives us a good indication of the usual length of a compact measure.

Measurement quality

The data for all the items were collected from individual respondents and are thus potentially subject to common method bias (CMB) (Podsakoff, MacKenzie, Lee, & Podsakoff, 2003). Although a recent study shows that 'in contrast to conventional wisdom, common method effects do not appear to be so large as to pose a serious threat to organizational research' (Lance, Dawson, Birkelbach, & Hoffman, 2010, p. 450), we have addressed this potential problem in various ways.

We enhanced construct validity by formulating questionnaire items about people management such that they refer to employees' perceptions of specific concrete behaviors of line managers. The items measuring employees' behavior all refer to specific concrete actions undertaken by individual employees, such as 'I listen...', 'I inform...' and 'I respect...'. To measure our dependent variable 'thoughtful care' we requested respondents to take a client's perspective, by formulating items starting with 'my clients...' (see also Results). By conceptually separating employees' behavior and the outcomes of these behaviors for clients, we tried to limit conceptual overlap between the variables. Moreover, in the survey design, we spread the items relating to different variables among various sections of the questionnaire. Further, we conducted two sets of CFAs to check for CMB in the data, comparing the hypothesized structure (CFI = .989; TLI = .987; RMSEA = .037) with a one-factor model (CFI = .737; TLI = .717; RMSEA = .177). The analyses provide evidence against there being a bias stemming from common method variance (Podsakoff et al., 2003).

One obvious risk of self-reporting measures is that respondents tend to inflate their ratings, and so the scores should be regarded with some caution. However, inflated self-ratings should not affect the relationships, and it is these in which we are most interested.

Data analysis

In the following section, we first describe the development and validation of the mediating and dependent variables based on the qualitative and quantitative parts of our study. Next, we provide the descriptive statistics and correlations for the variables used. Then, we present the results of the model tests, for which we used structural equation modeling (SEM) techniques. Because our respondents are nested in supervisor groups, the non-independence of observations was taken into account by using the 'TYPE = COMPLEX' analysis command in MPlus. In the model tests we controlled for age, tenure, gender, and educational level, which are frequently used as control variables in HRM research (Boselie, Dietz, & Boon, 2005).

Results

Developing measures for thoughtful care and related employees' behaviors

The mediating variable employees' behaviors required to provide thoughtful care consisted, according to the care workers interviewed, of three dimensions: paying attention to clients, acting respectfully, and treating each client as an individual person.

Attention

Employees providing thoughtful care pay attention to clients. They regularly talk to clients, listen to their problems, take the time to do some extra and if necessary, try to find a solution for clients' problems. From the exploratory study four items were developed to measure this dimension.

Interviewed care workers were unanimous that 'attention is always important for every client'. One care worker observes: 'For instance, when a client rings the bell for assistance, it is important that one of us reacts immediately so that the client feels he is listened to'. Another care worker says: 'One should take extra time for a client occasionally, for instance for trimming and painting her nails or putting on make-up. Another client may feel happy by making a walk together'.

Respect

Employees who show respect for their clients do not impose their own norms and values but respect their clients' norms and values and respect their clients' need for privacy. Moreover, they inform clients about their actions. For example, why clients have to wait or why they receive new medication. Another indicator of respect is living up to the promises made to clients. Five items were generated to measure this dimension.

Care workers agree that it is important to respect the personal values and lifestyle of each client. An example given by one care worker illustrates this. 'The room of one of our clients is spilling over with knick-knacks. I have to remind myself that she likes it this way and that I have to respect this. These are not my values but hers. I think that we always have to respect these'. Respect involves according to another care worker 'that you call them when you will be late. And when you tell them that you will be 10 minutes late, you shouldn't actually be there half an hour late, that is not honest'.

Individual approach

Taking an individual or personal approach—as opposed to a standardized or collective one—is another important type of behavior requisite for thoughtful care. This includes meeting the needs of individual clients, attending to their personal habits and routines, and involving them in decision making. Four items were taken from the exploratory study to measure this dimension.

One care worker gives the following answer to the question what makes a client smile: 'One should really do what clients ask and like. That is very different for clients. One client likes a joke, another a gentle stroke. You adapt yourself to each client'. Another care worker stresses the importance of care workers giving clients a choice. 'For instance, what sandwich filling they want, at what time they want to wake up or go to bed'.

Thoughtful care

The dependent variable in our study is thoughtful care. According to the care workers clients are happy in terms of thoughtful care when they are satisfied with the care they receive, feel that they are listened to, and treated respectfully, have a say in the care provided and can continue living their life as they were used to. Seven items were generated to measure this variable.

Interviewed care workers explain that it is sometimes difficult for them to know whether and when psychogeriatric patients are satisfied. But they know that preventing restlessness is important: 'In the morning when I help clients get up I am busy with one client and then another one wakes up.

This latter lady will have to wait. If it is only a few minutes that is not a problem, but if it takes more than 10 minutes she starts to cry and gets restless'. Generally, clients' satisfaction is regarded as the most important indicator of thoughtful care. 'Clients are happy when everything went to their satisfaction'. 'When you leave a client's room and they say "thank you" or smile… you know they are satisfied and happy'.

The items measuring thoughtful care relate to the three dimensions of public service performance distinguished by Boyne (2002) that we designated as the primary service quality interests of the service user, namely service outputs and outcomes, and responsiveness in terms of satisfaction by direct service users. These items reflect the interests of the stakeholder client. However, they are measured as employees' perceptions of clients' experience of thoughtful care. The use of employees' perceptions of service quality is not uncommon in studies of human service organizations (e.g. Agbényiga, 2011; Cronley & Kim, 2014). Also, employees' perceptions appear to be correlated with client perceptions (Cronley & Kim, 2014, p. 85). The specific reason in this survey for asking employees' perceptions of the thoughtful care experience of clients is that it would have been very difficult to ask clients themselves as the majority are psycho-geriatric clients.

Construct validation

Construct validation for these new scales was carried out using Mplus (Muthén & Muthén, 2012). First, we examined the dimensionality of employees' care behaviors and thoughtful care scales by performing an exploratory factor analysis (EFA). We used principal component factoring and direct oblimin rotation, because this allows for the factors to be correlated. We included all 20 items generated to measure these constructs in the analysis. We examined the number of factors extracted with eigenvalues greater than or equal to one. This indicated four factors, which together explained 57.3% of the total variance in the measure. The factor structure was as we expected. All items had factor loadings of .40 or higher.

Second, we performed CFAs. For the items measuring employees' care behavior, we tested a first-order model based on the results of the EFA, in which four items loaded on the dimension 'attention', five items on the dimension 'respect' and four items on the dimension 'individual approach'. The initial CFA showed unacceptable fit indices. Therefore, we excluded one item from each dimension, based on factor loadings and item errors. As a result, the fit increased substantially. Fit indices are as follows: CFI = .987; TLI = .982; RMSEA = .061. All items loaded significantly on the latent variables ($p < .001$). Factor loadings ranged from .650 to .890. Because we conceptualized that these three variables (attention, respect, and individual approach) are dimensions of the underlying construct employees' care behavior, we conducted a second-order CFA. The results of this test confirm the proposed structure. Factor loadings of the three sub-dimensions on the second-order construct vary between .811 and .979. Figure 1 displays the final factor structure of the items measuring employees' care behavior. In summary, the results of the CFA support a three-dimensional scale comprised of 10 items.

We also conducted a CFA for the items measuring thoughtful care. Initially, model results indicated a poor fit. Based on factor loadings and item errors we deleted two items. The resulting five items show good fit indices (CFI = .995; TLI = .990; RMSEA = .095). All items loaded significantly on the latent variable ($p < .001$). Factor loadings ranged from .766 to .886. Figure 2 displays the factor structure of the items measuring thoughtful care. Thus, the results of the CFA support a factor comprised of five items.

Third, we assessed the reliability of the scales by examining the coefficients Cronbach's alpha's. The three sub-scales of employees' care behavior all showed sufficient reliability. Cronbach's alphas were .721 for 'attention', .713 for 'respect', and .745 for 'individual approach'. The reliability estimate for the overall scale was .847, which is considered very good. The coefficient alpha estimate of

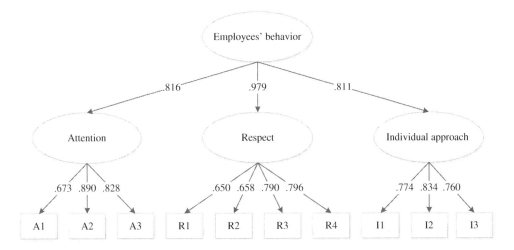

Figure 1. Factor structure employees' behavior.

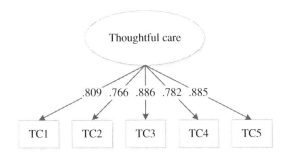

Figure 2. Factor structure thoughtful care.

reliability was also very good for the variable 'thoughtful care' (.859). Thus, the results of our analyses indicate that the employees' care behavior and thoughtful care scales are reliable measures.

A potential bias is introduced by the fact that we measure thoughtful care from a client perspective by surveying employees. We have addressed the potential problem of bias in various ways. We explicitly requested employees to take a client perspective, by formulating items starting with 'my clients…'. Further, we have data from the Consumer Quality Index (CQ-index), which provides information about the quality of care from the perspective of care users (or their relatives) at the level of homes. The index is an additive measure of various aspects of quality of care. We computed the mean score of thoughtful care at the level of a residential home from the scores of all employees serving one residential home. The correlation between the score from the CQ-index and our measure of thoughtful care is significant ($r = .516$, $p = .003$). This indicates that the scores obtained by surveying employees show similar patterns to client responses. This supports our claim that effects of this source of potential bias are limited.

Descriptive statistics and correlations

Table 1 presents the means, standard deviations, and correlations for the variables used in our quantitative study.

The results in Table 1 show that employees were moderately positive about the people management activities undertaken by their supervisors with all the average scores above the theoretical scale midpoint

Table 1. Descriptive statistics and correlations.

	Mean	SD	1	2	3
1. People management activities	3.60	0.56	1.00		
2. Employees' behavior	4.34	0.42	.439***	1.00	
3. Thoughtful care	4.11	0.49	.382***	.771***	1.00
4. Gender (1 = female)	n.a.	n.a.	−.075*	.014	−.045
5. Age	43.9	11.8	−.037	.008	.082
6. Tenure	10.3	9.3	−.063	−.078	.009
7. Educational level	n.a.	n.a.	.034	.015	.004

** $p < .001$; * $p < .05$; n.a. not applicable

(3.60, $SD = 0.56$). Employees reported high levels of thoughtful care-related behavior (4.34, $SD = 0.42$), indicating that they pay attention to the needs of clients, act respectfully, and take an individual approach. The score on the outcome variable 'thoughtful care' indicates that respondents report high levels (4.11, $SD = 0.49$).

The correlation analysis displayed in Table 1 shows that people management is significantly related to both employee behavior and thoughtful care. The correlation coefficients are .439 ($p < .001$) and .382 ($p < .001$) respectively. The results also show that employee behavior and thoughtful care are significantly related ($r = .771$, $p < .001$). With one exception, none of the control variables was related significantly to people management activities, employee behavior, or thoughtful care. Only gender was significantly related to people management activities ($r = .075$, $p < .05$): women reported slightly lower levels of people management support from their supervisors than men.

Model test

In order to test our model, we first analyzed whether a mediated model as developed in the theoretical framework produced the best model fit compared to a direct model. This analysis is based on the minimization of the Akaike Information Criterion (AIC) and the Bayesian Information Criterion (BIC). These fit indexes can be used to compare models, where lower scores indicate superior models (Schreiber, Nora, Stage, Barlow, & King, 2006). In the first model, we assumed that people management had a direct effect on thoughtful care. The AIC score was 31,954 and the BIC score was 32,410. In the second model, we tested the mediated effect of people management activities on thoughtful care through employee behavior (AIC = 31,822; BIC = 32,279). These results show that the mediated model had the lowest AIC and BIC scores, meaning that this model is the preferred one. Therefore, results from the mediated model are presented.

Table 2 presents the results of the model test. Fit indices show a good model fit (CFI = .983; TLI = .981; RMSEA = .033). People management is significantly related to employee behavior ($\beta = .513$, $p < .001$). In turn, employee behavior is significantly related to thoughtful care ($\beta = .802$, $p < .001$). This implies that the indirect path from people management through employee behavior on thoughtful care is also significant ($\beta = .411$, $p < .001$), meaning that we found support for our hypothesis. None of the control variables included in our model test (gender, age, tenure, educational level) was significant.

Table 2. Mediated SEM model.

	β	B	S.E.	p
People management → Employees' behavior	.513	0.496	.058	.000
Employees' behavior → Thoughtful care	.802	1.134	.102	.000
People management → Employees' behavior → thoughtful care	.411	0.563	.061	.000
R^2 Employees' behavior	.287			
R^2 Thoughtful care	.645			

[a] None of the control variables is significant
[b] Fit indices: CFI = .983; TLI = .981; RMSEA = .033

Overall, the levels of explained variance are quite high. The explained variance is 28.7% in the case of employee behavior. This can be attributed to the effect of people management. The level of explained variance for thoughtful care is 64.5%. This can be attributed to the mediated effect of people management through employee behavior.

Conclusion and discussion

This article set out to answer the question to what extent frontline managers' people management activities contribute to mission achievement through frontline workers' behaviors. Drawing on the case of elderly care, the results of our study provide support for our hypothesis that line managers' people management activities are positively related to mission achievement (i.e. thoughtful care performance in elderly care) mediated by care workers' behaviors. Our results also show that thoughtful care is a valid measure of the mission defined by elderly care organizations in the face of the current challenges of long-term care for older people. Moreover, the results reveal that care workers' behavior that contributes to thoughtful care consists of the following dimensions: paying attention, showing respect, and treating each client as an individual person.

This study's contributions

These results are of interest to the study of mission achievement of human service organizations and human service management in various respects. First, a valid measure of 'thoughtful care' is relevant for a number of reasons. The construct relates to the mission of elderly care organizations and is based on what organizational stakeholders regard as the essence of the care they provide with the client as the focal stakeholder. The mission achievement is assessed by a compact measure of five items that relates to three dimensions of public service performance conceptualized by Boyne (2002): service outputs and outcomes, and responsiveness in terms of satisfaction by direct service users. This compact measure helps to see the forest from the trees represented by the tens and hundreds of performance indicators suggested by performance studies. We regard the measure of thoughtful care as a sector-specific complement to generic measures of public service performance (Andrews et al., 2006). The importance of a context-specific construct is related, as we argued in the theoretical framework, to the fact that effectiveness means different things for different nonprofit and public organizations because of the specificity of their missions (Rainey & Steinbauer, 1999; Sowa et al., 2004). In this study, we also conceptualized the thoughtful care-related behavior of care workers, which pertains to the process of service provision while thoughtful care itself concerns the service product. Our context-specific measures of thoughtful care and related behavior of care workers increases the validity of research, because respondents better understand specific than generic survey questions (Meier & O'Toole, 2013), especially as we have distilled these questions from conversations with care workers. In this article, we developed a scale to measure mission achievement in elderly care. We hope that our endeavor will inspire others to do the same for mission achievement in other public and nonprofit sectors and that this piece provides directions how to tackle this task specifically with regard to contextualizing the scale using qualitative data as input.

Second, the results of our study are of interest because they demonstrate that people management matters and that line managers contribute to mission achievement by supporting employees' behavior. The notion that employee attributes are positively related to customer service quality and ultimately organizational performance is the basis of Heskett et al.'s (1994) service-profit chain model and is empirically corroborated in profit service industry studies (e.g. Yee, Yeung, & Cheng, 2010). Our study provides empirical support for the notion that employees' behaviors are vital for service quality and mission achievement in nonprofit human service organizations (see also Sowa et al., 2004). In addition, this study shows that frontline managers can make a considerable contribution to mission achievement by supporting the employees they supervise by their people management activities, that is their implementation of HR practices and their leadership behavior. This is a contribution to the public management literature which has questioned the efficacy of managers because of the constraints on managerial autonomy and the prevalence of detailed regulations in the area of personnel policies (Brewer & Walker, 2012; Feeney & Rainey, 2010). Our study shows that, at least in elderly care in the Netherlands, line managers can contribute to thoughtful care performance through their people management. As such our study contributes to systemizing knowledge on the management–performance relationship and ultimately to theory development as called for by Abner, Kim, and Perry (2017).

Limitations

We note that our study has some limitations. First, in our study we decided to concentrate on a context-specific measure of mission achievement because this adds to the current body of literature which generally focuses on the generic dimensions of performance. In follow-up studies, it would be interesting to include both types of measures (generic and context-specific) to examine to what extent these are related.

Second, in our study we used a subjective measure of thoughtful care. Because thoughtful care concerns the interior experiences and perceptions of older clients we believe that a subjective measure is apt (Andersen et al., 2016, p. 5) but also that the actor perspective in the survey should ideally align with this focal stakeholder. Although we explicitly requested employees to take a client perspective, and although our analyses showed that our measure of thoughtful care is significantly related to the score on the CQ-index, we recommend that in future studies, clients (or their relatives) are used as respondents expressing their perceptions of thoughtful care.

Third, the results of our study show that our measures of thoughtful care and related employees' behavior are highly correlated. This could point to conceptual overlap between our variables. In our operationalization of thoughtful care-related behavior we referred to specific concrete actions undertaken by individual employees, whereas in our measure of thoughtful care we captured (employees' perceptions of) clients' experience with the provided care. In follow-up studies, this potential overlap might be further reduced by focusing more specifically on client perceptions of the outcomes of care leaving out the process of care provision. Despite these limitations, our results provide substantial evidence for answers to the core issues addressed in the introduction.

Implications

We provided a compact context-specific measure of mission achievement in elderly care. Moreover, we showed that people management activities as perceived by employees have a significant impact on employees' behavior, which is the linking mechanism in the relationship between people management and mission achievement.

These findings also have important implications for practice. Our measures of mission achievement in elderly care and the related employee behaviors can be a used as a diagnostic tool in elderly care organizations. The measure can help to gain insight into the way clients experience the care that is provided to them, capturing the essence of service provision in this particular sector. This provides practitioners with a tool to benchmark organizational units' thoughtful care performance and locate units that deserve specific attention. Moreover, this scale can be administered to facilitate discussions between team members about the mission achievement and potential interventions aimed at improving the provision of thoughtful care. One such intervention is continuous investment in people management. Our study shows that people management matters, which implies that human service organizations can improve mission achievement by designated people management activities.

Acknowledgment

We want to thank Mandy Onwezen and Kimberley van Bijsteren for their assistance in the exploratory study.

Funding

This work was supported by the Nederlandse Organisatie voor Wetenschappelijk Onderzoek [451-15-002].

References

Abner, G., Kim, S., & Perry, J. (2017). Building evidence for public human resource management: Using middle range theory to link theory and data. *Review of Public Personnel Administration*, 37(2): 139–159. 0734371 × 17697248.

ActiZ. (2010). *Naar autonomie, verbondenheid en een gezond leven: Een nieuwe ambitie voor de langdurige zorg.* Utrecht, The Netherlands: Author.

ActiZ. (2012). *De verpleeg- en verzorgingshuiszorg en thuiszorg in kaart: Feiten, financiering, kosten en opbrengsten.* Retrieved from www.actiz.nl.

Agbényiga, D. (2011). Organizational culture-performance link in the human services setting. *Administration in Social Work*, 35(5), 532–547.

Alfes, K., Truss, C., Soane, E., Rees, C., & Gatenby, M. (2013). The relationship between line manager behaviour, perceived HR practices, and individual performance: Examining the mediating role of engagement. *Human Resource Management*, 52(6), 839–859.

Andersen, L., Boesen, A., & Pedersen, L. (2016). Performance in public organizations: Clarifying the conceptual space. *Public Administration Review*. doi:10.1111/puar.12578

Andrews, R., & Boyne, G. (2010). Capacity, leadership and organizational performance: Testing the black box model of public management. *Public Administration Review*, 70(3), 443–454.

Andrews, R., Boyne, G., & Walker, R. (2006). Subjective and objective measures of organizational performance: An empirical investigation. In: G. Boyne, K. Meier, L. O'Toole, & R. Walker (eds.), *Public service performance: Perspectives on measurement and management* (pp. 14–34). Cambridge, UK: Cambridge University Press.

Ang, S., Bartram, T., McNeil, N., Leggat, S., & Stanton, P. (2013). The effects of high-performance work systems on hospital employees' work attitudes and intention to leave: A multi-level and occupational group analysis. *International Journal of Human Resource Management*, 24(16), 3086–3114.

Aryee, S., Walumba, F., Seidu, E., & Otaye, L. (2011). Impact of high-performance work systems on individual- and branch-level performance: Test of a multilevel model of intermediate linkages. *Journal of Applied Psychology*, 97(2), 287–300.

Barney, J. (1991). Firm resources and sustained competitive advantage. *Journal of Management*, 17(1), 99–120.

Bentler, P. M. (1990). Comparative fit indexes in structural models. *Psychological Bulletin*, 107(2), 238–246.

Boon, C., Den Hartog, D. N., Boselie, P., & Paauwe, J. (2011). The relationship between perceptions of HR practices and employee outcomes: Examining the role of person-organisation and person-job fit. *The International Journal of Human Resource Management*, 22(1), 138–162.

Boselie, P., Dietz, G., & Boon, C. (2005). Commonalities and contradictions in HRM and performance research. *Human Resource Management Journal*, 15(3), 67–94.

Boselie, P., & Veld, M. (2012). Human resource management and commitment in Dutch child day care. *Administration in Social Work*, 36(2), 189–211.

Boyne, G. (2002). Concepts and indicators of local authority performance: An evaluation of the statutory frameworks in England and Wales. *Public Money & Management*, 22(2), 17–24.

Brewer, G., & Walker, R. (2012). Personnel constraints in public organizations: The impact of reward and punishment on organizational performance. *Public Administration Review*, 73(1), 121–131.

Brewster, C., Brookes, M., & Gollan, P. (2015). The institutional antecedents of the assignment of HRM responsibilities to line managers. *Human Resource Management*, 54(4), 577–597.

Carnochan, S., Samples, M., Myers, M., & Austin, M. (2014). Performance measurement challenges in non-profit human service organizations. *Nonprofit and Voluntary Sector Quarterly*, 43(6), 1014–1032.

Combs, J., Liu, Y., Hall, A., & Ketchen, D. (2006). How much do high-performance work practices matter? A meta-analysis of their effects on organizational performance. *Personnel Psychology*, 59(3), 501–528.

Cooke, F., & Bartram, T. (2015). Guest editors' introduction: Human Resource Management in health care and elderly care: Current challenges and toward a research agenda. *Human Resource Management*, 54(5), 711–735.

Coursey, D. H., & Pandey, S. K. (2007). Public service motivation measurement testing an abridged version of Perry's proposed scale. *Administration & Society, 39*(5), 547–568.

Cronley, C., & Kim, Y. (2014). The path to service quality: The mediating role of organizational commitment on the effects of strategic planning and technology access within the Salvation Army. *Human Service Organizations: Management, Leadership & Governance, 38*(1), 74–88.

Deusdad, B., Pace, C., & Anttonen, A. (2016). Facing the challenges in the development of long-term care for older people in Europe in the context of an economic crisis. *Journal of Social Service Research, 42*(2), 144–150.

DeVellis, R. F. (2003). *Scale development: Theory and applications.* Thousand Oaks, California, US: Sage.

Donabedian, A. (1980). *Exploration in quality assessment and monitoring.* Ann Arbor, Michigan, US: Health Administration Press.

Eisenberger, R., Huntington, R., Hutchinson, S., & Sowa, D. (1986). Perceived organisational support. *Journal of Applied Psychology, 71*(3), 500–507.

Feeney, M., & Rainey, H. (2010). Personnel flexibility and red tape in public and non-profit organizations: Distinctions due to institutional and political accountability. *Journal of Public Administration Research and Theory, 20*(4), 801–826.

Greenhaus, J., Parasuraman, A., & Wormley, W. (1990). Effects of race on organizational experiences, job performance evaluations, and career outcomes. *Academy of Management Journal, 33*(1), 64–86.

Guest, D. E. (2007). HRM: Towards a new psychological contract?. In: P. Boxall, J. Purcell, & P. Wright (eds.), *The Oxford handbook of human resource management* (pp. 128–146). Oxford, UK: Oxford University Press.

Guest, D. E. (2011). Human resource management and performance: Still searching for some answers. *Human Resource Management Journal, 21*, 3–13.

Hasenfeld, Y. (2015). What exactly is human services management? *Human Service Organizations: Management, Leadership & Governance, 39*(1), 1–5.

Heskett, J., Jones, T., Loveman, G., Sasser, W., & Schlesinger, L. (1994). Putting the service-profit chain to work. *Harvard Business Review, 72*(2), 164–174.

Huselid, M. (1995). The impact of human resource management practices on turnover, productivity, and corporate financial performance. *Academy of Management Journal, 38*(3), 635–672.

Jiang, K., Lepak, D. P., Hu, J., & Baer, J. C. (2012). How does human resource management influence organizational outcomes? A meta-analytic investigation of mediating mechanisms. *Academy of Management Journal, 55*(6), 1264–1294.

Knies, E., & Leisink, P. (2014). Linking people management and extra-role behaviour: Results of a longitudinal study. Human Resource Management Journal, 24(1), 57–76.

Knies, E., Leisink, P. L. M. & Van de Schoot, R. (2017), 'People management: developing and testing a measurement scale', International Journal of Human Resource Management, 1–33.

Lance, C. E., Dawson, B., Birkelbach, D., & Hoffman, B. J. (2010). Method effects, measurement error, and substantive conclusions. *Organizational Research Methods, 13*(3), 435–455.

Larsen, H. H., & Brewster, C. (2003). Line management responsibility for HRM: What is happening in Europe? *Employee Relations, 25*(3), 228–244.

Lynn, L. E., Heinrich, C. J., & Hill, C. J. (2000). Studying governance and public management: Challenges and prospects. *Journal of Public Administration Research and Theory, 10*(2), 233–262.

Meier, K., & O'Toole, L. (2013). I think (I am doing well), therefore I am: Assessing the validity of administrators' self-assessments of performance. *International Public Management Journal, 16*(1), 1–27.

Meier, K., O'Toole, L., Boyne, G., & Walker, R. (2007). Strategic management and the performance of public organisations: Testing venerable ideas against recent theories. *Journal of Public Administration Research and Theory, 17*(2), 357–377.

Moynihan, D., & Pandey, S. (2005). Testing how management matters in an era of government by performance management. *Journal of Public Administration Research and Theory, 15*(3), 421–439.

Muthén, B., & Muthén, L. (2012). *User guide MPlus.* Los Angeles, CA: Muthén & Muthén.

Nishii, L. H., Lepak, D. P., & Schneider, B. (2008). Employee attributions of the "why" of HR practices: Their effects on employee attitudes and behaviors, and customer satisfaction. *Personnel Psychology, 61*, 503–545.

Oldham, G., & Cummings, A. (1996). Employee creativity: Personal and contextual factors at work. *Academy of Management Journal, 39*(3), 607–634.

Paauwe, J. (2009). HRM and performance: Achievements, methodological issues and prospects. *Journal of Management Studies, 46*(1), 129–142.

Piening, E. P., Baluch, A. M., & Salge, T. O. (2013). The relationship between employees' perceptions of human resource systems and organizational performance: Examining mediating mechanisms and temporal dynamics. *Journal of Applied Psychology, 98*(6), 926–947.

Podsakoff, P. M., MacKenzie, S. B., Lee, J., & Podsakoff, N. P. (2003). Common method variance in behavioral research: A critical review of the literature and recommended remedies. *Journal of Applied Psychology, 88*, 879–903.

Purcell, J., & Hutchinson, S. (2007). Front-line managers as agents in the HRM-performance causal chain: Theory, analysis and evidence. *Human Resource Management Journal, 17*(1), 3–20.

Purcell, J., & Kinnie, N. (2007). HRM and business performance. In: P. Boxall, J. Purcell, & P. Wright (eds.), *The Oxford handbook of human resource management* (pp. 533–551). Oxford, UK: Oxford University Press.

Quality Framework Responsible Care (2010). *Den Haag: Stuurgroep Kwaliteitskader Verantwoorde Zorg.* Retrieved from www.zichtbarezorg.nl.

Rainey, H., & Steinbauer, P. (1999). Galloping elephants: Developing elements of a theory of effective government organizations. *Journal of Public Administration Research and Theory, 9*(1), 1–32.

Rhoades, L., & Eisenberger, R. (2002). Perceived organizational support: A review of the literature. *Journal of Applied Psychology, 87*(4), 698–714.

Riccucci, N. (2005). *How management matters: Street-level bureaucrats and welfare reform.* Washington DC, US: Georgetown University Press.

Richard, P., Devinney, T., Yip, G., & Johnson, G. (2009). Measuring organizational performance: Towards methodological best practice. *Journal of Management, 35*(3), 718–804.

Rowold, J., Borgmann, L., & Bormann, K. (2014). Which leadership constructs are important for predicting job satisfaction, affective commitment, and perceived job performance in profit versus non-profit organizations? *Nonprofit Management & Leadership, 25*(2), 147–164.

Schaufeli, W. B., Bakker, A. B., & Salanova, M. (2006). The measurement of work engagement with a short questionnaire: A cross-national study. *Educational and Psychological Measurement, 66*(4), 701–716.

Schreiber, J. B., Nora, A., Stage, F. K., Barlow, E. A., & King, J. (2006). Reporting structural equation modeling and confirmatory factor analysis results: A review. *The Journal of Educational Research, 99*(6), 323–338.

Schriesheim, C. A., Neider, L. L., Scandura, T. A., & Tepper, B. J. (1992). Development and preliminary validation of a new scale (LMX-6) to measure leader-member exchange in organizations. *Educational and Psychological Measurement, 52*(1), 135–147.

Selden, S., & Sowa, J. (2015). Voluntary turnover in non-profit human service organizations: The impact of high performance work practices. *Human Service Organizations: Management, Leadership & Governance, 39*(3), 182–207.

Sowa, J., Selden, S., & Sandfort, J. (2004). No longer unmeasurable? A multidimensional integrated model of non-profit organizational effectiveness. *Nonprofit and Voluntary Sector Quarterly, 33*(4), 711–728.

Van Rijn, M. (2015). *Waardigheid en trots. Liefdevolle zorg voor onze ouderen.* Den Haag, The Netherlands: Ministerie van Volksgezondheid, Welzijn en Sport.

Wright, P., & Nishii, L. (2013). Strategic HRM and organizational behaviour: Integrating multiple levels of analysis. In: J. Paauwe, D. E. Guest, & P. M. Wright (Eds.), *HRM & performance: Achievements & challenges* (pp. 97–110). Chichester, West Sussex: Wiley.

Yee, R., Yeung, A., & Cheng, T. (2010). An empirical study of employee loyalty, service quality and firm performance in the service industry. *International Journal of Production Economics, 124*(1), 109–120.

Appendix

		λ
	Supportive HR practices: employees' commitment	
	I experience the following HR practices as being implemented to support me:	
	●changes in job design	.728
	● vitality	.842
	● work-life balance	.672
	Supportive HR practices: employees' career development	
	I experience the following HR practices as being implemented to support me:	
	● training and development	.835
	● mobility	.792
	Implementation of tailor-made arrangements	
	My supervisor tailors employment conditions to my personal situation	.893
	My supervisor tailors employment conditions to my individual needs so I can do a better job	.914
	Support of employees' commitment	
	My supervisor shows an interest in how I do my job	.943
	My supervisor shows an interest in my personal functioning	.928
	If my supervisor appreciates the job done by me, he/she does not let this pass unnoticed	.908
	My supervisor asks me if I can manage my job	.877
	Support of employees' career development	
	My supervisor informs me about opportunities for training and development	.943
	My supervisor offers me opportunities to participate in training	.906
	My supervisor supports me in utilizing opportunities for vertical mobility	.839
	Attention	
A1	During my work I talk regularly with my clients	.673
A2	I listen to the problems of my clients	.890
A3	If problems occur I will look for a solution together with the client	.828
	Respect	
R1	I do not argue with clients about their norms and values (e.g. as regards expressions of religion or the design of the room)	.650
R2	I inform my clients about my actions (e.g. as regards new medication or delays in service)	.658
R3	I always live up to my promises	.790
R4	I respect my clients' need for privacy (e.g. as regards toilet use)	.796
	Individual approach	
I1	I meet the personal needs of my clients	.774
I2	I keep up the personal habits and routines of my clients	.834
I3	I involve my clients in decision making	.760
	Thoughtful care	
TC1	My clients are satisfied with the care they receive from me	.809
TC2	My clients can continue their lifestyle as I take care of them	.766
TC3	My clients feel that I listen to their needs and wishes	.886
TC4	My clients have a say in the care they receive from me	.782
TC5	My clients feel that I treat them with respect	.885

Policy fields, data systems, and the performance of nonprofit human service organizations

Lehn M. Benjamin, Amy Voida, and Chris Bopp

In a policy environment that demands evidence of effectiveness, data collection has now become a significant part of the work of many nonprofit human service organizations. One commentator in the Stanford Social Innovation Review lamented: "Nonprofits are often collecting heaps of dubious data, at great cost to themselves and ultimately to the people they serve" (Snibbe, 2006, p. 39). Since these demands will likely continue or even increase, we need to ask ourselves how these demands for evidence of effectiveness are impacting human service nonprofits: What data are nonprofits collecting? How do they collect, process, analyze, store, report, and share this information? What is influencing the structure of these performance data systems? And how do these systems shape the work of staff?

Existing research provides some answers to these questions. For example, many studies have examined nonprofits' adoption and use of outcome measurement, as one management and evaluation tool driving data collection. Other studies have examined why nonprofits adopt outcome measurement frameworks, finding that network partners and staff, not just funders, influence that decision (MacIndoe & Barman, 2012). Other studies have examined the types of data nonprofits collect—financial, output, and outcome—and found that many nonprofits do not collect outcome data but continue to rely on financial and output data (Carman, 2007; Innonet, 2016; LeRoux & Wright, 2010). Several studies have looked at how nonprofits use the data they collect and have found that reporting to funders is a primary use (e.g., Alexander et al., 2010; Bopp, Harmon, & Voida, 2017; Carnochan, Samples, Myers, & Austin, 2014; Ebrahim, 2003; Hwang & Powell, 2009; Stoecker, 2007; Zimmermann & Stevens, 2006). Other studies have documented some of the consequences of these outcome data demands for the work of nonprofits. For example, studies have found that performance measurement requirements can lead nonprofits to be less responsive to clients or to underinvest in community building work (e.g., Benjamin, 2008a; Smith & Lipsky, 1993). Along these same lines, studies have also examined the mismatches between types of data collected to understand outcomes and the actual work required to achieve outcomes (e.g., Benjamin, 2012; Benjamin & Campbell, 2015; Carnochan et al., 2014; Miller & Holstein, 1989; Parton, 2008; White, Hall, & Peckover, 2009).

But what do we know about the actual data systems in nonprofits? Some research studies have examined specific points in the workflows associated with data systems. For example, studies show that staff encounter problems inputting and extracting the data—which include everything from computer glitches, the time lag between collecting and inputting the data, and limited access to databases (e.g., Carnochan et al., 2014; Stoecker, 2007). This research found that these problems increased the staff time needed to use these systems, resulted in inaccurate data and led staff to create alternative systems, i.e., "workarounds," to manage information. These studies suggest that problems with data systems are the result of systems designed to meet funding requirements, to serve management needs, or by information technology vendors who have limited understanding of direct service work (Bopp et al., 2017; Carnochan et al., 2014; DeWitte, Declercq, & Hermans, 2016; Gillingham, 2014; Schoech, 2010; Stoecker, 2007).

Despite all this important research, we still lack a comprehensive picture of the data systems in nonprofit organizations, including the data practices, data tools, databases, and data flows, e.g., what forms and tools do nonprofits use to collect data, what happens to the data once they collect it, where do they store this information, how is it shared with external stakeholders, and so on. Consequently, we are not able to understand the nature of the duplication and overlap in these systems nor are we able to understand the degree of fragmentation across systems and what all of this means for the work of staff. Our study contributes to research on nonprofit data systems. We report on results from an ongoing study that examines the data systems in nonprofit human service organizations. Our work, unlike previous studies, examines nonprofits' data systems in the context of larger data ecosystems. By data ecosystem, we refer to the broader sociotechnical environment or information ecology of an organization's data systems (see, e.g., Star & Ruhleder, 1996). Examining nonprofit data systems within a larger data ecosystem enables us to develop a fuller understanding of these data systems, including both the causes and consequences of their implementation. We know that if we want to understand organizations, including their structure and work, we need to consider the environment in which they operate (DiMaggio & Powell, 1991; Meyer & Rowan, 1977; Pfeffer & Salancik, 1978).

This paper reports on our findings from in-depth case studies of the data systems used in two nonprofits—one in the HIV/AIDS field and the other in the homeless services field—and the larger data ecosystems in which these organizations and their data systems were situated. We examined how data entered the organization, were processed inside the organization, and then shared and/or reported outside the organization. These in-depth examinations of the data systems of two focal nonprofits were complemented by fieldwork carried out to understand the larger data ecosystems— including interviews with representatives from other service providers that were part of the focal organization's referral network and organizations responsible for aggregating data at the community level, such as local government funders. By looking at the larger data ecosystem of each focal organization, we were able to see that these systems were more fully explained by the larger policy field in which these organizations worked.

The paper proceeds by first summarizing what we know about the data systems and data work in nonprofit human service organizations. By data systems, we mean the systems organizations use to collect, process, analyze, store, report, and share data on the organization's performance. By data work, we include the work staff do to create and maintain these systems, including the work undertaken to gather, enter, clean, and use the data in these systems. After summarizing the existing literature, we describe our conceptual framework, methodology, and our two field sites. We then zero in on the data systems in each of the focal organizations, describe the consequences of these systems for the data work of staff, and then turn to examine their causes. Here, we show how the data systems in these nonprofit human service organizations are better understood as a consequence, not simply of funder requirements, but of the particular policy field in which these nonprofits work. The concept of policy fields recognizes that actors in a policy area share certain substantive knowledge about the issue, are shaped by the same legal and regulatory history, as well as local knowledge about particular people and organizations (see Sandfort & Stone, 2008). We describe three characteristics of the policy field that help explain our findings: the location of administrative authority, the funding tool, and assumptions about the policy problem. We conclude by discussing the implications of using policy fields as a lens for understanding nonprofit data systems as well as the limitations of our findings.

These findings extend existing research in two important respects. First, the findings provide a more comprehensive picture of the data systems in nonprofits than we have had to date. Second, by situating nonprofit data systems in their larger data ecosystems, the findings help us move beyond generic references to funders to understand these systems as reflections of the larger policy field in which human service organizations work. The policy field concept was not part of our original conceptual framework entering the field. While we were versed in this concept and the broader policy implementation literature, the validity of the policy field concept as an interpretive frame for the data systems became apparent in our comparative analysis of the two cases, undoubtedly facilitated by our attention to larger data ecosystems. The generalizability of these findings will need to be tested through replication with additional cases.

Existing literature

Literature examining accountability and performance issues in the nonprofit sector has grown tremendously in the last few years. Less attention has been paid to how these cumulative demands for evidence of outcomes shape the data systems in organizations and the data work of staff. We organize the existing literature around our main research questions: (1) what data do nonprofits collect? (2) how do they collect, process, analyze, store, report, and share these data? (3) what shapes these systems?, and (4) what are the consequences of these systems for the work of staff in human service nonprofits?

What data do nonprofits collect?

A number of studies help us understand the types of data—financial, client satisfaction, output, and outcome data—that nonprofits collect (Carman, 2007; Innonet, 2016; LeRoux & Wright, 2010). For example, Carman (2007) found that fewer human service organizations reported collecting customer satisfaction and outcome information, compared to disability organizations. Findings from a survey by Innonet (2016), an evaluation consulting firm, suggested that 91% of nonprofits surveyed collect outcome data. Other studies help us understand the time staff spend on data collection. For example, Stoecker (2007), who surveyed 80 nonprofits in Toledo, found that on average a staff person spent about six hours a week on data work including data collection, entry, analysis, and reporting. Another study of over 2000 human service professionals in the United Kingdom found that staff spend 60% of their time on administrative work, which included data entry, as opposed to direct client contact.

How do they collect, process, analyze, store, report, and share these data?

We did not find any studies that comprehensively examined the end-to-end work practices associated with the data systems of human service organizations. Studies have reported on different points in the workflow around these systems, however. For example, Stoecker (2007) found that 61% of the data nonprofits collect was in paper form. Carman and Fredericks' (2008) survey of nonprofits in Indiana seems to confirm this, with 79% of the nonprofits surveyed relying on written forms. Moving from data collection to data entry, De Witte, Declercq, and Hermans' (2016) study of child welfare workers in Belgium found great variability in how much of the electronic record social workers completed. This loss of information when moving from interaction to paper to computer is confirmed by other studies of record keeping in social work and health (see Huuskonen & Vakkari, 2015). De Witte et al. (2016) also found that the information collected early on in the social worker–client relationship was often incomplete or inaccurate, as client trust was lower, but that the system required staff to complete entries anyway, resulting in inaccurate data input. Carnochan et al. (2014) reported similar findings in their study of four large nonprofit human service organizations in the United States. Finally, De Witt et al. (2016) also found that prior to inputting data, staff used Microsoft Word to make a report and then copied this into the data system, resulting in double entry.

Once inputted, data can be aggregated and analyzed. Høybye-Mortensen's (2016) study provides some insight into this process. She looked at Danish municipalities providing disability services and found that small errors in entry can significantly affect accuracy in the aggregation process, as the data system would leave out entire records with missing fields. She also found that the informal systems staff used to aggregate data created problems because staff could not remember exactly how they aggregated the data year to year; consequently, variations were likely the result of changing aggregation practices in addition to the actual changes in the social phenomenon of interest. Voida, Harmon, and Al-Ani (2011) found that the data systems within nonprofit organizations were generally so fragmented across numerous, incompatible systems that aggregation and analysis often proved impossible. Schoech (2010) noted that human service organizations are entering into a world where data will be linked across organizations and services and notes one of the challenges to this is that data often reside in antiquated legacy systems that serve an intended purpose but hinder interoperability because data are isolated in unlinked information silos.

We could find no study that explicitly examined data coordination and aggregation outside of the organization. Stoecker (2007) did find that on the whole nonprofits did not share their data with other organizations because of a lack of standardization. A recent article in the Stanford Social Innovation Review provides some insight into the coordination work required by staff when organizations participate in collective impact initiatives. This article points to the privacy concerns that organizations have to address when engaging in such efforts and that interpreting data across organizations requires context and thus ongoing conversation among organizations participating in such efforts (Cooper & Shumate, 2015). Le Dantec and Edwards (2010) further suggest that competition between organizations for funding serves as a disincentive for collaborating in shared data initiatives.

Finally, while studies have asked how nonprofits use the performance data they collect, the findings are somewhat contradictory. Studies that rely on surveys report that nonprofits use performance data for a variety of purposes, including reporting to funders and making program decisions. For example, in the study by Carman and Fredericks (2008), 67% of the nonprofits surveyed said they used these data to assess whether they were meeting program goals and 71% of the nonprofits surveyed said they used this information to report to funders. These findings are relatively consistent with other surveys (see LeRoux & Wright, 2010 for a good summary of these studies). However, qualitative studies suggest that internal data use is limited. Researchers have identified several conditions that limit data use in human service organizations, including concerns about data quality, limited understanding of the software, limited support from vendors, and lack of leadership (Carnochan et al., 2014; Carrillo, 2007; Høybye-Mortensen, 2016; Lynch-Cerullo & Cooney, 2011; Stoecker, 2007).

What shapes these systems and what are the consequences of these systems for the work of staff?

The literature above suggests that data systems in human service organizations are influenced by several factors. Yet, existing research suggest that funding requirements are the primary cause explaining why nonprofit data systems look the way they do because data systems are developed to capture information that demonstrates accountability to funders for agreed upon tasks and goals. Plenty of empirical work supports this conclusion (e.g., Benjamin, 2008b; Bopp et al., 2017; Cutt & Murray 2000; Ebrahim, 2003; Stoecker, 2007; Smith & Lipsky, 1993). Other research has started to highlight the importance of staff and network partners, not just funders, in nonprofit managers' decisions to adopt specific performance management frameworks (MacIndoe & Barman, 2012); these stakeholders will also likely influence how nonprofits develop their data systems.

Existing research suggests several consequences of these data systems for the work of nonprofit staff. On the positive side, one study found that more diverse types of performance data collected by a nonprofit were associated with self-reported effectiveness in strategic decision making (LeRoux & Wright, 2010). Other researchers found that staff welcome data collection tools that help them assess clients' situations, as it enhances their professionalism (Robinson, 2003 cited in Bradt, Roose, Bouverne-De Bie, & De Schryver, 2011). Finally, data collection tools, to the extent they are standardized, can reduce arbitrary decision making by staff, although the findings here are mixed (White et al., 2009; Jorna & Wagenaar, 2007; DeWitte, Declercq & Hermans, 2016). But research also suggests some negative consequences of these data systems for staff. First, data collection, particularly when it is not used to inform decision making within the organization, is seen as an added burden on time and material resources (e.g., Gillingham, 2013; Parton, 2008). Second, data systems affect staff understandings of the problem and organizational learning more broadly. For example, increasing quantification of intake procedures affects staff understanding of the clients' issues (White et al., 2009). At an organizational level, data systems that focus on demonstrating accountability can inhibit organizational learning (Ebrahim, 2003). Finally, data systems can lead to goal displacement, as staff and organizations focus on what is measured (e.g., Benjamin, 2008a; Bopp et al., 2017).

Conceptual Framework

While existing studies go some distance in helping us understand the data systems in nonprofit organizations, these studies have not looked at nonprofit data systems as a whole nor have they considered how these data systems might shape or be shaped by the larger data ecosystem in which they are situated. But classic work in organizational theory suggests that if we want to understand organizations, and why they are structured and function in particular ways, then we need to consider the larger environment in which they operate (Meyer, Scott, & Deal, 1983; Meyer & Rowan, 1977; Powell & DiMaggio, 1991; Scott & Davis, 2007).

As noted above, existing research has identified one key environmental variable—funders' requirements—and how this variable has impacted nonprofit data systems. But as MacIndoe and Barman's research suggests, other stakeholders in the environment also play a role in nonprofit decision making. In our research, we anticipate that peer organizations and clients might also influence data systems and data work. More specifically, we anticipate that three environmental conditions will shape data systems in nonprofits and make data work more varied and intensive. These conditions are not hypotheses that we test but rather are criteria we use to select information rich cases to better understand the phenomena of interest: the data systems and data work in nonprofits. We describe these conditions here and then discuss how they informed our case selection in the 'Methodology' section.

First, as already noted, funding requirements have been found to shape data systems and data work in nonprofits. More specifically, research suggests that government funding will likely require more elaborate data systems to demonstrate accountability than other types of funding (see Smith & Lipsky, 1993). Private funders, particularly individual donors and independent foundations, do not necessarily require specific reports or detailed accountability information. Consequently, organizations receiving government funding will require that staff engage in data compliance work.

Second, policy efforts to achieve community-level outcomes, i.e., what has sometimes been called collective impact, will likely affect data systems and data work in nonprofits. Working toward community level outcomes requires coordination with other organizations, i.e., peer organizations that are addressing the same problem and providing similar services, to identify common metrics and aggregation processes. While we are not aware of studies that have looked at how nonprofits coordinate data collection across organizations, scholars like Schoech (2010) have predicted that the general trend toward big data will require human service organizations to develop greater interoperability of data systems and this requires "predetermined data definitions, standards, protocols" and "user authentication and identity management tools to ensure data security, client privacy and confidentiality" (Schoech, 2010, p. 8). Consequently, nonprofits involved in efforts to achieve community-level outcomes will require that staff engage in data coordination work.

Finally, the third environmental condition affecting data systems and data work is the client. Clients can be a significant cause of environmental uncertainty for organizations (Thompson 1962). To this point, Carnochan et al. (2014) and De Witte et al. (2016) found that collecting valid data depends on building a trusting relationship with clients so that clients are willing to fully disclose information about themselves. We anticipate this work to become more intense for populations facing some societal stigma (see Goffman, 1963; Sparks, 2010). Consequently, the validity of the data and the functionality of data systems require staff to engage in what we call data confidence work.

Methodology

The findings reported here are from two cases that are part of a larger ongoing study of data systems in nonprofit human service organizations. Here, we describe our case selection, data collection, and data analysis for these two cases.

Case selection

We used three criteria, based on the conceptual framework above, to select two information-rich cases where extensive data work would be visible. These criteria included (1) a nonprofit that received government funding to illuminate data compliance work, (2) a nonprofit located in a policy area where there was an effort to achieve community level outcomes to illuminate data coordination work, and (3) a nonprofit serving a population that faced some societal stigma to illuminate data confidence work. We chose case sites in two different social service areas, so we could understand the extent to which the findings were unique to the case or held across different service settings, with the plan to replicate the study to test the robustness and generalizability of the results. We also made sure that each focal organization was an established organization, as we could not be certain that a new organization would have data systems in place.

Data collection

Each case study included a focal organization where we conducted in-depth fieldwork. We interviewed a cross section of staff from each organization including frontline staff in different programs. We worked with the central staff person responsible for data oversight to develop data journey maps: drawings of how data flowed into, through, and out of their organization (Bates, Lin, & Goodale, 2016). We interviewed staff from other nonprofit service organizations that were part of the referral network for the focal organization. Finally, we interviewed key data stakeholders from organizations that were responsible for receiving and aggregating data across organizations. In the HIV/AIDS case, this included staff from the county and state and in the homeless services case, this included staff at one nonprofit intermediary and two county departments. In total, we conducted 24 interviews in the HIV/AIDS services case (16 in the focal organization, 4 with referral partners, and 4 with data aggregators) and 14 in the homeless services case (7 in the focal organization, 4 with referral partners, and 3 with data aggregators). We have described the interviewees and organizations in a way that will protect their confidentiality. Since we are reporting on the data systems of the focal organizations for this paper, we focus primarily on the those interviews, drawing on the outside interviews to better understand this focal organization's data systems, e.g., to what extent were the issues in the focal organization unique and to what extent were they evident of larger patterns in the service field.

In addition to conducting interviews, we reviewed a variety of documents to understand each organization's data systems. We reviewed the forms used to collect data in the focal organization. We reviewed data dictionaries and database user manuals that described what data staff should enter into a particular database, as well as the websites of the vendors providing the technical assistance and/or housing the data systems. In addition, we reviewed material on the history of the problem itself, including program implementation guidance, reports on prevalence of the problem (HIV/AIDS and homelessness), policy histories, along with policy documents on plans to address the problem (i.e., National HIV/AIDS strategy, Ten-Year Plan to End Homelessness). Finally, we observed coordinating meetings, where service providers and funders discussed service coordination across the locality.

Analysis

Our analysis was iterative and moved between inductive and deductive strategies to prioritize the experiences of interviewees alongside an analysis of the literature (see, e.g., Corbin & Strauss, 2007). We used both Microsoft Excel and Word to aid in our analysis, to avoid compatibility issues because we worked on two different operating systems. Here, we identify the steps we took to move from data to interpretation and give an example to make our process explicit. As with most studies, more than one interpretive frame can be used to understand the data, illuminating some aspects of a case while downplaying others (see Ragin & Ambroso, 2011). By including the examples, we show how our interpretation is supported by the data.

First, we read through the transcripts for each case separately, identifying instances of data work—whether compliance, confidence, or coordination work (deductive codes from our conceptual framework). For example, with data coordination work, we noted in the HIV/AIDS case that staff who used a state database were able to easily share data and coordinate services with staff in other sites, while staff who used the county database were severely constrained in doing coordination work. In iterative reads through of the transcripts, we also identified emergent themes. For example, the "external control" of databases was a strong emergent theme in both cases.

Second, we combed through data collection forms, documentation about the databases, as well as program policy documents and coupled this with the information from the interviews and the data maps drawn by staff in order to develop a fuller account of the data systems. For example, using the theme of external control in the HIV/AIDS case, the data maps showed the two primary databases that were externally controlled, but interviews revealed an additional three external databases. Staff conducting HIV tests were funded either by the state or the county. If they were funded by the state, they entered data in one database and if they were funded by the county, they entered data into a different system. This was true even though all reports of positive results were eventually reported to the state so they could monitor the prevalence of the disease. The two different databases had consequences for the compliance work of staff. For example, to locate a client's test results, staff had to know who had tested them in order to know which database to search and where to locate the paper file.

Third, while the staff interviews illuminated the consequences of these systems for their work, we turned to the interviews with partners and data aggregators (i.e., nonprofit intermediaries and public agencies) to better understand the origins of the data systems. We coupled the data from these interviews with documents about the history of the problem and the evolution of the policy detailed in 10-year plans, historical policy timelines, and so on. Again, taking a small example from the HIV case, the separate databases used by the testers could be partly explained by the historical separation of prevention and treatment into two separate federal agencies, the Center for Disease Control (CDC) and the Health Resources and Services Administration, respectively, each with their own databases. When the county, which primarily funded treatment services, also started funding testers, they required those testers to track that information in the database they used.

Finally, we compared and contrasted the data systems in the two cases. This comparison threw into sharp relief how the characteristics of the policy field influenced the configuration of the data systems in our two focal organizations. One of the characteristics of a policy field is the location of administrative authority. While some of the databases for the focal organization in both cases were externally controlled, the data systems in the HIV/AIDS case were more centralized at the federal level. Local organizations had some discretion, but the software, the overall configuration, and the data, itself, were controlled at the federal level. In contrast, in the homeless service case, the selection of vendors and information system implementation was delegated to the local level, although federal funders specified minimum data elements. The location of administrative authority in the policy field mirrored the nature of the problem: HIV/AIDS was an epidemic, requiring a coordinated and centralized national response.

Homelessness, while also a crisis, has been a long-standing issue addressed at the community level. Next, we describe our field sites, focusing on the features that we used to select the cases.

Fieldsites

HIV/AIDS services case

HIV/AIDS has gone from a death sentence to a communicable disease. When HIV first burst into national consciousness in the 1980s, individuals contracting HIV/AIDS were ostracized and often faced violent reactions from the communities in which they lived and worked. One of the earliest visible cases happened in Indiana when Ryan White, a boy who contracted the disease through a blood transfusion, was denied access to his school. As his family fought to reinstate him, Ryan became a national symbol of the fight against discrimination and in 1990 not only did Congress outlaw discrimination based on HIV/AIDS status in the American with Disabilities Act, but it also passed a major piece of legislation that bore Ryan's name, the Ryan White Comprehensive AIDS Resources Emergency Care Act (https://hab.hrsa.gov/about-ryan-white-hivaids-program/about-ryan-white-hivaids-program). While scientific and public understanding of the disease has dramatically improved over the years and HIV/AIDS status is often invisible today, persons with HIV/AIDS still face stigma.

Three primary agencies address HIV/AIDS at the federal level: (1) the Center for Disease Control focuses on prevention and tracking the incidence of new infections, (2) the Health Services Resource Administration (HRSA) provides funding for localities to provide care for those already infected, and (3) the National Institutes of Health supports research and clinical trials to develop new testing and treatment methods. All three agencies reside within the Department of Health and Human Services (HHS). HRSA administers the Ryan White grant, which is still the single largest source of support for treatment at the local level and is passed down to the states and counties and then contracted out to local service providers (see Figure 1). The CDC also has several grant programs that provide funding for prevention activities at the local level. A bulk of this funding are grants that pass through the states and then on to local nonprofits to support testing. Other federal agencies also have specialized programs. For example, the Department of Housing and Urban Development (HUD) provides housing assistance for persons living with HIV/AIDS. Figure 1 provides a very basic picture of funding flows from HHS, down to the focal organization, focusing on Ryan White funding. To protect confidentiality, the names are generic.

In 2009, the Obama Administration announced the first ever national strategy to address HIV/AIDS. The National Strategy was intended to coordinate efforts by public and private agencies at the federal and local levels and to drive toward specific outcomes, including reducing the number of new diagnoses by at least 25% and increasing the percentage of persons with HIV who are virally

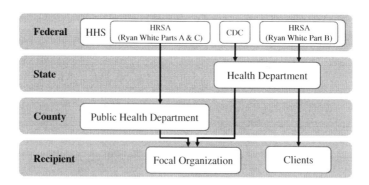

Figure 1. Government funding flows for HIV/AIDS services focal organization.

suppressed to 80% (National AIDS Strategy Update 2020, www.whitehouse.gov/onap). This focus on coordinating prevention and treatment to reduce community viral loads reflects the significant advances in the treatment of the disease. The introduction of highly active antiretroviral drugs in 1996 reduced AIDS-related deaths considerably. In 2010, the NIH announced a new drug to prevent HIV-negative individuals from contracting the disease, and in 2015, the results of a decade-long study showed that early intervention and treatment of those infected reduced their viral loads to undetectable levels and prevented transmission to an uninfected partner.

The focal organization in the HIV/AIDS case is a community organization that was founded in the late 1980s in response to the growing AIDS crisis. Located in a county with a population of approximately 1 million, the organization, like many other community-based organizations that popped up around the country in the 1980s, worked to care for those infected as well as advocated for their rights. Today, this organization provides a number of services to those diagnosed with HIV/AIDS, including case management, mental health and addiction counseling, medical services as well as employment support, housing assistance, and emergency assistance (e.g., food). In 2015, the organization had almost 50 staff, served approximately 1200 HIV-positive individuals, and provided 3500 free HIV tests. The organization received support from a wide range of foundations and individual and corporate donors but a majority of its funding (62%) comes from county and state government.

Homeless services case

Individuals experiencing homelessness also face societal stigma (Sparks, 2010, 2012). While homelessness is not a permanent condition like HIV/AIDS, it often is more visible. Shifts in social policy have also contributed to foregrounding the stigma of homelessness, shifting the blame from society to the individual (Sparks, 2010, 2012). Between the 1980s and the 1990s, for example, media coverage of homelessness shifted from stories depicting individuals who had been affected by various external circumstances that caused homelessness (e.g., economic downturns) to coverage emphasizing the deviance and disorder introduced by these individuals (e.g., littering, committing crimes, and panhandling) (Lee, Tyler, & Wright, 2010).

Homelessness, unlike HIV/AIDS, has been a long-standing issue in communities and addressed primarily at the local level. But in 1987, Congress passed and President Regan signed the McKinney Homeless Assistance Act (later named the McKinney–Vento Homeless Assistance Act). McKinney–Vento is largest source of federal support for homeless assistance and came on the heels of a sharp increase in the prevalence of homelessness. The legislation included 15 programs, housed in different federal agencies; the Department of HUD has the largest grant program. Initially, HUD made grants to individual organizational applicants from across the country but in 1994 it started requiring communities to develop and submit a single comprehensive plan, now called the continuum of care (CoC). With the CoC, one organization serves as the official applicant for the entire CoC; it facilitates the dispersal of awarded funding and is required to track data in compliance with federally established standards.

The CoC was an early effort to encourage coordination to achieve community-level outcomes. The focus on community-level outcomes solidified even further in early 2000 when Congress asked HUD to provide data about the effectiveness of the CoC grants (HUD, 2006, June). In response, HUD established and mandated data standards to be used in the collection of data about service provision and homelessness, which facilitated output data that could be compared at local, state, and federal levels. Around this same time, the National Alliance to End Homelessness began encouraging communities to formalize the coordination of regionally specific services into a document called a Ten-Year Plan to End Homelessness, including a data-supported, outcome-driven approach. The increased federal involvement in homeless assistance and the alliance shifted the focus of local providers toward regionally scoped program design, coordination, and data collection. Despite this, and perhaps reflective of the problem being viewed as a local issue, HUD never set specific national

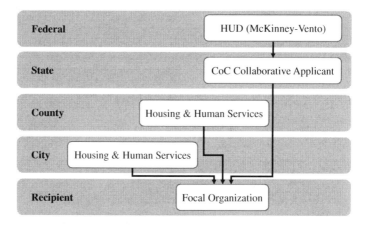

Figure 2. Government funding flow for homeless services focal organization.

performance targets around homelessness, like the Obama Administration did for HIV/AIDS. Instead, it assessed communities on progress toward their own locally defined goals for reducing homelessness (HUD, 2006, July).

The focal organization in the homeless case is located in a county with a population of about 400,000. The organization was founded in 1987 (the same year as the focal organization in the HIV/AIDS case). A census of individuals experiencing homeless suggested that in 2016, there were approximately 700 individuals experiencing homelessness in the county. This organization is one of three in the city that provides services to adults experiencing homelessness. These services included street outreach, overnight sheltering during the winter months, as well as transitional and permanent supportive housing year-round. Services were provided by approximately 50 staff members. The majority of its funding came from private sources (40%) and government grants (30%) through two city governments, the county government, and from HUD as passed through by the local CoC as depicted in Figure 2. Again, this is a very basic picture of one funding stream from HUD down to the focal organization. To protect confidentiality, names are generic.

Findings

In this section, we provide a general overview of the data systems in the two case sites, highlighting the fragmentation and duplication in these systems, and then briefly describe the data work required to use these systems, giving examples of confidence, compliance, and coordination work. We then discuss how the characteristics of the policy field help explain the structure and form of these data systems in these two cases. Because of space constraints, we focus on three characteristics of the policy field that shaped the data systems and data work in our two cases:

(1) *Policy authority*—Where does administrative authority lie? The United States has a federalist system of government where significant policy authority is vested in the states. Consequently, when the federal government addresses a policy problem, it often addresses the problem not by employing federal workers to address the problem directly but by delegating partial authority to state governments, local governments and nonprofits to address the problem (Salamon, 2002). In our study, the dispersed and decentralized nature of the policy implementation process helped to elucidate the data systems in our two focal organizations.

(2) *Policy assumptions*—What assumptions does the policy make about the problem, the causes of the problem, and the proposed solutions? Policies define problems and identify types of

interventions to address the problem (Schneider & Ingram, 1990). These problems and interventions rest on assumptions about the causes of the problem and the appropriate solutions, which in turn shape action in the policy field. In both our cases, changing definitions of the problem and shifting beliefs about appropriate solutions illuminated ways in which policy assumptions influenced the data systems.

(3) *Policy tool*—What kind of policy tool is used to achieve the policy objectives? Regulations, contracts, grants, tax credits, and loans are all examples of policy tools that governments use to incentivize organizations to help achieve public objectives (Salamon, 2002). These tools have different consequences for those entities receiving funding. For example, some tools, like contracts, are more coercive, have more restrictions and requirements than others, like grants. In our study, the coerciveness of the tool influenced the degree to which the formal data systems penetrated the daily routines of nonprofit staff (see Smith & Lipsky, 1993).

Other characteristics of the policy field may also be relevant—for example, the legal framework or vertical and horizontal networks; but again, given space constraints, we focus on these three.

HIV/AIDS services case

Overview of data systems

At the time of this study, the staff collected information using several paper forms (e.g., intake forms, applications, referrals, screening forms, verification forms, treatment plans, and surveys). We counted over 50 unduplicated distinct forms, although this number is an estimate because 20 page applications, which we counted as 1 form, often contained multiple forms. The data collected included demographic information, information to determine eligibility for services (e.g., income, employment), and information to determine need (e.g., housing status, mental health status, health diagnosis, including viral loads and CD4 counts, risk behaviors). If clients are already HIV positive, they can self-refer or may be referred from testing or from another service provider. Clients meet with a care coordinator, who asks them a series of questions necessary to complete an application and determines if they are eligible for services.

Once the staff collect this information, they input data, from the forms, into six main databases, although each staff person only reported entering data into one or two of these databases for his/her own work. Five of the databases were government-sponsored databases and were externally managed and controlled, i.e., service providers could customize certain fields to some extent, which they did, but could not make overarching decisions about the system. The only database that the organization controlled was its recently instituted electronic medical records system. In addition to these six databases, the organization also entered data into an Excel spreadsheet for a foundation that supported one particular program. Staff also checked external databases for other types of information (e.g., client insurance, comparable rental prices) when completing these forms.

In addition to these databases, the organization maintained up to five separate paper files for clients—depending on the services they access. The organization also managed electronic backups of clients' Ryan White applications and referrals for services, which were stored on an internal server. All the applications and referrals were also checked for completion and accuracy by management before being sent to the county. Finally, all of the staff that worked with clients reported using a variety of other tools and strategies to help them do their work and work around the limits of the databases. For example, one staff member created an electronically fillable PDF file to make data entry easier (Case 1, Interview 7). Other staff created separate spreadsheets to aggregate information because the spreadsheets were easier to work with than the databases. This meant that staff were double and triple entering data. One staff person explained,

> We made our own spreadsheets that we keep in a password protected network…. It's double, triple entry sometimes. You got a case manager funded by Ryan White, so they've got to enter into CareWare, got to enter

into HMIS per HUD, and then we have this other spreadsheet that you're going to enter everything into so that when it comes to report time, we can actually do things in an easy way. (Case 1, Interview 8)

When staff were asked what data they used and how they used these data, most staff reported that the data they collected from clients helped them get to know the clients and to know what to do next for them (e.g., what kind of insurance did they have, did they need mental health counseling, are they symptomatic). However, there seemed to be little use of these data in aggregate within programs (Case 1, Interview 12). Instead, staff spoke of putting together reports for organizational leadership, who ran analyses on a weekly, quarterly, monthly, and yearly basis for funders and to inform organizational management decisions (e.g., number of client contact hours by staff; wait times; number of tests conducted, demographic profile of clients).

Overview of data work

While the description of the formal data systems and the alternative tools and strategies staff used provides some indication of the data work of staff, this picture is incomplete. For example, when staff collected data, they discussed the strategies and tactics they used to help put clients at ease when answering questions, work we call confidence work. One staff member in testing explained:

> The first questions that people have when they're testing is, who is this information going to? [So] taking that time to explain to them about the information and why we need this information and that it is a reportable condition and that they need this information in case there is a reactive test so they can get in touch with you and make sure you get the help that you need and anyone that you have come in contact with to get the help that they need. And I think after like breaking it down and explaining those type things, it just takes time to do that. (Case 1, Interview 10)

Despite these efforts, staff reported that clients regularly gave inaccurate information. In testing, they would give false names, which staff attributed to the stigma of getting an HIV test and possible diagnosis. In other program areas, staff reported that clients would underreport or over report risk behaviors (Case 1, Interview 7).

In addition to confidence work, staff engaged in compliance work: they entered data into several external databases to meet funding requirements. This compliance work was extensive and affected the daily routines of staff, the flow of information through the organization, and the administrative structure of the organization. This organization had a dedicated unit to oversee compliance, reporting and billing to funders. Data that were to be shared externally with county and state funders went through the staff in this unit. These quality assurance and compliance staff ensured that approvals were in place before services were rendered, that electronic and paper files were complete, and that services were billed in a timely manner.

Finally, staff spent time engaged in data coordination work, which included data sharing and aggregation, inside and outside the organization. Most of this coordination work was vertical, sharing data between line staff and management or between the service provider and the funder. For example, the county required that organizations fax copies of applications for services, in addition to entering some of these data into the external database. In contrast, service providers opted to hand deliver paper copies of the applications to the state health department every week. Organizations were not required to hand deliver these materials to the state, like they were required to fax them to the County, but all the service providers we spoke to adopted this practice to ensure applications were received.

In contrast, horizontal data sharing among staff in a program area or among staff from different service providers was constrained, despite the federal and local emphasis on greater coordination to reduce community viral load. For example, the focal organization had testers who were funded by the county and testers who were funded by the state. The state testers entered their data into one database, while the county-funded testers entered their data into another. This was also true for the care coordinators, the non-medical and medical case managers. Among the network of service providers, sharing data about services and care was required in one database but prohibited in another, because one service provider made the decision early on, with the permission of the county, to include all their clients in the database, not just those funded by Ryan White. To protect the privacy of these individuals, who did not sign a waiver form, the privacy settings in the database were configured such that no service providers in the county could share case notes or details about service protocols.

Policy field

While it would be easy to look at the data systems in the HIV/AIDS organization and attribute them to funding requirements, we can better understand these systems by looking at the larger policy field. For example, administrative authority for addressing the problem and the resulting data systems were more centralized in this case compared to the homeless services case. This likely reflects the fact that HIV/AIDS was a national epidemic at the time that Ryan White was passed in the early 1990s (hiv.gov/timeline). This more centralized data system meant that nonprofits in the HIV/AIDS case had less decision-making authority over these data systems, compared to the nonprofit in the homeless service case. For example, the HIV/AIDS nonprofits did not work with other service providers at the local level to choose software vendors or work with other service providers to develop common data standards, which was possible with the Homeless Management Information System (HMIS). While nonprofit providers could tailor certain fields that were in their local domain of the federal database, which most nonprofits did to some extent, nonprofits tried to put the minimum amount of information into this database as possible (Case 1, Interview 18). At the same time, administrative authority was more visibly fragmented in HIV/AIDS case, a consequence of the fact that the authority to monitor and prevent a disease resided with the Center for Disease Control, while authority to treat those infected was given to HRSA. The CDC worked primarily with states, whereas HRSA delegated Ryan White funding not only to all states but also to counties and cities hardest hit by the disease. As already noted, this meant that staff carrying out the same function within the focal organization entered data into two separate databases, depending on which government unit funded their position.

Assumptions about HIV/AIDS, about the people infected, and how to best treat the disease also influenced the data systems of the focal organization and the larger data ecosystem. For example, at the time of this study, there was a movement to change the consent law, which criminalizes HIV-infected persons for not informing partners that they are infected. While HIV-infected persons could now effectively prevent the spread of the disease by ensuring their viral loads were below the level that was now proven to prevent transmission, the legal requirements were embedded in the data systems and data work. Staff were still required to inform HIV-positive clients of their responsibilities to inform potential partners of their HIV status, have them sign a form acknowledging their understanding of these responsibilities, include that documentation in the patient's file, and sign off that they had this documented in reports to the state. One staff person explained the problem, "They're based on either the archaic notions of the times or it is medically incorrect now" (Case 1, Interview 10). Take a similar example: new drug therapies changed HIV/AIDS from a death sentence to a communicable disease. This change opened up the possibility of managing the disease and preventing transmission by tracking high-risk individuals over time. It was now possible to track high risk individuals who were not yet infected to ensure they remained on preventative treatment as well as HIV-positive individuals to ensure they remained on treatment and their viral loads suppressed. Yet, the data systems both in the focal organization and at the state level did not allow for this. Data systems in the focal organization were bifurcated between point-in-time testing and treatment, making it difficult for the organization to monitor individuals' evolving status. There was a similar bifurcation at the state level. As one interviewee at the state explained,

You set the [data systems] up at the time when your life expectancy wasn't very long and I, I think a lot of these things just evolve … Now you've got your high-risk population and how do you get them into [prevention treatment] and how do you capture this population up here that really ultimately could affect the numbers that go into that box there so and that again there are so many different sources that we pull from. (Case 1, Interview 19)

In the HIV/AIDS case, most of the staff were funded through a contract from the county. Unlike the homeless case where the focal organization received a grant and was only required to report these services annually, getting paid through a contract required that the staff in the HIV/AIDS focal organization interact with government databases daily, reporting on activities, running reports, and certifying clients. One staff person summed up his experience providing social services as "just data collection" (Case 1, Interview 7). Even the clients learned the data routines, as one staff member explained, "A lot of my clients get to the point now where I'm not even asking the questions. I just say, 'hey how's it going?' and they're answering everything" (Case 1, Interview 5).

Homeless services case

Overview of data systems

The focal organization in the homeless services case collects a variety of data about their clients (e.g., name, prior living situation, medical conditions) for the many programs they administer (e.g., overnight shelter, permanent supportive housing), using at least 11 paper-based forms. Staff also use scraps of paper that they carry around to record data on the spot. These data are entered into numerous, completely independent data systems tailored for different audiences in the data ecosystem. For the internal workings of the organization, there exists one internal database, a local master spreadsheet, and another cloud-based spreadsheet. For external stakeholders, the focal organization also enters data into a manually aggregated spreadsheet for grassroots homeless services collaborations in the city, an online data portal and data warehouse for county-wide human services initiatives, and a paper-based intake form and database for the federally mandated HMIS.

Nearly, all data are initially collected for either the HMIS or internal organizational use. New clients are asked to complete an 8-page intake form, although completion of the paperwork is technically not required to access services. Clients are subsequently asked to fill out the form on an annual basis. The paper intake forms are put in a large stack and eventually entered into the HMIS when a staff member or volunteer is able to make time. Data are also collected for the internal database through a face-to-face conversation with a shelter staff member or volunteer at the front desk; these data are also used to check in clients and assign them a bed for the night. Initials and birthdates of clients who have been randomly selected for a bed every night are logged in a cloud-based Google spreadsheet and shared for clients to access from off-site.

While data collected for the HMIS are not used by the organization and are externally managed and controlled, the organization does use the data it collects for internal use in three ways. First, daily data from the internal database are combined with additional paper and digital data repositories—such as breathalyzer logs, TB screening records, chore tracking, logs of rule violations, and a narrative nightly shift log—to generate internal reports for the executive director and board via the local spreadsheet. Second, selected data from the internal database is exported annually into a standardized Excel format and merged with data from two other homeless services organizations in the city so that they can attempt to create a city-level count of individuals experiencing homelessness, outside of the HMIS system. Finally, at the time of this study, the organization was considering exporting a subset of its internal data to the county's data warehouse, which had an expanding roster of participating human services organizations. Since the internal data are more frequently updated and are perceived to have better data quality, the focal organization and the county decided to use the internal database over the HMIS. With a vision of using the data warehouse to create a more holistic repository of every interaction an individual has had with any participating human services organization, the county believes it will be an invaluable resource for community-level decision making.

Overview of data work

In the homeless services case, staff also engaged in multiple forms of data work—confidence, compliance, and coordination work. At the focal organization, frontline staff engage in confidence work, building trust by helping clients tell stories, which also serves as a means of eliciting more accurate data:

> There's the whole thing about bridges out of poverty [training] that people in poverty relate information through stories ... they get you this big long story but what's interesting is they probably give you more accurate information in the long run if you let them tell their story. (Case 2, Interview 9)

Even though storytelling might take longer time, which is difficult given case managers' limited time with clients, it elicits more accurate data and "in the process of extracting this data, we're learning more about our client" (Case 2, Interview 9). Walking the client through the process of self-evaluating their autonomy and independence (i.e., in income, relationships, employment) also requires confidence work. Using a survey instrument to help clients with this self-evaluation, another case manager adapted his data collection process, from starting at the highest level of vulnerability, "the negative end, the stigmatized end of in-crisis" (Case 2, Interview 9) to a more conversational approach, to prevent the data work from reinforcing stigma.

Despite the confidence work of staff, there is still high variability in the reliability of data—in particular, between the reliability of data in the internal systems and the reliability of data in HMIS. In the homeless services organization, compliance work undertaken for federal funders was minimal in comparison to the extent of the compliance work in the HIV/AIDS organization. As noted above, completion of the HMIS intake form was not required for receiving services at the focal organization; as a result, clients sometimes only partially completed the intake form before it was added to a stack to await data entry. Yet, the HMIS system required that some fields be completed when data were finally entered, so some staff members reported making a best guess about data for fields that a client had originally left blank. These data work, in service of compliance, introduced increased variability in the data but was carried out as a work-around to differences between internal data practices (i.e., completion of the intake form is not required) and the requirements embodied by the HMIS system (i.e., that certain fields in the system are required). In contrast, the organization spends more time and effort ensuring data quality for its own internal data that are used both for supporting the organization's workflow as well as for reporting to other funders. More specifically, the consistency of data between the internal Access database and the focal organization's paper forms is manually checked on a daily basis—this is carried out to make sure that, for example, someone entered in the system with a gender of male is not accidentally enrolled into a program for women—before the data are summarized manually in reports to the executive director, board, and funders. For this organization, the variability in compliance work for different stakeholders affected the accuracy of data for these stakeholders (Case 2, Focal Organization Site Tour).

Despite the emphasis on tracking and ending homelessness at the community level, the homeless services focal organization did not participate much in the CoC coordination work around HMIS. This is hardly unique. Other similar organizations in the CoC and other homeless services organizations, as reported in the literature, also did not participate (see also Le Dantec & Edwards, 2008). Instead, management-level staff in the focal organization and at other nonprofits in the county discussed data coordination in the context of the county data portal and data warehouse projects—which would require extensive, ongoing negotiations to align diverse stakeholder needs for data sharing agreements. Staff also discussed how efforts to coordinate and share data among the three homeless services organizations in the city took more than a year. Data sharing and coordination work within the focal organization was not discussed much by interviewees beyond providing summarized data up to managers, the board, and funders. In fact, one project that had been brought up a number of times internally, but never carried out partially due to technology limitations, was tracking individuals across programs within the organization. The lower priority of this project among staff highlights the lower prioritization of internal coordination work.

Policy field

In the end, navigating among different stakeholders, needs, and collaboration initiatives contributed to the fragmentation of data systems in the focal organization. Yet, in the homeless services case, administrative authority was less centralized and less fragmented. For example, while programs supported by the McKinney–Vento Act were spread across several agencies, HUD coordinates with other organizations (e.g., Veteran's Affairs and the HHS) to require the use of a single data system instead of the multiple systems in the HIV/AIDS case. At the same time, while HUD retains the authority to specify the minimum data that need to be uploaded to HMIS and the technical standards for data collection, privacy, and security, the state-level CoC had the authority to select the particular software vendor and HMIS that service providers would be required to use if they received federal funding. The authority for deciding how to configure the selected HMIS system resided with the coordinating nonprofit organization in each region. While this did not always mean that the local nonprofits had the ability to restructure the HMIS to meet their specific organizational needs, they did have a voice in the selection and configuration of the system within their CoC. This seemed to result in less fragmentation of data systems compared to the data systems in the HIV/AIDS case but this did not mean that the data system was more useful to the focal organization. Moreover, the data systems in the homeless services case were still somewhat fragmented, in part because of grassroots city- and county-data initiatives.

In the homeless services case, we also see evidence of how a shift in policy assumptions created tensions in the use of data systems. The introduction of the housing-first model to the CoC around 2005 created the need for a centralized waiting list so that the community's most vulnerable individuals were given priority for extremely limited permanent supportive housing units. However, the need for a community-wide waiting list was not identified until the community had already designed their HMIS earlier in the decade. Coupled with technology limitations, this shift in policy assumptions means that the waiting list is currently maintained in a system disconnected from HMIS or any other database. Under this configuration, staff must enter an individual's details in two systems which, in part, leads staff to only enter details for individuals who they believe will be put high enough on the list to have a good chance of getting a unit.

The extent to which the policy tool structured the daily routines of staff in the HIV/AIDS case stands in contrast to the homeless services case, where we did not see the data systems shape the day-to-day routines of staff and clients to the same extent. While there is a requirement to "use" HMIS, the focal organization sees space for its own interpretation of what it means to "use" the system:

> The regional group is really meeting the requirement that's set forth by HUD. So they say: '[focal organization] if you want your [program] money, you have to use HMIS'. We say: 'okay, we'll use HMIS.' (Case 2, Interview 1)

While organizations receiving federal funds are required to use HMIS, they are not required to collect and report data in order to get reimbursed for services. So in the focal organization's case, "using" HMIS has been interpreted, at least in the case of the overnight shelter program, as updating a client's demographic information annually, not entering day-to-day service level information. However, at the time of this study, the organization coordinating the HMIS began working with the focal organization to look at how to support more data intensive use.

Conclusion and Implications

As the demand for evidence of nonprofit effectiveness continues, considering the effects of these data demands on nonprofits is timely. Nowhere is this more pressing than in the nonprofit human service organizations. This study was unique in its comprehensive look at the data systems in the focal organizations, the data work required to maintain and use these systems, as well as in its examination of the larger data ecosystem in which these data systems were situated. The nonprofit human service organizations in our study worked in a fragmented data environment, where their authority over data systems was partial, duplication was common, and regular workarounds were necessary. On the face of it, these systems seem irrational, creating more work for staff, preventing greater coordination and thwarting the use of data to manage for outcomes. Consequently, staff used workarounds, which often involved duplicate data collection and entry, to manage their work while at the same time facing obstacles to using the data to improve performance.

While existing literature attributes these problems to funding requirements, we find that this assessment is accurate but incomplete. Our examination of the broader data ecosystem, including our interviews with those who collect and aggregate these data as well as other service providers, revealed the significance of the broader policy field in shaping these data systems. By understanding the data systems in these nonprofits through the interpretive lens of the policy field, the findings help us move beyond the common causal story to consider how the characteristics of the policy field—including the funding tool, the policy assumptions about the nature of the problem and the location of the administrative authority to administer the policy—all have consequences for the data systems and the data work of nonprofits. These findings suggest that solutions to address the fragmentation and duplication of data systems in nonprofits may not rest with individual funders but may require policy field solutions.

We see a stronger role for nonprofit intermediaries in a policy arena to convene stakeholders and map the existing data ecosystem and then compare these data mapping to data maps from other locations. For example, one could compare the data map for HIV/AIDS in Boston and Washington DC, to understand how federal data requirements may be managed differently across locations and the consequences of this for local nonprofit organizations. Nonprofit intermediaries might also identify the localities where there seems to be greater cooperation among stakeholders to address data issues to learn from their efforts. Several interviewees mentioned movements to look more comprehensively at these data systems at the federal and local levels and organizations at the local level were a part of convenings with relevant stakeholders that could work toward these ends, but the focus, instead, was often on funding, service protocols, and clarifying requirements, not the larger data ecosystem.

For human service managers, the findings suggest a need to look beyond their own organization and the specific data demands they face, to come together with other organizations in a policy field to better understand where data needs align and diverge. The findings suggest value in any efforts that would facilitate greater alignment of data across organizations and institutions with the caveat that honoring essential local data practices is also important as when external data practices trump local data needs, we have observed greater redundancy of systems and duplication of data work. We also recognize that confidentiality of individual data is a critical concern that can make such efforts challenging.

For researchers, we see three immediate lines of inquiry. First, our findings need to be tested in other social service fields, as well as against other HIV/AIDS and homeless services cases to understand how unique characteristics of the locality may affect these data systems. Second, relatedly, there is a real need to look at the relationship between the data ecosystems and the characteristics of the policy field. For example, do all policy fields that rely on contracts penetrate the daily routines of nonprofits in the same way? Or how have changing policy assumptions impacted data systems for nonprofits within a particular policy field? Does the belief that the problem requires local solutions or a national response impact the character of the data systems in these organizations? Third, researchers could play a real role by working to develop comparative data maps that would help nonprofits in similar policy domains, as noted above, see how their data systems compare with others working in the same substantive area but in a different location.

Acknowledgments

We would like to thank all of the individuals who participated in this research at our local fieldsites. We also want to thank Dr. Thomasina Borkman for her comments on an earlier draft and the anonymous reviewers and the special issue editors for their feedback.

Funding

This work was supported by the Lilly Family School of Philanthropy [NA].

References

Alexander, J., Brudney, J. L., Yang, K., LeRoux, K., & Wright, N. S. (2010). Does performance measurement improve strategic decision making? Findings from a national survey of nonprofit social service agencies. Nonprofit and Voluntary Sector Quarterly, 39(4), 571–587. doi:10.1177/0899764009359942

Bates, J., Lin, Y. W., & Goodale, P. (2016). Data journeys: Capturing the socio-material constitution of data objects and flows. Big Data & Society, 3(2). doi:10.1177/2053951716654502

Benjamin, L. M. (2008a). Bearing more risk for results: Performance measurement and nonprofit relational work. Administration & Society, 39(8), 959–983. doi:10.1177/0095399707309357

Benjamin, L. M. (2008b). Account Space: How accountability requirements shape nonprofit practice. Nonprofit and Voluntary Sector Quarterly, 37(2), 201–233. doi:10.1177/0899764007301288

Benjamin, L. M. (2012). Nonprofit organizations and outcome measurement: From tracking program activities to focusing on frontline work. American Journal of Evaluation, 33(3), 431–447. doi:10.1177/1098214012440496

Benjamin, L. M., & Campbell, D. C. (2015). Nonprofit performance accounting for the agency of clients. Nonprofit and Voluntary Sector Quarterly, 44(5), 988–1006. doi:10.1177/0899764014551987

Bopp, C., Harmon, E., & Voida, A. (2017). Disempowered by data: Nonprofits, social enterprises, and the consequences of data-driven work. To appear in Proceedings of the ACM Conference on Human Factors in Computing Systems. New York: ACM Press.

Bradt, L., Roose, R., Bouverne-De Bie, M., & De Schryver, M. (2011). Data recording and social work: From the relational to the social. British Journal of Social Work. bcr131. doi:10.1093/bjsw/bcr131

Carman, J. G. (2007). Evaluation practice among community-based organizations: Research into the reality. American Journal of Evaluation, 28(1), 60–75. doi:10.1177/1098214006296245

Carman, J. G., & Fredericks, K. A. (2008). Nonprofits and evaluation: Empirical evidence from the field. In J. G. Carman & K. A. Fredericks (Eds.), Nonprofits and evaluation. New Directions for Evaluation, 119, 51–71.

Carnochan, S., Samples, M., Myers, M., & Austin, M. J. (2014). Performance measurement challenges in nonprofit human service organizations. Nonprofit and Voluntary Sector Quarterly, 43(6), 1014–1032. doi:10.1177/0899764013508009

Carrillo, T. E. (2007). Using client information systems in practice settings: Factors affecting social workers' use of information systems. Journal of Technology in Human Services, 25(4), 41–46. doi:10.1300/J017v25n04_03

Cooper, K. R., & Shumate, M. (2016). Sharing data in collective impact efforts. Stanford Social Innovation Review. Retrieved from https://ssir.org/articles/entry/sharing_data_in_collective _impact_efforts

Corbin, J. M., & Strauss, A. C. (2007). Basics of Qualitative Research: Techniques and Procedures for Developing Grounded Theory (3rd ed.). Thousand Oaks: Sage Publications.

Cutt, J., & Murray, V. (2002). Accountability and Effectiveness Evaluation in Nonprofit Organizations. London and New York: Routledge.

De Witte, J., Declercq, A., & Hermans, K. (2015). Street-level strategies of child welfare social workers in Flanders: The use of electronic client records in practice. British Journal of Social Work, 46(5), 1249–1265. doi:10.1093/bjsw/bcv076

DiMaggio, P. J., & Powell, W. W. (1991). The new institutionalism in organizational analysis (Vol. 17). Chicago, IL: University of Chicago Press.

Ebrahim, A. (2003). NGOs and organizational change: Discourse, reporting, and learning. Cambridge, U.K; New York, NY: Cambridge University Press.

Gillingham, P. (2013). The development of electronic information systems for the future: Practitioners, 'embodied structures' and 'technologies-in-practice'. British Journal of Social Work, 43(3), 430–445. doi:10.1093/bjsw/bcr202

Gillingham, P. (2014). Repositioning electronic information systems in human service organizations. Human Service Organizations: Management, Leadership & Governance, 38(2), 125–134.

Goffman, E. (2009/1963). Stigma: Notes on the Management of Spoiled Identity. New York, NY: Simon and Schuster.

Høybye-Mortensen, M. (2016). Performance information in human service organizations: Quality and usefulness. Human Service Organizations: Management, Leadership & Governance, 40(5), 486–499.

HUD. (2006, June). HMIS: A History. Retrieved from https://www.hudexchange.info/resource/1643/hmis-a-history/

HUD. (2016, July). Has HUD set any performance benchmarks or targets for the System Performance Measures?. Retrieved from https://www.hudexchange.info/faqs/2883/has-hud-set-any-performance-benchmarks-or-targets-for-the-system/

Huuskonen, S., & Vakkari, P. (2015). Selective Clients' trajectories in case files: Filtering out information in the recording process in child protection. British Journal of Social Work, 45(3), 792–808. doi:10.1093/bjsw/bct160

Hwang, H., & Powell, W. W. (2009). The rationalization of charity: The influences of professionalism in the nonprofit sector. Administrative Science Quarterly, 54(2), 268–298. doi:10.2189/asqu.2009.54.2.268

Innonet. (2016). State of Evaluation 2016: Evaluation Practice and Capacity in the Nonprofit Sector. Washington DC: Innovation Network.

Jorna, F., & Wagenaar, P. 2007. The "Iron Case' Strengthen? Discretion and Digital Discipline. Public Administration. 85 (1): 189–214.

Le Dantec, C. A., & Edwards, W. K. (2008). The view from the trenches: Organization, power, and technology at two nonprofit homeless outreach centers. In Proceedings of the 2008 ACM conference on Computer Supported Cooperative Work. (pp. 589–598). ACM.

Le Dantec, C. A., & Edwards, W. K. (2010). Across boundaries of influence and accountability: The multiple scales of public sector information systems. In Proceedings of the 2010 SIGCHI Conference on Human Factors in Computing Systems (pp. 113–122). ACM.

Lee, B. A., Tyler, K. A., & Wright, J. D. (2010). The new homelessness revisited. Annual Review of Sociology, 36, 501–521. doi:10.1146/annurev-soc-070308-115940

LeRoux, K., & Wright, N. S. (2010). Does performance measurement improve strategic decision making? Findings from a national survey of nonprofit social service agencies. Nonprofit and Voluntary Sector Quarterly, 39(4), 571–587. doi:10.1177/0899764009359942

Lynch-Cerullo, K., & Cooney, K. (2011). Moving from outputs to outcomes: A review of the evolution of performance measurement in the human service nonprofit sector. Administration in Social Work, 35(4), 364–388. doi:10.1080/03643107.2011.599305

MacIndoe, H., & Barman, E. (2012). How organizational stakeholders shape performance measurement in nonprofits: Exploring a multidimensional measure. Nonprofit and Voluntary Sector Quarterly, 42(4), 716–738. doi:10.1177/0899764012444351

Meyer, J. W., & Rowan, B. (1977). Institutionalized organizations: Formal structure as myth and ceremony. American Journal of Sociology, 83(2), 340–363. doi:10.1086/226550

Meyer, J. W., Scott, W. R., & Deal, T. E. (1983). Institutional and technical sources of organizational structure: Explaining the structure of educational organizations. In: J. W. Meyer, & W. R. Scott (Eds.), Organizational environments: Ritual and rationality. Beverly Hills, CA: Sage.

Miller, G., & Holstein, J. A. (1989). On the sociology of social problems. Perspectives on Social Problems, 1, 1–16.

Parton, N. (2008). Changes in the form of knowledge in social work: From the 'social' to the 'informational'? British Journal of Social Work, 38(2), 253–269. doi:10.1093/bjsw/bcl337

Powell, W. W., & DiMaggio, P. J. (eds.). 1991. The New Institutionalism in Organizational Analysis. 232–263.Chicago: University of Chicago Press.

Pfeffer, J., & Salancik, G. R. (1978). The external control of organizations: A resource dependence perspective. New York: Harper & Row.

Ragin, C. C., & Amoroso, L. M. (2011). Constructing Social Science (2nd ed.). Thousand Oaks: Sage Publications.

Salamon, L. M. (2002). The New Governance and the Tools of Public Action: An Introduction. Chapter 1. In Salamon, L. (Ed) The Tools of Government: A Guide to the New Governance. Oxford: Oxford University Press.

Sandfort, J., & Stone, M. (2008). Analyzing policy fields: Helping students understand complex state and local contexts. Journal of Public Affairs Education, 14(2), 129–148.

Schneider, A., & Ingram, H. (1990). The Behavioral Assumptions of Policy Tools. Journal of Politics, 52(2), 510–529.

Schoech, D. (2010). Interoperability and the future of human services. Journal of Technology in Human Services, 28 (1–2), 7–22. doi:10.1080/15228831003759539

Scott, W. R., & Davis, G. (2007). Organizations and Organizing: Natural, Rational and Open Systems. Pearsons Prentice Hall.

Smith, S. R., & Lipsky, M. (1993). Nonprofits for hire: The welfare state in the age of contracting. Cambridge, Mass: Harvard University Press.

Snibbe, A. C. (2006). Drowning in data. Stanford Social Innovation Review, 6(1), 39–45.

Sparks, T. (2010). Broke not broken: Rights, privacy, and homelessness in Seattle. Urban Geography, 31(6), 842–862. doi:10.2747/0272-3638.31.6.842

Sparks, T. (2012). Governing the homeless in an age of compassion: Homelessness, Citizenship, and the 10-Year plan to end homelessness in King County Washington. Antipode, 44(4), 1510–1531. doi:10.1111/anti.2012.44.issue-4

Star, S. L., & Ruhleder, K. (1996). Steps toward an ecology of infrastructure: Design and access for large information spaces. Information Systems Research, 7(1), 111–134. doi:10.1287/isre.7.1.111

Stoecker, R. (2007). Research practices and needs of non-profit organizations in an Urban Center. Journal Social & Social Welfare, 34, 97.

Thompson, J. D. (1962). Organizations and Output Transactions. American Journal of Sociology, 68(3): 309–324.

Voida, A., Harmon, E., & Al-Ani, B. (2011). Homebrew databases: Complexities of everyday information management in nonprofit organizations. In Proceedings of the ACM SIGCHI Conference on Human Factors in Computing Systems. New York: ACM Press, pp. 915–924.

White, S., Hall, C., & Peckover, S. (2009). The descriptive tyranny of the common assessment framework: Technologies of categorization and professional practice in child welfare. British Journal of Social Work, 39(7), 1197–1217. doi:10.1093/bjsw/bcn053

Zimmermann, J. A. M., & Stevens, B. W. (2006). The use of performance measurement in South Carolina nonprofits. Nonprofit Management and Leadership, 16(3), 315–327. doi:10.1002/nml.109

What counts? Quantification, worker judgment, and divergence in child welfare decision making

Emily Adlin Bosk

ABSTRACT

In an effort to manage risk under chronic resource constraints, information uncertainty, and accountability pressures, U.S. child welfare organizations have embraced the structured decision-making (SDM) model, which combines actuarial-based risk assessment with clinical decision making. Although 33 states have adopted the SDM to impose greater rationality and precision to child welfare decision making, little is yet known about how actuarial-based risk assessment interacts with child welfare workers' own judgment in implementation, and to what effect. Drawing on original data from a case study of four child welfare agencies in one state, this article examines the nature of this interplay, and its implications for the quality of worker decision-making, child welfare, and worker job satisfaction.

Introduction

Errors in judgment in child welfare can have lasting consequences for the children the system intends to protect and the families it is charged to serve. At their most severe, flawed assessments allow children to remain in unsafe situations that can result in severe injury or death (false negatives [FN]) or lead to unwarranted separations between children and their caregivers with all the attendant trauma that accompanies them (false positives [FPs]). Over the past 20 years, child welfare agencies have embraced quantified decision-making strategies under intense pressure to enhance performance, reduce error, and avoid the accompanying tragic outcomes that have often been associated with the low reliability of worker clinical judgment (Camasso & Jagannathan, 2013; Gainsborough, 2010).

To date, more than 33 states and multiple countries have now implemented the structured decision-making model (SDM), a series of standardized tools to improve child welfare decision making. The SDM addresses the low reliability of clinical decision making through the integration of standardized and actuarial-based risk assessments with clinical judgment (Children's Research Center (CRC), 2012). By systematizing the process, the SDM creates a template from which it can be expected that any worker assessing a specific case will arrive at a similar conclusion.

Actuarial-based risk assessments (RA) are considered the gold standard for conducting child welfare assessments because they use a validated algorithm to determine the likelihood that a child who has been found to be maltreated will reexperience abuse or neglect in the future (Baird & Wagner, 2000; Baird, Wagner, Healy, & Johnson, 1999; Schwalbe, 2008). This probabilistic determination of risk is based on analysis of case characteristics that are highly associated with the reoccurrence of maltreatment. Because one of the most fundamental goals of risk assessment in child protective services is to minimize the potential for decision-making errors that lead to fatality or severe harm to a child, developers of the SDM's RAs have been transparent that the balance of the tool is tilted toward FPs (Baird & Wagner, 2000). That is, when it errs, the RA may be more likely to find that a child is at a high risk of future maltreatment, when she is not (FP), than to err by finding a FN.[1] According to its developers, however, the RA's bias toward FPs should be "moot" because it is designed to classify cases according to levels of risk, and is not meant to be used as a sole means for predicting outcomes (Baird & Wagner, 2000, p. 850). That is, integrating "clinical"—or workers'—judgment into the use of the RA mitigates the chances of FPs and thus optimizes decision making as a whole (Baird & Wagner, 2000).

Prominent child welfare scholars also describe the need for comprehensive systems of decision making that balance a rational, systematic approach with the application of worker judgment to reduce errors (Pecora, Chahine, & Graham, 2013; Shlonsky & Gambrill, 2001). Despite this widespread recognition, however, there are no formal guidelines for agencies or their workers on how specifically to go about integrating the RA tool with workers' own sense of a given case as derived from their combination of training and experience (Schwalbe, 2008). At the same time, social and economic demands for increased productivity and accountability, the desire to create transparent bases for decision making, and the fiscal constraints that necessitate more streamlined operating procedures in child welfare agencies, all exert organizational pressure for increased dependence on quantified forms of decision making that are efficient and clearly defensible (Espeland & Vannebo, 2007; Porter, 1995; Power, 1997).

In this article, I examine three key questions. First, what are the sources and nature of conflicts arising between risk that is automatically scored by these newer, highly rationalized decision-making tools (like RA) and risk as identified by workers' own judgment? Second, how do workers handle those conflicts, by potentially adjusting (downgrade or upgrade) risk assessments and in making final decisions about the trajectories cases will take? And finally, how do workers feel about their jobs in the face of navigating such conflicts? In other words, how do workers integrate their judgment into the use of standardized risk assessment tools in practice, and to what effects?

In line with new research on the decision-making ecology in child welfare (Fluke, Yuan, Hedderson, and Curtis, 2014), I draw on data from a case study of child welfare decision making involving 35 workers affiliated with four urban and suburban, midwestern child welfare agencies. Using this case as a foundation, I examine two particular scenarios of decision making that arise when RA scores and worker judgments conflict: first, when RAs indicate high risk but workers assess low risk (worker-perceived "FPs"), and, second, when RAs indicate low risk but workers assess high (er) risk (worker-perceived "FNs"). The midwestern state in which the case study was completed offers a particularly helpful context for this investigation. As will be elaborated on below, the SDM approach and RA tool are legally mandated, thus enforcing the integration of a highly rationalized, quantified risk assessment strategy with workers' instinct and experience, with limited accompanying guidance on that integration.

Emergence of standardized decision making in child welfare

Research on child welfare decision making prior to the introduction of actuarial-based assessments highlights the critical and consistent deficits of clinical decision-making, demonstrating that case outcomes were more dependent on which worker (and agency) a family was assigned to than other relevant case factors. Lindsey's (1992) research on the reliability of clinical decision making found that, when given an identical set of facts, child welfare workers agree on a case trajectory only 25% of the time. In separate studies, Rossi, Schuerman, and Budde (1996) and Davidson-Arad and Benbenishty (2010) also found large levels of disagreement among child welfare workers evaluating the same case. More broadly, ample research in psychology details the kinds of errors to which clinical decision making is prone, such as the use of heuristic biases and other cognitive shortcuts that widely lead to incorrect assessment (Gilovich, Griffin, & Kahneman, 2002; Kahneman & Frederick, 2002; Tversky & Kahneman, 1974). These heuristics include confirmation bias where

---

1. Conversely, a false negative (FN) finds a child is at a low risk of future maltreatment when she is not.

ambiguous evidence is interpreted as supporting their initial belief, the representativeness heuristic where risk is under- or overestimated based on a misunderstanding of how common an actual occurrence is, and the conjunction fallacy where events that are not necessarily related are assumed to be linked (Tversky & Kahneman, 1974). Incomplete or missing information, as is common in child welfare cases, can lead a worker to draw a faulty conclusion (Gambrill & Shlonsky, 2001; Van de Luitgaarden, 2009). Agency characteristics such as the task environment and workers' personal orientation to casework also influence decision making, leading researchers to conclude that it is really a subjective rather than objective process (Chu & Tsui, 2008; Loughlin, 2008; Regehr, Bogo, Shlonsky, & LeBlanc, 2010). In the absence of standardized criteria, Stein and Rzepnicki (1983) observed, "it appears that vague laws and knowledge deficits create a void for decision-makers, which they tend to fill by interjecting personal values and biases" (as cited in Wilson and Morton, 1997 p. 3). Rossi et al. (1996) were early in those calling for new modes of decision making in child welfare, stating, "It seems reasonable to assert what happens in cases should not be a crap shoot".

Taken together, these studies offer a decisive picture of the weaknesses of clinical decision making and how, without additional aid, clinical decision making is likely to result in error. In response to these issues, actuarial-based assessments have come to prominence (Gambrill & Shlonsky, 2000, 2001; Schwalbe, 2004). Quantifying child welfare decision making through actuarial-based RAs offers the potential to enhance the consistency and evidence base of child welfare decisions. More specifically, actuarial-based RA explicitly seek to improve low reliability and reduce subjective or biased judgments that contribute to inconsistent case outcomes and clinical mistakes by providing schemas for decision making grounded in an analysis of case characteristics that are highly associated with the risk of reabuse. Easy to review and track, actuarial-based RAs also provide a clear system for holding individual workers and organizations accountable for the decisions they make. The broad consensus is that actuarial-based decision-making outperforms clinical judgment across fields (Baird & Wagner, 2000; Baird et al., 1999; CRC, 2008; Dawes, 1988; Dawes, Faust, & Meehl, 1989). A meta-analysis of more than 100 studies found that "mechanical prediction techniques were about 10% more accurate than clinical predictions" (Grove et. al 2009, p. 19). As a result, actuarial-based risk assessments are considered to be the "gold standard" for case decisions and are now used in the majority of child welfare cases (Schwalbe, 2008, p. 205).

Child welfare decision making under uncertainty

Child welfare decision making comprises multiple smaller decisions, each made in an overall context of uncertainty (Gambrill & Shlonsky, 2001). Figure 1 describes the distinct decision-making points in each case and their possible consequences.

The focus of this case is decision making related to the integration of worker judgment and the actuarial-based RA for cases that have been substantiated (the allegation of child maltreatment is found to be true). The purpose of the RA is to accurately classify cases, specifically those that are at a high risk for future maltreatment, so appropriate intervention can take place with families and fatal or severe injury to children avoided. Some of the mechanisms utilized to protect children in cases deemed high risk are removal from the home, court ordered in-home supervision where any noncompliance by the caregiver is grounds for subsequent removal, intensive treatment of the caregiver, placement of the caregiver on a Central Registry for Abuse and Neglect (explained in more detail below) and frequent visits from Child Protective Service (CPS).

The RA comprises a list of items related to neglect (in one column) and abuse (in a separate column) that are that are empirically associated with the risk of reabuse. Points are assigned to each item a worker determines to be accurate and then summed. The highest number of points in either the neglect or abuse column is then used to determine the final risk score. The neglect and abuse inventories include a mix of objective and subjective indicators. Objective factors include demographic items about the caregiver such as number of children in the home and information about the caregiver's previous involvement in the child welfare system. These items are understood by workers

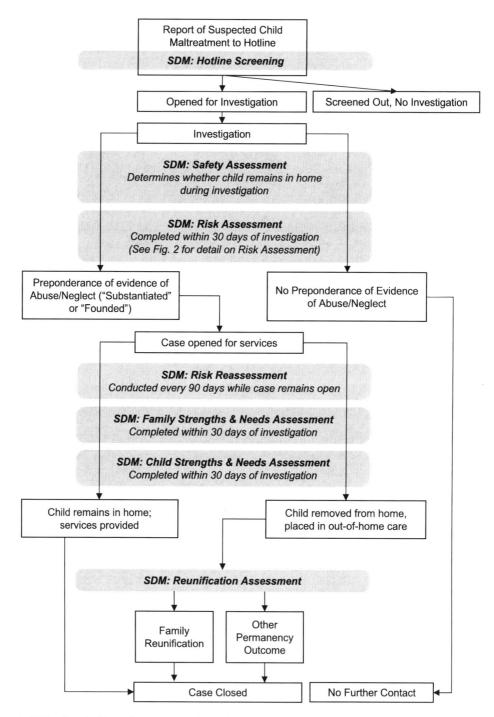

Figure 1. Child welfare decision-making points in relationship to the SDM .

to be fixed, requiring little of their own judgment in their assessment. More subjective factors included in the RA are related to current case information such as whether the caregiver is cooperating with CPS. Workers' understand these items to require some judgment. Although the RA is not used to determine whether a case is substantiated, it is intended to be filled out during the investigative process. When a case is denied (the allegation found to be untrue), the RA does not inform its trajectory because the case is automatically closed. Functionally, this means that a case could score as High or Intensive risk without these categorizations being pursued.

Designing risk assessments involves a balance between considerations of sensitivity and specificity which, in turn, necessitates embedding tradeoffs in decision-making rules. In the context of the RA, "sensitivity refers to the degree to which true cases of maltreatment are correctly identified and specificity refers to the degree to which non-abusing families are correctly identified" (Shlonsky & Wagner, 2005, p. 416). Choices about whether to favor sensitivity or specificity necessarily reflect choices about what types of error (FPs or FNs) to avoid, and which types of error should be afforded a greater degree of tolerance. The fact that these decisions are grounded in empirical data about risk factors for child maltreatment does not remove the values embedded in choices about cutoff points.

Validation studies of the RA demonstrate that its design privileges avoiding FNs (Baird & Wagner, 2000). Using a hypothetical example, Baird and Wagner (2000) note that a high rate of FPs on the RA, even of "56%," would not be problematic as long as the tool improves the identification of cases that need more intensive services (p. 850). Baird and Wagner state:

> Despite the high proportion of FPs, cases that were rated high risk experienced maltreatment at a 44% rate, while only 5.3% of those rated at lower risk levels had subsequent maltreatment reported. The ratio of "failures" in the high risk group to "failures" in the low risk group is more than 8: 1. Such results help agencies identify which families are more likely to abuse or neglect their children. In addition, 11 of the 15 cases (73.3%) where subsequent maltreatment occurred were correctly identified (a relatively high rate of specificity). (p. 850)

The benefits of weighting RAs to prevent fatalities or serious harm are clear. However, an unintended consequence of this tradeoff is that when FP errors occur, the costs to families are largely unexamined and unacknowledged. Scheff (1963) highlights that these unintended consequences are an unavoidable result of basing decision-making rules on averting one kind of suffering. When doing so, other kinds of suffering will always be obscured. Camssasso and Jagannathan (2013) assert that risk assessments in child welfare policy in general, and in child welfare decision making in particular, are formulated around the principle of avoiding FPs. They note that lawsuits filed against child welfare agencies and a "zero tolerance" policy for errors where children are severely harmed have caused more cases to be screened into the system, and higher rates of FPs at every decision point in a case.

As noted above, worker judgment is a mechanism intentionally built into the SDM to avoid error in general and FPs in particular. When the RA score is integrated with worker judgment, four separate scenarios are possible as indicated in Table 1.

An RA score and a worker's sense of risks in a case can diverge in two key ways: where the RA identifies high risk, but a worker interprets low risk (a worker-perceived potential FP); and conversely, where the RA scores as low risk, but a worker believes there to be high (or higher)

Table 1. Potential Convergence and Divergence of Risk Assessment (RA) Score and Worker Judgment.

		Worker Judgment	
		Low	High
RA score	Low	Convergence: no need to negotiate between RA score and worker judgment	Divergence: need to negotiate between RA score and worker judgment (worker-perceived potential false negative)
	High or Intensive	Divergence: need to negotiate between RA score and worker judgment (worker-perceived potential false positive)	Convergence: no need to negotiate between RA score and worker judgment

risk (a worker-perceived potential FN). Resolving any worker-perceived potential FP (or FN) is dependent on how this divergence is negotiated.

Although there is broad agreement that actuarial-based RA improves decision making, few studies have examined how RAs are used in practice in a U.S. context (Schwalbe, 2008). As a result, we have little knowledge about what workers and agencies do—by harnessing their clinical expertise—to make sense of divergence in RA scores in light of their potential for high rates of FPs. Prominent child welfare scholars all make clear that the success of risk assessment instruments is predicated on the integration of professional judgment alongside them (Gambrill & Shlonsky, 2000; Munro, 2004; Pecora et al., 2013; Shlonsky & Wagner, 2005). However, work from Australia suggests that the SDM is being used in ways that blunt critical thinking in case assessments or that worker judgment is not used at all (Gillingham, 2006; Gillingham & Humphreys, 2010). In an experimental study, Regeher and colleagues (2010) found that use of an actuarial-based RA did not standardize worker assessments of the same case, and that decisions were still variable. Additionally, Munro (2004) documented that workers are not adequately trained in probability theory, leading them to overestimate the accuracy of actuarial-based RAs and an insufficient understanding of their FP rates. This study offers unique insight into the conditions under which divergence between the RA and worker judgment happens, identifying recurring patterns of chronic stress between RA and worker assessments.

Method

This article uses the case study method to examine child welfare decision making utilizing the SDM in one state. Case studies are useful for sorting out the complex relationship between a policy's theoretical grounding, intentions, and implementation (Flyvbjerg, 2006; Greenwood & Lowenthal, 2005). Employing a critical case approach allows for an examination of the layered manner in which divergence between worker judgment and the RA are managed in the specific policy environment in which both operate.

Case selection: The SDM in midwest state

I chose to investigate Midwest State (a pseudonym) because of the state policies that connect child welfare decision-making to quantified processes (Flyvbjerg, 2006: 230). Midwest State's legislature mandates the use of the SDM for all child welfare casework and relies on the RA score to determine a case's trajectory once it has been substantiated. Figure 2 below details the relationships between risk score, case category, and the use of overrides:

In practice, this Midwestern State policy ties the risk score to a number of case decisions such as whether a parent or caregiver is placed on the Central Registry for Abuse and Neglect (CRAN, a centralized list of offenders of child maltreatment searchable by public and private employers and others), the intensity of services a family will receive, whether those services will be voluntary or mandated, and the frequency of contacts with the CPS. For some caregivers, RAs that are rated high do not result in the removal of their children but do result in their placement on the CRAN. Placement on the CRAN is automatic for all cases that score as intensive or high and can result in termination from employment as well as prohibit participating in activities with their children (such as attending school functions), so there are serious consequences that can last long after a maltreatment case has been concluded. Tying the risk score to case trajectory runs contrary to the intentions of SDM's developers who stress that the SDM is not designed to replace clinical judgment but rather "help to structure decisions by bringing objective information to bear on these critical questions" (CRC, 2008, p.16).

In Midwest State, there is no policy mechanism to lower risk scores and the subsequent trajectory that the score determines. The inability to lower a risk score functionally means that there is no mechanism to remove a caregiver from the CRAN. Over-rides to raise the risk score can be made, in contrast, and are either discretionary or mandatory. Discretionary over-rides permit a worker to

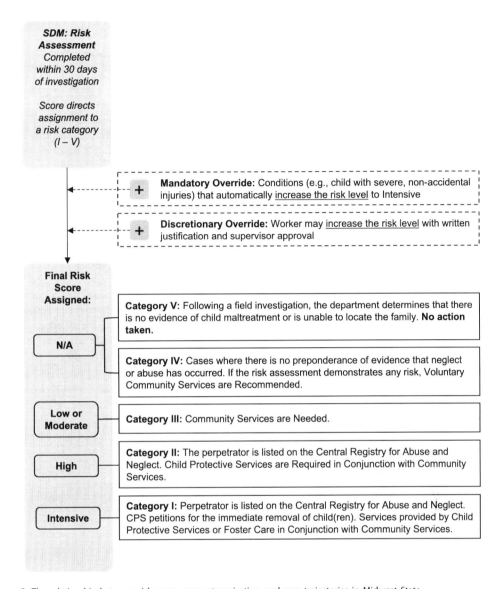

Figure 2. The relationship between risk score, case categorization, and case trajectories in Midwest State.

increase the risk level with written justification and supervisor approval. Mandatory over-rides are a series of policy conditions that require the risk level to be raised to intensive (which would automatically mean the child is removed from the home during the investigation period), such as a child with severe nonaccidental injuries. When it comes to cases that require a child to be quickly removed from their caregiver due to safety concerns, failures of the RA are assumed to occasionally occur.

In sum, Midwest State stands out from the other states for its explicit connection of the RA score to how a case is managed and is therefore helpful for understanding the process and the unintended consequences of child welfare decision making that combines highly structured risk assessment tools with workers' judgment—and to what effects on the process for determining case actions.

Data and data analysis

Data come from interviews, documents, and brief observation related to the decision-making procedures. Interviews were conducted with 35 CPS workers working at four agencies across the state who were responsible for the initial case investigation and following families until a case was closed. The agencies were selected to represent a mix of urban and suburban counties. Workers were recruited via e-mail, a presentation at an all agency staff meeting, fliers, and at (CEU, Continuing Education Unit) trainings geared toward child welfare workers, and interviews were conducted in a confidential location of the worker's choosing. On average, interviews were 90 minutes in length and ranged from 45 minutes to 3 hours, all were single sessions. Interviews were recorded and professionally transcribed. Review of documents included texts related to the case site such as the CPS manual for the state, the legal statute for use of the SDM in Midwest State, and all publicly available materials about the SDM released by its developers. Brief observations took place when workers allowed me to sit with them at their desk and witness their administrative work.

The semistructured interview protocol for this study was designed to ground data about participants' beliefs through their behaviors (Charmaz, 2006). Following an initial discussion, I asked participants "to walk me through" their most recent case, a challenging case, and a case where they felt good about their decision. By collecting data on decision making across a continuum of affective states and challenges, I was able to get a rich sense of how a worker made case decisions (Weiss, 1995). After collecting these accounts, I turned the focus of the interview to the SDM tools. Once again, I collected information on attitudes through questions about behaviors. I asked workers how they used these tools in their everyday practice and asked each worker to "walk me through" the RA for any or all of the cases they described. These questions allowed me to collect data on the weight these assessments were given in the final disposition of the case and how they influenced decision making. Throughout the interview, I followed up every question with probes specific to the conversation. All names of offices, agencies, and people are pseudonyms.

I began analyzing data during the observation and interview phase of my fieldwork (Charmaz, 2006). Using NVivo 10, I coded interviews and documents based on the emergence of patterned regularities within them as well as my knowledge of the literature (Emerson, Fretz, & Shaw, 1995). That is, my reading of the data was informed by current debates about the strengths and weaknesses of actuarial-based and clinical decision making, the goals of the SDM as stated by its developers, and sociological work on quantification. Therefore, I was sensitized to the tensions inherent in integrating actuarial and clinical judgment and alert to these themes during coding but also allowed for the emergence of other, unrelated themes. Once I identified core themes, I then coded interviews at the aggregate level.

Throughout, memoing was used as a strategy for recording observations and insights gained through all types of data collection. To ensure confirmability and independence of the findings, two research assistants analyzed the data deductively using a codebook based on the themes and categories I initially identified. Any discrepancies between coders were noted and resolved in a consensus coding process. The data presented below represents larger themes found in the data, except where noted. Quotes from the data are edited for clarity (e.g., repeated "Ums" removed), but no words have been changed or reordered. Institutional Review Board approval was granted for this study.

Findings

Results examine patterns of chronic divergence and points of stress in worker and RA understanding of cases. Two key scenarios of conflicted decision making that workers faced in the agencies studied are considered: divergence in risk assessment in which the RA scored high but a worker rated the risk lower and divergence in which the RA scored low but a worker observed greater risk. Findings consider how these divergences occur. Broadly, workers report that divergence originates from two sources: (1) items on the RA that they believe are not sufficiently nuanced in relationship to presenting case information and (2) state policy that prohibits workers from downgrading a risk score. The final section describes the impact on morale when case workers believe decisions are being made in error with limited options for correcting them.

When risk diverges: How it happens

Demographic factors

The RA in Midwest State contains a series of questions on a set of demographic factors, such as number of children in the home and children's age, used to assess risk for child maltreatment based on established research. Focus on demographic factors means that it is possible for an RA to score high through the presence of these indicators rather than the behaviors of the caregiver in question. Angela describes how this can occur:

A: Well sometimes with the outcome of the RA I don't agree with; like 'cause you know when it comes to high and it's open, it's gonna be a Category 2. And sometimes I feel like it shouldn't be 'cause sometimes it's just for having four or more kids in the home...

E: So like that might be something that throws it over the edge?

A: That throws it over the edge and it shouldn't; like or either there'll be like there were four or more kids in the home and they had... and the children had mental health issues. Then that throws it over the edge to make them be a Category 2 and put them on the unfit list; even when it's like a first-time offense.

As it is currently constructed, the Midwest State RA weighs having more than 2 children, children under the age of 7 and a previous child maltreatment complaint (not necessarily a substantiation) as factors that will raise the risk level for a family. This risk factor is based on clear evidence demonstrating that more children and younger children in the household are at higher risk for maltreatment (MacKenzie, Kotch, & Lee, 2011). However, many workers reported feeling that families who, in their estimation, were low risk for child maltreatment have often been penalized on the basis of demographic rather than relational or behavioral factors related to the complaint.

Alternately, demographic items that seem without any controversy as to their relationship to child maltreatment, such as N2. Number of prior assigned neglect complaints and/or findings and A2. Number of prior assigned abuse complaints and/or findings, can be more problematic in practice. The more past complaints (whether denied or substantiated) a caregiver has, the riskier the current situation is likely to be and the greater the probability of future maltreatment (Hussey, Chang, & Kotch, 2006). However, workers object to measuring the number of complaints rather than only the number of "substantiated" complaints. Investigators report that reasons for multiple complaints vary and are not necessarily indicative of the parent or caregiver's past actions. Frequently, workers described how parents engaging in custody battles can use the CPS system as a way to bolster their case for receiving custody. Filing an anonymous complaint with CPS is also a way of settling scores between neighbors, and of exacting revenge when relationships between parents change (breakups, divorce) and when new people (girlfriends, boyfriends,) enter the picture. Because unsubstantiated complaints are treated the same as substantiated ones, they can and do inflate the risk score. As Ashley describes:

You'll have some families that the neighbors will continually call on them or there'll be like one RP [Reporting Person] that continually calls on them and makes up a new allegation every time and we have to go out and investigate and deny the case repeatedly. But let's say they have four kids and one's young. So then they got a bunch of previous CPS history, the young kid and the four kids in the home, they're already at a very high-risk level. So even if it's a small issue because of all those risk points, there's a very good chance they'll be put on Central Registry and Cat 2.

In general, workers believed that the RA treats the suspicion of maltreatment by others and the presence of confirmed incidents of maltreatment as the same event or at least as events that predict the same amount of risk, when they should be kept separate in practice.

The presence of the past: How caregivers' personal history impacts current assessments

Playing out within the RA form are larger discussions about the role that a parent's experience of maltreatment has to the current complaint. Question A5 asks workers to record whether either caretaker was abused or neglected as a child. If the question is endorsed, 2 points are added to the RA. Workers assert that, in combination with other demographic questions, adding past history into the mix can be enough to move caregivers into a high-risk category and onto the CRAN without regard to other factors that should influence the case such as the severity of the substantiated maltreatment and how those under investigation understand and are addressing the problem. Jennifer asserts:

> I mean there's cases all the time that score out as high, you have parents participating throughout the whole thing…. You know one of the biggest questions we have to ask in policy is; does the family … have you ever been abused or neglected as a child? They self report that. Well again, if you clicked yes, parent self reports they were sexually abused as a minor, you know again that just raised their risk level, but that doesn't mean that they're at [risk] … it could've been over something of a dirty house you know.

Although a parent's history of child maltreatment is a risk factor, Jennifer notes that it might not affect the current complaint in a meaningful way. Workers note that as the item is written there is no way to gain a more sophisticated understanding of how a parental history of maltreatment as a child affects the current situation. The inventory thus interprets a history of maltreatment uniformly to be negative and static, collapsing events that workers' understand to be dynamic and multilayered into a singular meaning. Lauren recounts how an RA scored as high even when her investigation revealed no risk to the children:

> There was a family who had previous CPS history a lot of it, which bumps it up on the risk scale. You know here was previous domestic violence, previous substance abuse, and the father I think was abused or neglected as a child. So the risk level kind of scored through the roof, but the allegations we got were that the children they didn't have food or clothing. And I went to the house and everything was perfect. All the kids, they didn't disclose anything concerning and there was plenty of food; they had tons of clothes. So it was kind of bogus allegations I think, so obviously I wasn't going to substantiate the family, but the risk level did score through the roof because of everything that had happened in the past … (short laugh) … so and you can't bump it down a risk level, you can only bump it up so in those cases you just got to leave it as a high risk and deny it.

Although a negative outcome for the family is prevented because the case was denied, the family would have had a very different outcome if Lauren had found maltreatment that needed to be addressed but was not severe. This leaves little room for workers to intervene in a maltreatment complaint that might need to be substantiated, but where the severity of maltreatment does not, in their opinion, match the imposed consequences for being high risk (according to state policy).

When analyzed collectively, one of the main critiques that CPS workers in Midwest State have about the RA is the way that it can penalize caregivers for being "a victim of circumstance." Workers view demographic items that document facts or events differently than those that encode agency or behaviors, interpreting them to be more "unfair" because they may not be related to the maltreatment allegation. As a result, CPS workers assert that the resulting case actions can unfold in ways they feel are unjustified. Ironically, the demographic factors on the risk assessment are considered by researchers to be the fairest way to assess risk because they are objective indicators that do not require subjective assessment that opens the door to all the issues inherent in clinical decision making that the RA is designed to avoid.

Subjectivity within mechanical objectivity

In addition to the demographic questions, the RA also includes questions that necessitate some degree of interpretation given their inherent subjectivity. N11. Primary caretaker able to put child needs ahead of own is one such question, answering which requires a different level of skill than a demographic question such as A2. Number of prior assigned abuse complaints and/or findings. Questions that are open to interpretation have the potential to lead to exactly what the RA is designed to avoid: disparate assessments of the same case by different workers. Rob believes that individual workers understand the same evidence differently, producing wide variation in case categorization:

> You know I tell people this all the time. If you had one CPS case and it has a borderline complaint, you know could be, couldn't be. And you gave it to 50 different workers, all throughout the state with different supervisors, you'll probably get 20 Cat 4s, 20 Cat 3s, a couple Cat 2s and then maybe one or two guys will give it a Cat 5.

Justine details how different scoring of the same question can occur:

> I mean its how you interpret that question you know…. You know like "primary caretaker puts child's needs ahead of her own." That night she didn't but say two days later she's saying all the right things and she's showing, she's willing to put her kids above others … a worker might say "okay, she's willing to do what she did but that one instance she didn't so"; it's kind of like depending on how the worker interprets it all.

As Justine's observations highlight, all RA questions are cross-sectional data points, recording information about a caregiver at one moment in time. Workers who attempt to carefully complete the RA can struggle with how to endorse items where the caregiver has behaved differently throughout the investigation. Lila describes the dilemma:

> L: I put no [to whether the caregiver has a substance abuse problem].
> E: Okay, you seem embarrassed?
> L: Right, well I don't know because I'm like thinking to my supervisor should it be like, you know she tested positive? Like I know, but I tested her again and she tested negative so I don't think she has a problem because if she did she would've tested [positive].

Lila wants to be as accurate as possible in her assessment, but there is no way to record the varied nature of the caregiver's engagement with substances during the course of the investigation. Whether the caregiver has a substance abuse problem is open to some amount of interpretation, with some workers using the evidence of a single positive drug screen to confirm and others using the evidence of a single negative drug screen to deny a finding of substance abuse. Divergence occurs between workers and the RA and across workers depending on how they manage issues of interpretation in their assessment.

To manage issues of subjectivity as they relate to scoring the risk assessment, Midwest State has created a policy manual that outlines exactly how questions should be interpreted and what criteria should be used in answering each question. Policy manuals are accessible by clicking on a question when a worker is filling out the risk assessment and through the smart phones that workers carry with them during the workday. Even with these measures and a significant amount of training on how to complete the RA, some workers report that they do not ever consult the policy manual, leaving a wide range of responses to the RA open and multiple possibilities for divergence. Workers who do consult the policy manual also recognize that there are individual differences in how workers respond to questions that affect whether the risk assessment is truly standardized. In practice, the presence of a policy manual that answers these questions is not functionally enough to standardize worker interpretation of questions (Bosk, 2015).

Keeping it simple is not less complicated

Kelly finds that the lack of context that Casey refers to on the RA makes it difficult to complete it accurately:

> It's either—it is this or it isn't this. There's no grey area you know, so it's like, and that's what makes it hard going through this. You know it's like; am I gonna want to put another thing on the RA or is it not to that point where I really need to put it on the RA? Its just not so straightforward, you know.

Like all standardized assessments, the RA in Midwest State is designed to mediate the gray areas of cases by creating a more objective reading of the facts of the case. William describes how flattening the complexity of cases can actually invite more complication and produce divergence between worker and RA assessments:

> We have kids that beat up their parents. I know we're here to protect the kids, but we, when I in foster care we had kids that were [in] 7 and 8 old in residential placements. They come back to the community they're out of control. Their parents are sitting on them holding their hands down because they've busted everything up and they're hurting everyone in the house, and they don't know what else to do, and the child may have a bruise on his wrist from being held down. That's a bruise, that's substantiation. We need the discretion to say; how did that bruise get there? Was mom protecting the child? Was mom protecting another child from a child? Those things go on.

William is asserting that cases presenting as straightforward (e.g., corporal punishment by a parent that results in a mark, which is not only grounds for a mandatory substantiation but also against the law) are often anything but clear in practice. An unintended consequence of abstracting concepts into numerical forms can be an outcome that violates the principle of the rule, prompting divergence between worker and RA assessment.

Lack of a transactional perspective on risk

Although research clearly identifies the individual risk factors associated with a higher likelihood of future maltreatment, what is less clear is how these individual factors come together to affect risk. The risk assessment captures the cumulative burden of risk (e.g., more risk factors, equal a higher likelihood for future maltreatment) but is less able to account for the transactional and interactive effects of the items on the risk assessment. Pecora et al. (2013) note that: "safety and risk assessment tools generally contain discrete factors, yet, it is the interactions of these factors ... that are likely to figure in the causal processes leading to the lethal assaults of young children" (p. 145).

Workers believe that collecting information only on the presence or absence of risk factors without a more dynamic understanding of their relationship to the presenting complaint can overestimate risk. In its current form, the RA itself does not distinguish between risk factors and protective factors (e.g., a parent that is addressing substance abuse issues vs. one that is not; or a caregiver that was abused as a child and has received treatment for this experience vs. one who has not). Because clinical judgment is meant to account for the ways that the RA by nature is probabilistic not deterministic, these issues are not taken into account in its design. In an implementation of the SDM that uses the RA to drive case decision making, the absence of more finely grained assessments of risk have profound implications and make divergence between worker and RA assessment more likely.

Policy limitations as a driver of divergence

As Shlonsky and Wagner (2005) observe, child welfare decision making is highly dependent on context. The construction of the RA and the items described above have far more limited impact on decision making when the RA risk score is not determinative for decisions about removal, in-home supervision, and placement on the CRAN, and when workers are permitted to lower those scores based on their clinical judgment. Midwest State's decisions to tie the risk score to case trajectories and to not allow worker over-rides to lower the risk score establish a particularly strict context for SDM's implementation (and one that that runs counter to the intent of SDM's designers). That is, in other states where workers can infuse their clinical judgment into case decisions by either adjusting automatically generated RA scores or simply taking the RA score into account: the two sources of information about risk—RA and worker expertise—are able to be far more integrated in the process of tool implementation. This is not so in Midwest State child welfare decision making.

Casey explains her perception of how punitive consequences can escalate a case when context is excluded from the assessment in Midwest State:

> It was a neglect case and that's one of the ones I ended up having to do in-home ward with the courts. Mom is, I believe, between 24 and 26 and she has mental health issues of her own, and she comes from a very difficult relationship with her parents; a difficult relationship with her family. I think her mother is also undiagnosed bi-polar so I can only imagine how bad they, you know don't get along. And she has 3 children, an 8-year-old, a 5-year-old and a 1-year-old, I think she's like 13 months. And she was living with the father of the two youngest and for some reason she decided to let the oldest boy live with her parents and so she was only living with the two youngest and the father.

> And it was a domestic violence relationship and the house was in disarray partially because the landlord hadn't cared for, like the water main broke. So between that and a little bit of them knocking around and throwing things and her being, her mental health issues, … when the police came out for a domestic violence incident they filed because the house was dirty.

> I came out and she ended up getting evicted from the house within a couple of weeks because they weren't paying rent, I guess because the landlord wasn't fixing the issues. And when, you know, I looked at the case because of mom's mental health issues, because she has three children and one of, her youngest baby was special needs. She was a domestic violence victim, she had CPS history as a victim; all of these things made her have a high risk and made us have to go to the point where we had to file in-home (supervision).

> But she was completely willing to work with services. She was so happy to have someone to help her get out of the domestic violence situation. To help her get her own housing because she's always relied on her mom or a man and this was her first opportunity to support herself and we were helping her and she went to counseling and you know, she went with Families First and this was all before we filed. And just because her RA was so high; we had to file.

In this case, Casey believes that while multiple risks exist, the outcome for the case is unnecessarily punitive. The divergence occurs not between Casey and the RA's assessment of risk but in her disagreement with Midwest State's policy of how that risk should be managed. Casey observes that the mother in this case is working hard to attend to the issues present in the referral. In her estimation, these efforts are enough to mitigate the higher risk assessed by the RA. Casey sums up:

> And I totally agreed with the allegations and that somebody needed to you know address her mental health, address why she is doing this, and give her parenting classes to address the fact that she can't parent her kid and she just wants to medicate them to deal with them.

> But I didn't think that it was to the level that we had to take her job away and make it so she couldn't care for her four children, because then if she can't, you know that's just going to make the whole situation worse. And, I mean, I don't know I just felt that the way that, if she is a risk to children I feel like she should be a risk to children because of the actions and decisions she made, not because of the things that happened to her.

An unintended consequence of linking the risk score to the CRAN is that placement on the CRAN might actually make it more likely that child maltreatment will occur in the future, by leading the mother to lose her job and in turn creating the conditions for physical neglect. Gambrill and Shlonsky (2000) clearly discuss the importance of incorporating individualized risk assessment into case judgments to ensure that these kinds of nuances are taken into account in case decision making.

Although the RA is designed to protect families from the harmful consequences of subjective assessments that are incorrect, rooted in bias, or based on erroneous beliefs, the flip side of an implementation of the SDM that limits discretion from casework as described here is that when, in the worker's opinion, the assigned case trajectory diverges from the case dynamics, caseworkers have almost no recourse to redress the situation (with the exception of denying a case).

A risk score that is deemed inappropriately high by a caseworker would not be of much consequence if there were processes in place to manage the case in another way (such as not placing a parent on the CRAN) or to confirm that the caseworker was not erroneously interpreting the score as being too high.

Two sides to every story: Contested approaches to practice and restrictive policy

Another consequence of prohibiting workers to lower the risk score is that this policy limits responses to divergence between the RA and worker judgment when there are debates about how certain types of case should be handled. Cases that involve a child's exposure to domestic violence (DV) exemplify this issue. Ample empirical evidence supports the fact that the presence of DV presents a risk of future child maltreatment (Fantuzzo & Lindquist, 1989; Levendosky, Huth-Bocks, Shapiro, & Semel, 2003). At the same time, there is an ongoing debate about whether substantiating women for child maltreatment due to the presence of DV is itself a process of blaming the victim (Rivett & Kelly, 2006; Rogerson, 2012). This issue has not reached an empirical or policy consensus, making it far from settled. Kate believes that the RA treats this complex and unresolved concern in the field as overly simple leading to unnecessarily high risk scores and their attendant consequences for domestic violence victims—typically mothers:

> Like there's a lot of times like I'm surprised like when it comes out as high. I think that it's not so accurate 'cause there's two different questions regarding domestic violence; one if there's a history; one if the person's in a harmful relationship. So if there's any domestic violence they're scored negatively on two areas, whereas everything else is just one question. So I feel like it's a little skewed when it comes to that.

The way intimate partner violence is captured on the risk assessment may actually serve to create confusion about how to evaluate the role of intimate partner violence in a case. As Kate explains, official policy for the substantiation of cases is supposed to take a more nuanced view of DV cases that incorporates current debate about the issue:

> I mean there's a couple pages of very specific things and how you can't substantiate a parent. Like if there's domestic violence, a lot of people don't realize like if Mom's allowing the dad to beat her instead of the children, that's a protecting measure and you can't substantiate Mom for that. She's doing what she can within her means to protect the kids. . ... A lot of people interpret that differently because obviously you're still exposing your child to domestic violence, but that's an effort that she's making to protect them.

In practice, workers report that substantiated failure to protect cases may result in punitive consequences for these caregivers because of the weight that DV is given on the RA.

Neglecting emotional neglect and abuse

Although the case examples above highlight patterns of divergence that workers perceive to result in a potential FP not all divergence occurs in this direction. I find that policy requiring independent validation of mental injury (as represented on the RA) from external professionals works to lower risk scores and therefore is one area where divergence occurs that might lead to worker-perceived potential FNs for emotional abuse or neglect.

Although some items on the RA are heavily weighted, such as DV and past history of maltreatment, other potential sources of risk are functionally left out of the assessment process despite their official presence on the RA tool. One such item is emotional abuse and neglect. Workers are explicitly directed to assess on risk for this form of maltreatment in the RA through the following question: A1: Current complaint and/or finding includes mental injury. Midwest State's policy regarding mental injury is that only a mental health professional can identify it. Because of the inconvenience this requirement imposes, workers report that they rarely, if ever, endorse a finding of mental injury, answering the question negatively as a matter of routine. Casey and Monica detail this process;

M: Mental injury; No. I don't think I've ever marked that one.

C: And so for the other one mental injury. Mental injury, we don't assess that it's kind of going be assessed by psychiatrist, yeah and so anytime we have an allegation of mental injury we have to send them for an assessment and we wait for their [evaluation]... so I almost always hit zero on this one.

The majority of workers report endorsement of mental injury by a professional is important because cases involving emotional maltreatment are difficult to identify and outside their expertise. Casey articulates, "I don't think that we should be able to assess that … I'm not qualified to make that assessment…. I definitely think we should refer it out to other people." However, workers also report that they almost never actually seek out a psychiatrist to do this assessment. As a result, assessments of mental injury are omitted from regular consideration during the investigative process even though their inclusion on the RA asks workers to attend to its presence or absence. This means that emotional neglect and abuse are rarely substantiated or addressed by CPS workers in Midwest State.

William is one of the few workers who objects to having a mental health professional assess the presence of mental injury because he believes that the lack of ability to do so leads to exclusion of the presence of emotional maltreatment in risk assessments. William describes a case where he disagrees with his supervisor about whether mental injury is occurring:

A case where the mother, I think as part of discipline to get her kids in line, "I'm sending you back to foster care and I'm never taking care of you again, and you're never gonna see me again." That's mental injury. I also think that that's a poor use of discipline to try to get her kids in line. Right?

[The supervisor says:] "No, that's not inappropriate discipline and I can't call it mental Injury because it's gotta be substantiated by a therapist, who says this particular thing has really made this child emotionally unstable. All these kids aren't even in therapy for the most part. Why do they have mental injury? Call it something else."

I think it's mental injury, [DHHS administrators are] saying "no, you can't use it." And I'm like, when a kid hears I'm going to foster care, and has experience in foster care that maybe wasn't so good, what else could it be? Do I really need a therapist to confirm that?

Ultimately unable to convince his supervisor of the presence of mental injury, William is forced to omit that factor in assessing risk in this case.

When risk diverges: How workers feel

Lacking official recourse to address cases that are scored as higher risk than workers believe is warranted, or facing a mandatory assessment of high risk for cases that sets of a service trajectory that feels unnecessarily punitive, workers' morale suffers. Approximately two-thirds of the participants described the negative impact that relying on the RA risk assessment to the exclusion of their own clinical judgment to determine case trajectories had on their feelings about their jobs. Angela summarizes a general sentiment, "Sometimes you just feel bad. That's all … you just feel bad and you try to look … like you try to go over the risk assessment again and see maybe if you did something wrong if you clicked on the wrong button." Casey articulates how the ability to lower risk scores would resolve many of her issues with the RA:

But I feel like our overrides should be able to able to go both ways. I feel like, cause I know people, you know in my own personal life that meet a lot of these things, and maybe they'll be a high, intensive risk, but you know, just because you're a victim of domestic violence or because your children have issues or because you have, you know four children or mental injury, you know things like that; you don't always have to fall into the statistic of what's likely to happen. You know you can overcome those odds and be a good person and be a good parent. So I just wish that we had the ability to override both ways, that's all.

Policy that bases consequences for substantiated cases solely on risk score left multiple workers questioning the utility of the RA in their work. Without discretion related to case context, the majority of workers reported feeling their decision making had devolved to a computational process that they carried out but could not influence, with the exception of denying a case (Bosk, 2015). It is important to note that one third of workers felt extremely positively about the RA and the SDM, seeing it as a critical intervention against subjective decision making, which also removed the responsibility (and terror) of making a mistake (Bosk, 2015). These workers reported few, if any, instances where their assessment diverged from the RA.

Discussion

The cases described here identify patterns of divergence between the RA and worker judgment. The majority of divergence occurs under two conditions: (1) when workers perceive the RA is over-estimating risk or (2) when workers perceive the consequences of the risk score to be more more punitive than the situation warrants. In the first scenario, divergence primarily happens when workers believe that the RA score is an FP. Many workers perceive these FPs to occur due to the static nature of questions and their inability to take more nuanced contextual information into account. The phrasing of questions on the RA could be altered to address workers concerns and be more dynamic. For example, questions on the presence of substance abuse could be reframed from a binary to to be more reflective of a continuum. Possibilities for revisions could include (1) primary caretaker has had a positive substance abuse screening during the course of the investigation (with points given to reflect the number of positive screenings), (2) primary caretaker is currently in treatment to address substance abuse treatment, (2b) if primary caretaker is not currently in treatment to address substance abuse, primary caretaker is willing to participate in services. Demographic questions could also be reformu-lated to contextualize the presence or absence of documented risk factors within the current case. For example, questions about the number of children in the house could be revised as follows: There are more than three children in the house Y/N. If Y, Primary caretaker is overwhelmed by meeting the needs of all the children. Phrasing questions in this way has the potential to respond to workers' concerns by making the presence of risk factors directly related to the current complaint and the assessment process. When it comes to emotional maltreatment, the question and the policy could be adjusted. Instead of having a professional verify the presence of mental injury, the RA could instead assess for the presence of emotionally abusive language.

Although the SDM developers highlight the need for further discussion when workers' assess-ments diverge from the RA score, Midwest State's policy does not allow for these conversations to take place. Prohibitions to lower risk scores functionally mean that the RA supercedes worker judgment when they perceive a FP. Agency policy works to account for these situations through mandatory over-rides, yet no such accounting is made for scenarios where the RA understands the situation to be more severe than a caseworker believes. In this way, state policy views the RA to be infallible when it comes to overestimating risk and fallible when it comes to underestimating it. State policy that prohibits workers from lowering a risk score, whereas building in procedures to raise it reflects the organizational and moral costs of a FP. At a moral level, a child suffering a fatality or serious harm is always to be avoided. At an organizational level, high-profile fatalities often lead to very public excoriations of child welfare agencies. It makes sense, then, that a larger organizational focus is on catching FNs. An unintended consequence of this construction is that there are no structural mechanisms in place to account for the sensitivity of the RA and no organizational policy to guide workers when they perceive a FP has taken place.

Although FN cases receive a high level of scrutiny, the opposite is true for the impact of FP cases. Yet the impact of FPs are also consequential for those who experience them. FPs become real positives in any future case. Removals when they are unwarranted can be devastating to children and their caregivers. For young children, disruptions in care may profoundly alter relationships with life-long consequences for their emotional, social, and cognitive development

(Bowlby, 1973, 1979, 1980). For caregivers, extensive involvement with the child welfare system comes with costs related to time, money, energy, self-esteem, and well-being. Competent legal representation may be necessary to facilitate a reunification, and access to these services may not be available to all who require it. The child welfare system also loses when families are incorrectly sorted into risk categories. Intensive services for high-risk families are costly and time consuming. Caseworker time may be inappropriately spent attending to needs that do not require such a high level of services.

In Midwest State, when workers diverge from the RA's assessment because of the punitive consequences that accompany a high risk score, they often discuss the impact of the CRAN. Midwest State's decision to utilize the RA score to determine placement on the CRAN is likely a conflation of concepts of risk. The RA is designed to consider the likelihood of a reoccurrence of maltreatment and not issues related to whether the allegation should be substantiated, or, when it is, the severity of the offense. In practice, the risk score is being used as a proxy for maltreatment severity, and as a result two separate concepts are merged into a single policy. Much of workers' discomfort with the RA could be resolved by using another mechanism to establish placement of a caregiver on the CRAN.

Conclusion

In this article, I identify six distinct areas of the RA that likely contribute to divergence in worker and RA assessment. These areas of divergence primarily cause concern among workers that a FP will occur. To strengthen the integration of actuarial-based decision making and clinical judgment, it may be useful to develop structured questions related to these areas, which are informed by clinical evidence and validated through further empirical testing. Specifically, supervision of caseworkers could include a more nuanced (1) assessment of the meaning of demographic factors in relation to case evidence, (2) discussion of the impact of the caregivers' history of previous maltreatment on their caregiving, (3) assessment of any disagreement a worker has with the risk score based on contextual case factors, (4) consideration of how domestic violence is being accounted for and understood by the caregiver and worker, (5) discussion of how the caseworker interpreted questions on the RA and what evidence the caseworkers used to arrive at their endorsement of specific items, and (6) probing for the presence of abusive language in parent-child interactions.

Structured conversations between supervisors and caseworkers that explicitly address areas of concern from caseworkers have the potential to be an important site for making sense of the risk scores in the context of case information. Further, standardizing how workers are asked to make meaning of the RA in relationship to their assessment would create a clear process for grounding how divergences are handled in research about risk factors and ecological evaluation of cases. Procedures to strengthen the integration of clinical and actuarial-based judgment will also necessitate the creation of policies for reviewing divergence when it arises. As discussed above, over-ride review panels composed of child welfare experts could be one way to ensure that CPS workers are not erring in their objection to the RA's assessment.

The results of this study should be interpreted with care as these findings are based on a small sample of workers in a specific policy setting. Many of the case examples presented here represent instances where caseworkers believe the risk score was high in error. However, there is no way to know whether their assessments are correct. It may be that some of these examples demonstrate the reason that structured risk assessment is so important: because workers may downplay specific risk factors to which they should pay close attention. Additionally, the issue of FP and FN are not restricted solely to divergence between worker and RA assessments. There may be instances in which there is convergence but still a FP or FN error.

Debates about the the utility of mechanical versus clinical approaches have been at the center of social work for the last 20 years. Recognition that mechanical and clinical decision making are mutual rather than exclusive has, perhaps unsurprisingly, not yet fully translated into their reconciliation on the ground. Hirschman, Berrey, and Rose-Greenland, (2016) note that "numbers, even bad numbers, tend to drive out no numbers. Once in place, quantification does not seem to yield easily except to perhaps a 'better' quantification no matter how bad the critics allege the system to be" (p. 8). Other case studies of decision making across fields demonstrate that numbers become "self-vindicating" (Porter, 1995, p. 45). When a measure is established as important, it not only evaluates but also shapes behavior related to the original indicator (Espeland & Sauder, 2007; Porter, 1995).

Scholarship on quantification quite clearly predicts how difficult it will be for clinical judgment to be integrated alongside actuarial-based assessments like in Midwest State. In the context of a policy culture that incentivizes mechanical forms of decision making and accountability, more research is needed on how actuarial-based tools are being combined with worker judgment in practice across settings and fields. Further investigation is also needed about what specific practices would support integration of worker judgment with actuarial-based assessments and how frontline workers and child welfare agencies can be guided in analyzing cases when the RA and worker are not in agreement.

Acknowledgements

The author gratefully acknowledges Anna Haley, Karin Martin, Renee Anspach, Mary Ruffolo, Michael MacKenzie, Jerry Floersch, Donna Van Alst, Sheridan Miyamoto, Holly Thurston, Ethan Schoolman and the two anonymous reviewers, for their keen comments. Additionally, the author thanks Christopher Luoma and especially Morgan Purrier, for research assistance.

Funding

Funding for this work was provided by the National Science Foundation: Law and Social Sciences Division (SES – 1323916), The Doris Duke Fellowship for the Promotion of Child Wellbeing, and the Fahs-Beck Fund for Research and Experimentation.

References

Baird, C., & Wagner, D. (2000). The relative validity of actuarial and consensus based risk assessment systems. *Children and Youth Services Review, 22*, 839–871.

Baird, C., Wagner, D., Healy, T., & Johnson, K. (1999). Risk assessment in child protective services: Consensus and actuarial model reliability. *Child Welfare, 78*(6), 723–748.

Bosk, E. A. (2015). *All unhappy families* (doctoral dissertation). University of Michigan, Ann Arbor.

Bowlby, J. (1973). *Attachment and loss: Separation: Anxiety and anger* (Vol. 2). New York,NY: Basic Books.

Bowlby, J. (1979). *The making and breaking of affectional bonds*. New York, NY: Basic Books.

Bowlby, J. (1980). *Attachment and loss: Loss sadness and depression* (Vol. 3). New York, NY: Basic Books.

Camasso, M. J., & Jagannathan, R. (2013). Decision making in child protective services: A risky business? *Risk Analysis, 33*(9), 1636–1649.

Charmaz, K. (2006). *Constructing grounded theory: A practical guide through qualitative analysis*. Thousand Oaks, CA: Sage.

Chu, W. C., & Tsui, M.-S. (2008). The nature of practice wisdom in social work revisited. *International Social Work, 51* (1), 47–54.

CRC. (2008). *The structured decision-making model: An evidenced-based approach to human services*. Madison, WI: Author.

CRC. (2012). *Structured decision-making (SDM). The SDM system in child protection*. Madison, WI: Author.

Davidson-Arad, B., & Benbenishty, R. (2010). Contribution of child protection workers' attitudes to their risk assessments and intervention recommendations: A study in Israel. *Health & Social Care in the Community, 18*, 1–9.

Dawes, R. M. (1988). *Rational choice in an uncertain world*. Orlando, FL: Harcourt, Brace, Jovanovich.

Dawes, R. M., Faust, D., & Meehl, P. E. (1989). Clinical vs. actuarial judgment. *Science, 243*, 1668–1674.

Emerson, R., Fretz, R., & Shaw, L. (1995). *Writing ethnographic fieldnotes*. Chicago: University of Chicago Press.

Espeland, W., & Sauder, M. (2007). Rankings and reactivity: How public measures recreate social worlds. *American Journal of Sociology, 113*(1), 1–40.

Espeland, W., & Vannebo, B. (2007). Accountability, quantification, and law. *Annual Review of Law and Social Science, 3*, 21–43.

Fantuzzo, J. W., & Lindquist, C. U. (1989). The effects of observing conjugal violence on children: A review and analysis of research methodology. *Journal of Family Violence, 4*(1), 77–94.

Fluke, J., Yuan, Y., Hedderson, J., & Curtis, P. (2003). Disproportionate representation of race and ethnicity in child maltreatment: Investigation and victimization. *Children and Youth Services Review, 25*.

Flyvbjerg, B. (2006). Five misunderstandings about case-study research. *Qualitative Inquiry, 12*(2), 219–245.

Gainsborough, J. (2010). *Scandalous politics: Child welfare policy in the States*. Washington, DC: Georgetown University Press.

Gambrill, E., & Shlonsky, A. (2000). Risk assessment in context. *Children and Youth Services Review, 22*(11/12), 813–837.

Gambrill, E., & Shlonsky, A. (2001). The need for comprehensive risk management systems in child welfare. *Children and Youth Services Review, 23*(1), 79–107.

Gillingham, P. (2006). Risk assessment in child protection: Problem rather than solution? *Australian Social Work, 59*(1), 86–98.

Gillingham, P., & Humphreys, C. (2010). Child protection practitioners and decision-making tools: Observations and reflections from the front line. *British Journal of Social Work, 40*(8), 2598–2616.

Gilovich, T., Griffin, D., & Kahneman, D. (Eds.). (2002). *Huerstics and biases: The psychology of intuitive judgment*. New York, NY: Cambridge University Press.

Greenwood, D., & Lowenthal, D. (2005). Case study as a means of researching social work and improving practitioner education. *Journal of Social Work Practice, 19*(2), 181–193.

Hirschman, D., Berrey, E., & Rose-Greenland, F. (2016). Dequantifying diversity: Affirmative action and admissions at the University of Michigan. *Theory and Society, 45*(3), 265–301.

Hussey, J. M., Chang, J. J., & Kotch, J. B. (2006). Child maltreatment in the United States: Prevalence, risk factors, and adolescent health consequences. *Pediatrics, 118*(3), 933–942.

Kahneman, D., & Frederick, S. (2002). Representativeness revisited: Attribute substitution in intuitive judgment. *Heuristics and Biases: The Psychology of Intuitive Judgment, 49*, 49–81.

Levendosky, A. A., Huth-Bocks, A. C., Shapiro, D. L., & Semel, M. A. (2003). The impact of domestic violence on the maternal–child relationship and preschool-age children's functioning. *Journal of Family Psychology, 17*(3), 275–287.

Lindsey, D. (1992). Reliability of the foster care placement decision: A review. *Research on Social Work Practice, 2*(1), 65–80.

Loughlin, M. (2008). Reason, reality and objectivity–Shared dogmas and distortions in the way both 'scientistic'and 'postmodern'commentators frame the EBM debate. *Journal of Evaluation in Clinical Practice, 14*(5), 665–671.

MacKenzie, M. J., Kotch, J. B., & Lee, L.-C. (2011). Toward a cumulative ecological risk model for the etiology of child maltreatment. *Children and Youth Services Review, 33*(9), 1638–1647.

Munro, E. (2004). A simpler way to understand the results of risk assessments. *Children and Youth Services Review, 26*, 873–883.

Pecora, P. J., Chahine, Z., & Graham, J. C. (2013). Safety and risk assessment frameworks: Overview and implications for child maltreatment fatalities. *Child Welfare, 92*(2), 143–160.

Porter, T. (1995). *Trust in numbers: The pursuit of objectivity in science and public life*. Princeton, NJ: Princeton University Press.

Power, M. (1997). *The audit society: Rituals of verification*. Oxford, England: Oxford University Press.

Regehr, C., Bogo, M., Shlonsky, A., & LeBlanc, V. (2010). Confidence and professional judgment in assessing children's risk of abuse. *Research on Social Work Practice, 20*(6), 621–628.

Rivett, M., & Kelly, S. (2006). 'From awareness to practice': Children, domestic violence and child welfare. *Child Abuse Review, 15*(4), 224–242.

Rogerson, S. (2012). Unintended and unavoidable: The failure to protect rule and its consequences for undocumented parents and their children. *Family Court Review, 50*(4), 580–593.

Rossi, P. H., Schuerman, J. R., & Budde, S. (1999). Understanding decisions about child maltreatment. *Evaluation Review, 23*(6), 579–598.

Scheff, T. J. (1963). Decision rules, types of error, and their consequences in medical diagnosis. *Systems Research and Behavioral Science, 8*(2), 97–107.

Schwalbe, C. (2004). Re-visioning risk assessment for human service decision making. *Children and Youth Services Review, 26*, 561–576.

Schwalbe, C. (2008). Strengthening the integration of actuarial risk assessment with clinical judgment in an evidence based practice framework. *Children and Youth Services Review, 30*, 1458–1464.

Shlonsky, A., & Gambrill, E. (2001). The assessment and management of risk in child welfare services. *Children and Youth Services Review, 23*(1), 1–2.

Shlonsky, A., & Wagner, D. (2005). The next step: Integrating actuarial assessment and clinical judgment into an evidence-based practice framework in CPS case management. *Children and Youth Services Review, 27*, 409–427.

Stein, T., & Rzepnicki, T. (1983). Decision-making in child welfare: Current issues and future directions. In: B. McGowan & W. Meezan (Eds.), *Child welfare: Current dilemmas and future directions*. Itasca, IL: Child Welfare League of America.

Tversky, A., & Kahneman, D. (1974). Judgment under uncertainty: Hueristics and biases. *Science, 185*, 1124–1131.

Van de Luitgaarden, G. M. (2009). Evidence-based practice in social work: Lessons from judgment and decision-making theory. *British Journal of Social Work, 39*(2), 243–260.

Weiss, R. (1995). *Learning from strangers: The art and method of qualitative interview studies*. New York, NY: Free Press.

Wilson, D., & Morton, T. D. (1997). Issues in CPS decision making. Decision making in children's protective services: Advancing the state of the art, 1–16. Atlanta Georgia: Child Welfare Institute.

Levels and consequences of embeddedness among private human service organizations: National survey evidence from child welfare

Alicia C. Bunger 🄳, Bowen McBeath, Crystal Collins-Camargo, Emmeline Chuang, and Monica Perez-Jolles

ABSTRACT

Strong ties with and dependence on public agencies for service contracts can influence private human service organizations' operations. Using data from the National Survey of Private Child and Family Serving Agencies (NSPCFSA), this study assesses the degree to which private child welfare organizations report fiscal and relational embeddedness with public agencies and the influence of embeddedness on organizational functioning overall and in four specific domains: finances, service programming, staffing, and performance. Results showed that embeddedness may positively influence organizations' operations. The quality of private organizations' relationships with their public agency counterparts, and collaboration frequency may be especially important for improving organizational programming and performance.

Although public governmental agencies are responsible for administering programs to identify and address child maltreatment in the United States, private organizations deliver a substantial proportion of services to children and their families through purchase of service contracts (Flaherty, Collins-Camargo, & Lee, 2008). To achieve their mandates to promote child safety, permanency, and well-being, public child welfare agencies contract out a broad range of services which may encompass traditional core child welfare functions (e.g., case management, parent training, supervision of foster care placements), as well as complementary services like behavioral health care (Wells, Jolles, Chuang, McBeath, & Collins-Camargo, 2014).

In recent decades, the private sector role in delivering public human services has expanded in response to New Public Management reforms and pressures to contain costs. These reforms emphasize smaller government and bureaucratic innovation (Graaf, Hengeveld-Bidmon, Carnochan, Radu, & Austin, 2016; Radu, Carnochan, & Austin, 2015) through the outsourcing of public services to the private sector. In principle, private organizations compete for public contracts with clearly specified expectations, and public agencies select the private provider(s) with the highest quality product or service while containing costs. The expansion of public contracting with private child welfare organizations has been accompanied by growing use of performance-based contracting as a way to link financial reimbursements to achievement of performance targets. These contracting approaches are intended to leverage competition in the private sector to incentivize performance – a major change from human service funding approaches in the past, which provided robust support for service expansion with little competition or performance expectations (Smith, 2016). Under current performance-oriented contracting approaches, ties between public agencies and private child welfare organizations may be purely contractual, based only on economic transactions, and governed by formal strategies like monitoring, auditing, and outcome based assessments (Dicke, 2002).

In practice, however, the ties between public agencies and private child welfare organizations may be deeper than a typical "arms-length" relationship (Austin, 2003; Rosenthal, 2000). Public agencies are to some extent dependent on the private sector to deliver services that public agencies do not have the capacity to provide or cannot provide (Salamon, 1987). Limited provider markets can prevent public agencies from easily diversifying their contracts across a broad group of providers or switching from one provider to another in the case or poor performance or high costs, driving public agencies to work through contractor performance problems (Johnston & Romzek, 2008; Van Slyke, 2007). The ambiguous nature of services and difficulty of measuring many child welfare outcomes in a timely fashion also makes it challenging for public agencies to select, hold accountable, or terminate contractors based only on price and quality (2016; Brown, Potoski, & Van Slyke, 2010; Wulczyn, Chen, & Orlebeke, 2009). Instead, contracts may focus on process indicators or program outputs (e.g., number of service units), or rely on close monitoring. As a result, the contractual relationships between public agencies and private organizations can be close, reflecting ongoing negotiation and collaboration. These ties can evolve into enduring relationships, where public agencies and private providers work together on more than one contract, collaborate intensively, build trust, and learn and adjust in response to one another (Amirkhanyan, Kim, & Lambright, 2012; Austin, 2003; Holloway & Parmigiani, 2016). These strong relational ties between public and private organizations can facilitate better coordination across sectors (Kapucu, 2006) and better overall performance (Fernandez, 2007).

Based upon this understanding of the evolution of human service contracting, we argue that the linkage between public and private agencies is not simply economic in nature, but reflects a social dimension as well. These types of ties are considered "embedded," whereby social processes are interwoven within economic relationships (Granovetter, 1985) Similar to other types of interorganizational relationships, embedded ties with public agencies may have direct consequences for private organizations as well as distal effects on individual outcomes (Bunger, Cao, Girth, Hoffman, & Robertson, 2016; Chuang & Wells, 2010; Hurlburt et al., 2004; McBeath & Meezan, 2010). However, any consideration of these downstream consequences for service users must first consider the relationship between embeddedness and organizational outcomes for private human service organizations, which is the focus of this study.

Organizational embeddedness

Granovetter's seminal work (1992, 1985) has shaped modern-day embeddedness theory, which emphasizes the multidimensional and nested nature of relationships among actors. Drawing on economic sociological traditions (Swedberg, 1991, 1997), social and economic behavior are inextricably linked because economic transactions like contracting are situated within a social and institutional context. Thus, social norms, expectations, culture, politics, and cognitions inform and contextualize these ties (Zukin & DiMaggio, 1990); over time, multiple interactions generate shared norms, a common understanding of how resources should be used, joint problem solving, interdependence, and communal benefit. As a result of such tight coordination, embedded relationships often confer a variety of long-term organizational benefits including survival, competitive advantage, capacity, and efficiency, as illustrated in research on organizational relationships in other industries (Dacin, Ventresca, & Beal, 1999). Embedded relationships achieve collective goals and are governed by social norms (at least in part), which stands in contrast to arms-length relationships which are market-based economic exchanges driven by organizational self-interest, and governed primarily via formal contracts (Dacin et al., 1999).

Because an organization's relationships with others can also shape the larger social context, embeddedness is sometimes examined structurally from a network perspective (e.g., Uzzi, 1996). However, the quality of the relationship that results from repeated interactions between two partners over time may be as important for explaining organizational performance as the structure of networked relationships within a population of organizations (Moran, 2005; Nahapiet & Ghoshal, 1998). Therefore, this paper departs from a strict structural perspective, and instead focuses on the social and fiscal dimensions of dyadic ties to better understand the consequences of embeddedness in human services, specifically private child welfare organizations.

Embeddedness may be particularly strong within human service contexts, such as child welfare, with heightened benefits and disadvantages for these organizations. Within the human services, private organizations rely heavily on governmental funding, develop strong relationships with public agencies, and consequently might experience substantial embeddedness (Amirkhanyan et al., 2012; Salamon, 1987). These strong ties between public funders and private organizations reflect several trends including the historical evolution of public–private relationships in human service delivery systems (Austin, 2003; Flaherty et al., 2008); the lack of substantial competition for service contracts in some markets (Lamothe, 2014; Savas, 2002); and the presence of stable private provider bases, often leading to contract renewal and the development of long-lasting contractual relationships (Gronbjerg, 1993).

Some private organizations may experience greater embeddedness with public agencies than others, depending on the services they deliver. For instance, within child welfare contexts, private organizations that deliver core child welfare services (e.g., maltreatment investigation, foster care placement, family reunification, and congregate care placement) are typically located within the child welfare institutional context, and may have especially strong relationships with the public child welfare agency because it serves as their primary source of clients. As compared to these more traditional child welfare–oriented organizations, organizations that deliver complementary services to child welfare populations (e.g., behavioral health services), and operate within the behavioral health and health care systems institutional context, may experience less child welfare-specific embeddedness. These possibilities are themselves premised upon the strength of institutional ties between funders or patrons and private providers, and reflect the central tenets of institutional isomorphism (DiMaggio & Powell, 1983).

In the human services, embedded relationships with public agencies may confer substantial benefits for private organizations. Sustained relationships with a public agency partner may promote the development of shared norms, expectations, and efficient collaborations. Embedded relationships can also facilitate development of collective operational and service capacities, and alignment of services. These organizational benefits may in turn have a positive downstream impact on service users.

Yet, embedded relationships with a public agency may also be detrimental to organizational performance. Embededness may constrain an organization's behavior whereby organizations may act against their own self-interest to preserve their current relationship with their partner. Private human service organizations may be especially responsive to the needs, demands, and expectations of public agencies to secure future contracts (the economic dimension of the relationship), and to strengthen their legitimacy and stature (the social dimension of the relationship) (DiMaggio & Powell, 1983). Yet public agencies may use their contractual relationships to require private organizations to alter their service delivery strategies (e.g., requirements to implement specific evidence-based practices (EBPs) or experiment with new service approaches) even when such organizational changes may not align with their mission or may be perceived of questionable benefit to client populations. The classic literature on contract-based private human service delivery emphasized the challenges involved in adapting to purchase of service contracting, as contracts often required private providers to modify service approaches, serve different and/or unfamiliar client populations, discontinue provider-preferred modalities, and respond to other "strings attached" to public funds (Grønbjerg, 1993; Smith & Lipsky, 1993). These concerns with undue influence of public agencies on private service delivery parallel arguments concerning the possible cooptation of private organizations that are dependent fiscally and institutionally on public funders (Kramer, 1994). In child welfare where outcomes are often in question and the need for accountability is high, embedded private agencies may be reluctant to challenge the status quo. In short, while embedded relationships may enhance organizational capacity and performance, they may also lead to service delivery challenges, loss of organizational independence, and mission drift (Hasenfeld, 2015; Hasenfeld & Garrow, 2012).

Although scholars have examined embeddedness in a variety of industries, the level and impacts of embeddedness between public and private human service organizations has received little empirical attention, limiting our understanding of the complexity and best approaches for managing these relationships. How embedded are private human service organizations with public agencies? Do private organizations situated in different organizational fields experience similar levels of embeddedness? And what are the internal consequences of these relationships for private human service organizations?

The current paper addresses these questions in two ways. First, we analyze national-level survey data of private child welfare organizations to assess the degree of embeddedness experienced by individual organizations. Specifically, we develop a multidimensional understanding of embeddedness capturing economic and social dimensions of the exchange relationship between public and private organizations. Second, we examine the relationship between embeddedness and overall functioning of private child welfare organizations. To provide a more nuanced understanding about how embeddedness may influence private organizations, we follow up with an exploration the relationship between embeddedness and four domains critical to organizational functioning: finances, service programming, staffing, and performance. This attention to describing the level of embeddedness at the level of individual private service providers, and considering its operational consequences, distinguishes our analytical effort. In the next section, we review available theoretical and empirical literature to examine how embedded human service relationships inform the operations of private human service organizations. Although our focus concerns child welfare agencies, our arguments are developed to apply broadly to all human service fields of practice.

The influence of embeddedness on organizational functioning in child welfare

How might the development of strong, embedded relationships with public child welfare agencies influence private organizations' functioning? Child welfare services are governed by strong regulations and professional norms (Wells et al., 2014) that are conveyed to private organizations that work with the public system. In particular, prolonged, collaborative, and embedded relationships with the public child welfare agency expose private organizations to these formal and informal institutional demands. Drawing from institutional theory, private organizations adjust their structures, practices, technology, and behavior in response to strong institutional pressures to maintain legitimacy and secure resources from the public agency (DiMaggio & Powell, 1983).

For example, as a function or condition of working together, private organizations may be asked by the public child welfare agency to use a particular outcome measure, management information system, or billing procedures that require additional infrastructure investments. Private organizations may also be asked to modify, expand, or limit eligibility criteria for programs to align their programming with the needs of the public agency (Kramer, 1994). Private organizational leaders are likely to comply with these demands to avoid losing legitimacy and funding from the public agency.

Exactly how embedded relationships influence private organizations' overall functioning has not been explicated fully. On one hand, organizations might benefit from such strong relationships, whereby trust and familiarity with the public child welfare agency may confer legitimacy to private organizations, leading to future contracts, program expansion, improved performance, leading to a clear survival advantage over time (Baum & Oliver, 1992). On the other hand, such close embedded ties might oblige organizations to consider one another's needs and make decisions that may run counter to their interests (Hasenfeld, 2015; Hasenfeld & Garrow, 2012).

Influence on finances

Sufficient financial resources to support staff, programming, and administrative infrastructure are critical for organizational performance and long-term survival (Bowman, 2011; Calabrese, 2012; Carroll & Stater, 2009; Tuckman & Chang, 1991). Private child welfare organizations depend on public agencies for substantial revenue, and close, embedded relationships may help them secure additional funding. The more contracts secured and/or the greater the overall revenue received, the more resources flow from the public to the private organization (Baum & Oliver, 1992), and the more opportunities arise to deepen and improve the relationship between public and private organizations. Together these strong embedded relationships have been associated with greater revenue for the private organization in the short-term (Holloway & Parmigiani, 2016) and a survival advantage in the long-term (Baum & Oliver, 1992).

Although embedded relationships with public agencies may improve organizational finances for private organizations, these relationships may also have negative consequences. Public human service contracts often fail to cover the full costs of service delivery. Many do not fund start-up expenses and limit administrative costs; also, payments are frequently delayed, leading many private organizations to dip into their financial reserves or take on debt which may have lasting consequences for an organization's financial health (Behn & Kant, 1999; Marwell & Calabrese, 2015). Also, by contracting with public child welfare agencies, private organizations may take a loss when delivering Medicaid-covered services (since children in foster care or other out-of-home placements are Medicaid-eligible), which reimburses providers at a uniform rate that may be lower than the actual service cost (Smith, 2016). Further, repeated contracting and ongoing working relationships with the public child welfare agency may generate heavy dependence on a single source of funding (a public child welfare organization), leaving private organizations vulnerable to funding fluctuations and destabilization (Carroll & Stater, 2009). As a result, close ties with public agencies can generate substantial financial uncertainty and risk for private child welfare agencies.

Influence on staffing

Private child welfare organizations also depend on well-trained and professional staff to deliver services to maltreated children and families. Embedded relationships with the public child welfare agency may influence how private organizations are able to recruit, hire, manage, and retain personnel (Akingbola, 2004). More specifically, public contracts may contain stipulations about staff caseloads, qualifications (e.g., level of education or licensure), and service responsibilities that directly influence whom private agencies recruit and hire. The funding attached to contracts directly influences levels of compensation and opportunities for professional training for frontline professionals, which tend to be lower for staff employed by private organizations than public agencies, creating substantial retention problems (United States Government Accountability Office [GAO], 2003). Moreover, heavy dependence on public agencies leaves organizations vulnerable to funding fluctuations, which can be stressful for frontline professionals whose salaries are funded through contracts. For instance, a recent case study of changes in one state's child welfare procurement procedures found that the transition to performance-based contracting generated substantial uncertainty and job security concerns among staff at private organizations, leading to poor morale and influencing some workers to seek alternative employment (Willging et al., 2016). Consequently, embedded relationships with public agencies may challenge private agencies to recruit and retain a stable and high-quality workforce amidst ongoing demands of frontline child welfare practice, uncertain job security, high turnover and field desertion, poor salaries, and limited professional support.

Influence on service programming and outcomes

Embedded ties are also useful for joint problem solving because organizations may be willing to trust one another enough to share detailed information, expertise, and resources that might otherwise be kept guarded (Uzzi, 1996). These resources may act as drivers of innovation at the managerial and organizational levels (Meyers, Sivakumar, & Nakata, 1999), leading to adjustments in the service programs delivered by private child welfare organizations. Intense collaboration and collective problem solving can support joint learning – which can spark innovative programs, expand service offerings, and improve the quality of services (Amirkhanyan et al., 2012; Uzzi, 1997).

Yet, service expansion driven by embeddedness can be risky if new programs are inconsistent with an organization's mission, vision, and core expertise (Alexander, 2000). For example, when service contracts stipulate client eligibility criteria, time frames, and specific services or EBPs, private organizations may have limited discretion over program design (Bunger, et al., 2016). Considering how embedded relationships often evolve into long-term partnerships, private organizations may become locked into delivering specific services and programs, thereby limiting their flexibility to respond to emergent community needs as well as the demands of other organizational stakeholders (Kim, 2016). Therefore, embedded relationships with public child welfare agencies have the potential to constrain program expansion and management in the absence of careful consideration.

In sum, embedded relationships may influence private child welfare organizations' overall functioning. Repeated contracts and strong collaboration between public and private organizations can support organizational learning and innovation (Uzzi, 1997), which may be expected to have downstream effects on outcomes for children and families. But embedded relationships with the public agency may limit private organizations' discretion over service programming, impact their finances, and impact their ability to retain a diverse, qualified staff pool. These contingencies imply that embeddedness may have complex influences on private organizational operations.

Methods

Data and sample

To examine embedded relationships between public and private child welfare organizations, and the impact on private agency functioning, we drew on data gathered in the National Survey of Private Child and Family Serving Agencies (NSPCFSA). NSPCFSA was conducted in 2011 in partnership with the Child Welfare League of America (CWLA), the Alliance for Children and Families, and state-level associations involved with the National Organization of State Associations for Children (NOSAC), which collectively represented all the major associations for private child and family serving agencies. NSPCFSA was the first national survey of these organizations, and gathered comprehensive information in seven domains: director characteristics, organizational demographics, financing, services, internal and external pressures, interorganizational relationships, and performance management.

Organizations in the sampling frame included for-profit and nonprofit organizations that belonged to at least one of the partnering membership associations. To protect organizations' privacy, these associations emailed each of their organizational members an invitation to participate in the study containing details about the voluntary and anonymous nature of the study, risks and benefits, and a survey link. Because organizations could belong to multiple associations, the size of the sampling frame could not be determined. However, based on 2011 membership numbers, the sampling frame was estimated to include between 600 and 1000 unique organizations. A total of 446 agency directors in 38 states responded to the survey, representing a response rate ranging from 46% (assuming no overlap in membership) to 74% (under the assumption that there existed some overlap in involvement in state and national membership associations). Subsequent analyses determined that roughly 40% of responding agencies were members of their state association, as well as one or both national membership associations. Further methodological details are published elsewhere (McBeath et al. 2012).

Of the 446 respondents, 20 represented organizations that did not deliver any child welfare or behavioral health services either in house or via contract. Because our questions are rooted in the assumption that embeddedness has consequences for organizational functioning, service delivery, and ultimately outcomes for children and families, we did not include these organizations in our analysis. Thus, our resulting sample included 426 private organizations that deliver or contract out for services.

Measures

Dependent variables – effect of the relationship on organizational functioning

Eight survey items assessed directors' opinions about the effect of their organization's relationship with the public child welfare agency on *overall organizational functioning* along a five-point likert scale ranging from "It's made it much worse" (one) to "It's made it much better" (five). Together these eight items were intended to capture the overall impact of the public agency on the private organization ($\alpha = .9420$), and factor analysis generated a one-factor solution suggesting that the scale has good internal consistency. Responses were averaged across items to generate a continuous measure for our main dependent variables.

However, these items were designed to correspond to four domains that theoretically may respond differently in the context of embedded relationships with a public child welfare agency. As a result, we also created dependent variables that reflect these four domains to allow a more nuanced exploration of the relationship between embeddedness and four domains: financing, staffing, service programming, and performance. *Organizational financing* was measured using three survey items (e.g., perceived effect on overall financial outlook, level of financial risk, and financial outlook of agencies you contract with) ($\alpha = .8731$). *Staffing* was assessed with one item (recruitment and retention of staff). *Service programming* was measured using two items (e.g., development of new programs, and delivery of long-standing programs) ($\alpha = .8787$). Finally, *performance* was measured via two items (e.g., ability to serve children and families well, and ability to meet key agency performance outcomes) ($\alpha = .8719$). To examine the relationship between embeddedness and organizational functioning, responses to the respective items were averaged, although not all of the distributions for the four domain measures were conducive to linear regression approaches. As a result, and to facilitate analysis, ordinal measures were created. Because of a low frequency of responses in the lowest and highest response categories, we collapsed these responses into three categories: "It's made it worse" (one), "Neutral" (two), and "It's made it better" (three).

Independent variable – embedded relationships with public child welfare agencies

Two indicators of *fiscal embeddedness* were measured: number of contracts in different programmatic areas and overall dependence on government funding. First, since organizations with multiple contracts with public child welfare system are likely to interact repeatedly over time, develop stronger relationships with the public child welfare agency (Uzzi, 1996), and thus be more exposed to the demands of these public institutions than those with only one or no contracts, we accounted for the number of contractual relationships. Directors indicated whether their agency had a contract from a public child welfare agency to provide any of up to 11 distinct services, including programming such as from child abuse prevention, foster care placements, adoption, and independent living services. Thus, *contracts* represent the number of programming contracts an agency reported. Second, private organizations often rely on public funding as a primary resource for service delivery, which directly influence how organizations operate. Directors reported on the percentage of their annual revenue derived from public funding sources. *Dependence on public funding* was operationalized as a dichotomous variable set equal to one if more than 80% (the median response) of the agency's revenue came from government sources. Although this variable was initially intended to be a continuous measure (M = 69.1%, SD = 29.9%), responses were highly skewed to the left (skew = –.89) and neither squared nor cubic approaches were sufficient for transformation. The distribution of this variable, and our treatment of it, are not unusual: for instance, Boris, de Leon, Roeger, & Niklova (2010) note that a general sample of human service nonprofit organizations derived an average of 65% of their annual revenue from government sources. Because our data were so skewed, we dichotomized using a median split. This approach is similar to other studies that have modeled the dependence of private organizations on government funding (Guo & Acar, 2005; Murphy & Waters Robichau, 2016).

Two indicators of *relational embeddedness* were captured. First, high-quality partnerships tend to be stronger, and indicative of trust-based relationships compared than those that are poor and based on conflict and mistrust. The *perceived quality of the relationship* with the public child welfare agency was measured based on directors' rating of perceived quality on a 5-point Likert scale ranging from one ("It is very poor") to five ("It is very good"). Second, intensive collaboration is an indicator of embedded relationships and can lead to the adjustment of agency functioning. To measure *collaboration*, directors reported on the frequency of four types of collaboration with the public child welfare agency (data sharing, staff cross training, joint service delivery, and joint budgeting) along a five point Likert scale ranging from zero ("none") to four ("constant"). Responses were aggregated to create a scale representing the total collaborative intensity.

Control variables

Four control variables that may also be associated with agency operations were measured. We controlled for organizational *size*: As compared to small organizations, large organizations tend to receive a higher proportion of their revenue from government sources (Stone, Hager, & Griffin, 2001) and may have more capacity to face the challenges of embeddedness, and innovate in response to external pressures (Damanpour, 1992). Size was measured in terms of the number of full-time employees; directors responded to one categorical survey item with response categories that ranged from one (fewer than or equal to 10 full-time employees) to nine (more than 1000 full-time employees). Also organizations with *organizational infrastructure* dedicated to financing, quality, and information technology may be more prepared to respond to shifting demands of public child welfare agency partners (Alexander, 2000). As a result, the partnership may have a more neutral or positive effect on the organization than those without this capacity. Organizational infrastructure was operationalized as a count of the number of four types of specialized administrative staff employed at the time of data collection: a full-time chief financial officer, a program evaluation department or manager, a quality assurance/improvement unit or manager, and an information technology department or manager. We accounted for whether an organization was a branch agency or office that belonged to a larger *network organization*, as such organizations tend to have strong relationships with public agencies, and thus benefit more from their relationships with the public agency, perhaps due to their ability to leverage economies of scale (Amirkhanyan et al., 2012). Network membership was operationalized as a dichotomous variable set equal to one if the organization was a branch of a larger network. We also accounted for the organization's sector using a dichotomous variable set equal to one if the organization was for-profit.

Finally, private organizations that serve children and families vary in terms of the services they provide. Some deliver core child protective services and may have stronger relationships with the public child welfare agency. However, given the prevalence of mental health and substance use issues among children and families involved in the child welfare system (Burns et al., 2004; Horwitz et al., 2012), many private organizations that partner with public child welfare agencies offer behavioral health services and thus may be located in a different institutional context (i.e., the behavioral health and health care system). To explore the relationship between levels of organizational embeddedness vis-à-vis organizational location in different organizational fields, the types of services provided currently by the agency were used to categorize organizations into three distinct organizational fields: (1) child welfare only (reflecting an emphasis on foster care placement services, maltreatment investigations, ongoing services for cases where children are in a placement, services to promote reunification, and adoption-related services); (2) behavioral health only (i.e., substance abuse or mental health services for children or adults); or (3) hybrid organizations that deliver child welfare and behavioral health services.

Analysis

To address our first aim, we used basic univariate analyses to examine the responses to the four indicators of fiscal and relational embeddedness analyses. Variations in embeddedness across the three organizational fields (reflecting differences in service types) were explored using chi-square and analysis of variance (ANOVA) tests. Post-hoc analyses were conducted to further explore differences in the characteristics of private providers in different organizational fields.

To address our second aim, we prepared our analysis by first conducting basic univariate analyses of our main dependent variable (overall impact on organizational functioning), and bivariate tests examining associations with each independent and control variable. Next, we tested relationships among embeddedness and overall organizational functioning using linear regression. There were no issues with multicollinearity or heteroskedasticity

To explore whether embeddedness has differing consequences depending on the type of organizational functioning, we followed up with similar procedures for exploring our four domains (financing, staffing, programming, and performance). Given the ordinal nature of these four domain variables, we conducted non-parametric tests at the bivariate level (i.e., frequency tabulations, Spearman correlations, and Kruskall-Wallis tests) and examining associations between our five dependent variables and each independent and control variable. Next, relationships among embeddedness and the effect on organizational functioning were examined using multivariate ordered logistic regressions. During analysis, one model (programming) violated the proportional or parallel odds assumption as indicated by a significant Brant test. These results indicate that the independent variables had differing effects at different levels of the dependent variable (O'Connell, 2006). As a result, partial proportional odds (PPO) models, which relax the parallel odds assumption, were run for the programming variable using the gologit2 command (Williams, 2006, 2016). These models estimate the odds of each independent variable across each pair of dependent variable categories (e.g., the probability of a neutral versus worse influence, and the probability of a good versus neutral influence on organizational functioning).

Due to missing data, 47 organizations were dropped from analysis using list-wise deletion. Among these organizations, organizations that belonged to a larger networked organization were overrepresented (25%) compared to those in the analytic sample (13.46%) (X^2 = 3.88, p < .05). Organizations with missing data also reported significantly lower collaborative frequency (M = 7.32, SD = 5.18) (F(1, 424) = 27.01, p = .0000) than organizations with complete data. On other indicators, however, there were no significant differences in organizations by the degree of missingness. All analyses were conducted using Stata 14 (StataCorp, 2015).

Table 1. Sample characteristics.

	N	%/Mean (SD)	Range
Main Dependent Variable			
Influence on Overall Functioning	407	2.94 (.85)	1–5
Focal Independent Variables			
Relational Embeddedness			
Relationship quality	417	4.05 (.90)	1–5
Total collaboration	426	10.24 (4.21)	0–20
Fiscal Embeddedness			
CW contracts	426	3.52 (2.92)	0–11
>80% revenue from public sources	416	50.9%	0–1
Control Variables			
Organizational Features			
Staff Size	426	4.46 (1.76)	1–9
Part of a larger network	419	14.6%	0–1
Organizational infrastructure	420	2.67 (1.34)	0–4
For Profit	416	8.7%	0–1
Service Type			
Child Welfare & Behavioral Health	426	74.4%	0–1
Child Welfare Only	426	17.1%	0–1
Behavioral Health Only	426	8.5%	0–1

Results

Organizational characteristics

Descriptive information is presented in Table 1. Within this national sample of private child welfare agencies, organizations employed on average 50–99 FTEs (mean = 4.46, SD = 1.76), and reported employing staff in an average of 2.67 (SD = 1.34) of the four assessed administrative specialties. Most were independent organizations, with only 15% connected to a larger network. The majority (74.4%) of responding organizations were considered hybrid organizations that delivered both child welfare and behavioral health services, whereas 17.1% provided only child welfare services, and 8.5% only delivered behavioral health care.

Embeddedness with public child welfare agencies

Organizations reported a moderate degree of embeddedness with public child welfare agencies (Aim 1). With regard to relational embeddedness, respondents rated the quality of their relationship with their public counterparts as "good" (mean = 4.05, SD = .90), and collaborated somewhat intensively (mean = 10.24, SD = 4.21). Respondents also reported having strong fiscal relationships with their public counterparts; on average, organizations maintained 3.52 (SD = 2.92) child welfare contracts, and half (51%) relied on public sources for almost all of their annual revenue.

Variations across service types

Results of bivariate analyses examining differences in level of embeddedness by service type are presented in Table 2. Collaboration, an indicator of relational embeddedness, varied across organizational service types [$F(2, 423) = 4.83$, $p = .009$]. Post hoc analyses indicated that behavioral health only agencies (m = 8.25, SD = 3.32) collaborated with public child welfare agencies significantly less than child welfare-specific (m = 10.79, SD = 5.04, p = .009) or hybrid child welfare-behavioral health organizations (m = 10.34, SD = 4.04, p = .014). The number of child welfare contracts, an indicator of fiscal embeddedness, also varied across organizational fields [$F(2, 423) = 12.20$, $p = .008$]: hybrid child welfare-behavioral health organizations reported managing significantly more contracts (m = 4.33, SD = 2.97) than child welfare only (m = 3.49, SD = 2.46, p = .033), and behavioral health only organizations (m = 2.03, SD = 2.06, p = .00).

Additional differences across the three types of services were observed (Table 2). In terms of size, child welfare-only organizations (m = 3.51, SD = 1.48) were significantly smaller than hybrid child welfare-behavioral health organizations (m = 4.76, SD = 1.78, p = .00) or behavioral health-only organizations (m = 4.44, SD = 1.36, p = .021) [$F(2, 423) = 16.19$, $p = .00$]. Also, hybrid child welfare-

Table 2. Embeddedness, and organizational features by service type.

	CW & BH (n = 317)		CW (n = 73)		BH (n = 36)		
	M	SD	M	SD	M	SD	ANOVA/Chi2 results
Relational Embeddedness							
Relation. Qual.	4.02	.88	4.20	.98	3.97	.88	NS
Collab (total)	10.34	4.04	10.79	5.04	8.25	3.32	F(2, 4223) = 4.83, p = .009
Fiscal Embeddedness							
CW Contracts	4.33	2.97	3.49	2.46	2.03	2.06	F(2, 423) = 12.20, p = .008
>80% revenue	49.35%		54.17%		55.56%		NS
Organizational Features							
Infrastructure	2.77	1.31	2.18	1.48	2.69	1.08	F(2, 417) = 5.75, p = .0034
Size	4.76	1.78	3.51	1.48	4.44	1.36	F(2, 423) = 16.19, p = .00
Part of a Network	15.65%		12.33%		9.09%		NS
For Profit	6.77%		14.29%		13.89%		NS

Table 3. Linear regression results: overall organizational functioning (n = 379).

	b	SE	
Embeddedness			
Relationship Qual.	**.41**	**.045**	**
Collaboration	**.02**	**.01**	+
Contracts	.02	.02	
>80% Rev. is Public	.10	.08	
Control Variables			
Size	**−.06**	**.03**	+
Network Member.	.17	.12	
Infrastructure	.06	.04	
For Profit	**−.30**	**.15**	+
Service Type (CW only, ref)			
CW & BH	.13	.11	
BH Only	−.00	.17	

**p < .001
*p < .01
+p < .05

behavioral health organizations reported employing staff in a greater number of administrative specializations (m = 2.77, SD = 1.31) as compared to child welfare-only organizations (m = 2.18, SD = 1.48, p = .002), [F(2, 417) = 5.75, p = .0034].

Relationships between embeddedness and overall organizational functioning

Linear regression result examining the relationship between embeddedness and overall functioning are presented in Table 3. Relationship quality, an indicator of relational embeddedness was positively associated with the perceived effect of the relationship with the public child welfare agency on overall functioning (b = .41, SE = 0.45, p < .001). Collaboration, our second relational embeddedness indicator, was also positively associated with the perceived effect of the public agency on overall organizational functioning (b = .02, SE = 0.01, p < .05). Although both relational embeddedness indicators were significant, neither of the fiscal indicators was significantly associated with organizational functioning

However, two control variables were associated with the perceived influence of the public agency. Organizational size (b = −.06, SE = 0.03, p < .05) and for-profit status (b = −.30, SE = 0.15, p < .05) were negatively associated with overall functioning suggesting that smaller, and nonprofit organizations may perceive a more positive influence of their relationship with the public child welfare agency.

Relationships between embeddedness and financing, staffing, programing and performance

We continued to explore whether embeddedness may differentially influence four domains that make up overall organizational functioning: financing, staffing, programming, and performance. Table 4 breaks down the distribution of responses across these four domains. Ordered logistic regression results (examining financing, staffing, and performance) are presented in Table 5, and PPO model estimates (examining programming) are presented in Table 6. Consistent with the results from the overall model, relationship quality was consistently and positively associated with each specific organizational domain. High-quality relationships with public child welfare agencies were associated

Table 4. Response distribution: organizational functioning subdomains.

	Financing (n = 407)	Staffing (n = 404)	Programming (n = 406)	Performance (n = 406)
It's Made It Worse	34.4%	27.5%	23.7%	23.7%
Neutral	45.2%	54.0%	35.5%	37.7%
It's Made it Better	20.4%	19.6%	40.9%	38.7%

Table 5. Ordered logistic regression results.

	Finance (n = 379)			Staffing (n = 376)			Performance (n = 378)		
	OR	SE		OR	SE		OR	SE	
Embeddedness									
Relationship Qual.	2.41	.33	**	1.92	.25	**	**2.62**	**.36**	**
Collaboration	1.03	.03		1.03	.03		**1.08**	**.03**	+
Contracts	1.05	.04		1.06	.04		**1.09**	**.05**	+
>80% Rev. is Public	1..4	.28		1.25	.26		1.32	.28	
Control Variables									
Size	**.86**	**.07**	+	1.63	.51		**.79**	**.06**	*
Network Member.	1.25	.38		1.63	.51		1.42	.45	
Infrastructure	1.16	.11		1.13	.10		1.16	.11	
For Profit	.48	.18		.56	.22		**.40**	**.16**	+
Service Type (CW only, ref)									
CW & BH	1.47	.42		.99	.28		1.52	.44	
BH Only	1.57	.71		1.04	.47		.73	.34	

**p < .001
*p < .01
+p < .05

Table 6. Partial proportional odds model results.

	Programming (n = 378)					
	From Worse to Neutral			From Neutral to Better		
	OR	SE		OR	SE	
Embeddedness						
Relationship Qual.	**2.70**	**.45**	**	2.54	.46	**
Collaboration	.93	.04		**1.09**	**.04**	+
Contracts	1.04	.06		**1.13**	**.06**	+
>80% Rev. is Public	.73	.20		**1.95**	**.47**	*
Control Variables						
Size	.87	.09		.90	.08	
Network Member.	1.50	.65		1.49	.55	
Infrastructure	1.21	.14		1.14	.12	
For Profit	.89	.41		**.34**	**.16**	+
Service Type (CW only, ref)						
CW & BH	.79	.19		.71	.19	
BH Only	1.33	.53		1.33	.53	

**p < .001
*p < .01
+p < .05

with a more positive perceived effect on organizational financing (OR = 2.41, SE = .33, p < .001), staffing (OR = 1.92, SE = .25) and performance (OR = 2.62, SE = .36, p < .001). The same results were observed for programming: relationship quality was positively associated with a neutral (OR = 2.70, SE = .45, p < .001), and a better influence on programming (OR = 2.54, SE = .46, p < .001).

Collaboration, our second relational embeddedness indicator, was also positively associated with the perceived effect of the public agency on performance (OR = 1.08, SE = .03, p < .05), and programming (OR = 1.09, SE = .04, p < .05) (compared to a neutral influence). However, collaboration was not associated with financing or staffing. These results suggest that the stronger the relational embeddedness with public child welfare agencies, the more agencies perceived beneficial effects of these relationships on service delivery.

Although neither of our fiscal embeddedness indictors was associated with overall functioning, our analysis of the domains highlight more nuanced findings about the relationship between fiscal ties and organizational programming and performance. The number of child welfare contracts was positively associated with benefits for performance (OR = 1.09, SE = .05, p < .05) and programming (OR = 1.13, SE = .06, p < .05). Relying on public sources for greater than 80% of revenue was associated with a better influence on programming (OR = 1.95, SE = .47, p < .01). Neither fiscal embeddedness indicator was associated with financing or staffing. These results suggest a limited role for fiscal embeddedness in regards to private child welfare organizations' programming and performance.

Similar to the results for the overall model, organizational size and for-profit status were negatively associated in our domain-specific analysis although this relationship was not uniform across all domains. Staff size was negatively associated with the perceived effect on finance (OR = .86, SE = .07, p < .05), and performance (OR = .79, SE = .06, p, .01). These findings suggest that smaller organizations may experience more positive effects of their relationship with the public child welfare agency on financing, and performance, but not staffing or programming. Also, for-profit status was negatively associated with performance (OR = .40, SE = .16, p < .05), and a better influence on programming (OR = .34, SE = .16, p < .05). These results suggest that nonprofit organizations might experience a negative influence specifically on programming and performance, but not on staffing or financing. Belonging to a networked organization, infrastructure, and type of services provided were not associated with the influence of the public child welfare agency on overall organizational functioning or on any of the domains.

Discussion

Embeddedness refers to the multidimensional relationships among organizations, often reflecting overlapping economic and social domains (Granovetter, 1985; Uzzi, 1996). In the human services, the evolution of public-private partnerships through purchase of service contracting has generated significant research on the manner in which fiscally dependent private providers relate to public funders. This research has tended to concentrate upon the fiscal ties between public and private agencies, and as a result has reinforced an economic orientation to service contracting. Yet recent research drawn from the human services and other fields suggests that the contractual relationship between public and private agencies may be facilitated through the presence of strong social relationships and norms (Amirkhanyan et al., 2012). This perspective implies that contract-based linkages between public and private human service organizations may be characterized as much by social linkages as economic dependencies.

The current study examined how embedded relationships are manifested in the human services, specifically within the child welfare field. Analyses drawn from NSPCFSA found a moderate degree of embeddedness present among private child welfare organizations. Specifically, private organizations rated their relationship with their public child welfare agency to be "good" in general and collaborated relatively intensely. Private organizations also had contracts for about 4 of 11 services typically delivered in child welfare systems, and most organizations relied on public funding for nearly all of their annual revenue, consistent with prior findings (Salamon, 1987; Smith & Lipsky, 1993). Considering how multiple contracts may be awarded to a private organization over time as they demonstrate accountability and performance, and given the overall size and maturity of sample agencies, these findings may imply that the relationships captured in our data may be somewhat established, reflecting possibly decades of successful contracts with the public child welfare agency and other public funders (Van Slyke, 2007). Embeddedness was also fairly comparable across private organizations, although child welfare-only organizations tended to have more collaborative relationships. Also, hybrid child welfare-behavioral health organizations tended to have more service contracts, perhaps because of their capacity to deliver a wide array of services.

These descriptive findings suggest that relationships between public and private child welfare agencies can be characterized as positive, complex, and essential. Due to their fiscal dependence on service contract-based revenue, the presence of multiple contracts with public funders suggests that private organizations must manage complex dependencies actively. The generally positive cross-sector relationship perceived by private organizational directors might not be surprising, as private child welfare managers may invest significant resources in maintaining an effective relationship with the public child welfare agency (Austin, 2003). However, as compared to the classic literature on purchase of service contracting in the human services, these overall positive findings suggest that the influence of embeddedness on organizational operations may be more positive than previously expected since such close working relationships have potential to negatively influence organizational operations. From an institutional perspective, these descriptive findings may be a reflection of successful prior strategic adaptations by managers in response to earlier contract-based challenges.

Our multivariate analyses sought to identify the influence of embeddedness on organizational functioning. Private providers with stronger, more positive relationships with the public child welfare agency reported that the public agency had a more beneficial impact on organizational functioning. In addition, we found that the influence of collaboration may also benefit organizational functioning although this influence may be weaker. Our analysis of the functioning domains indicate how collaboration strength was not associated with improved finances or staffing; but was associated with perceived organizational functioning in the domains of programming and overall performance. Thus, results suggest that collaboration may be especially important for shaping private organization's programming and performance compared to financing or staffing.

These findings, which reflect the first multivariate analysis of the influence of embeddedness controlling for organizational characteristics and organizational field, highlight the importance of the social dimension of embeddedness on private human service organizational behavior, particularly for organizational programming and performance. Our effort to distinguish agency responses to embeddedness across organizational fields is important because private human service organizations often contract to provide services in multiple fields of service, each of which may have different institutional norms and pressures.

Our results also reinforce findings from studies of the relational aspects of human service contracting, in implying that stronger public-private relationships may be associated with more positive outcomes for private providers (Fernandez, 2007). The relational contracting literature has emphasized the role of informal norms of trust and reciprocity in supporting contract-based interpersonal relationships between public and private managers (Bertelli & Smith, 2010; Romzek, LeRoux, & Blackmar, 2012). Our findings suggest that these social bonds may not only be commonplace, but may also buffer private organizations from the more challenging aspects of human service contracting.

Turning to the fiscal dimensions of embeddedness, our findings were mixed. As seen in the PPO models, fiscal dependence was associated with improved programming and overall performance. This finding may suggest that such partnerships with the public agency may have the greatest impact on the services offered by private human service organizations and their ability to meet the needs of the community and responsiveness to those perceived by their public agency partner. Such dependence on public agencies suggests that private organizations have a lot at stake; in order to preserve their relationship with (and secure resources from) public agencies, private organizations may be especially attuned to changing their programs to meet the needs of public agencies and their clients. However, the number of contracts held by private organizations was generally unrelated to agency functioning. With additional contracts, private organizations have the potential to collaborate more intensively with their public agency partner, build trust, and overall improve their relationship quality (Amirkhanyan et al., 2012; Holloway & Parmigiani, 2016). Our findings may suggest that once these social dimensions are accounted for in our models, the fiscal aspect of the relationship is less influential for organizational operations.

Study limitations

These results should be understood in relation to limitations in the study design. First, although the current study reflected national survey data, findings may not be representative of all private child welfare agencies. In particular, smaller agencies, as well as agencies with weaker connections to public child welfare agencies, may have been less likely to participate in NSPCFSA given that its sample reflected agencies that were members of state and/or national level federations of private child and family serving agencies (which may be more likely to draw well-funded private organizations given the expenses of associational membership). Second, because study data were gathered using a cross-sectional research design, we cannot draw causal inferences. Rather the relationship between embeddedness and organizational functioning as associational as opposed to causal in nature. Third, findings reflect the perspectives of organizational administrators; the perspectives of other organizational staff may or may not comport with these executive perceptions. Fourth, we dichotomized our measure of dependence on government funding based on a median split (80%) because of extreme skewness. However, in so doing, we masked potential variation among the half of the sample that derived less than 80% of their revenue from public sources. Finally, although our multivariate models controlled for a range of agency characteristics and organizational contexts, it is possible that other factors were of importance to organizational functioning. For example, information as to the historical evolution of contract-based relationships between the private agencies and their public funders, as measured by the number of prior purchase of service contracts, was unavailable; similarly, it was not possible to determine the intensity of prior agency adaptations to purchase of service contracting requirements. Because these factors were unavailable for analysis, their influence contributed to possible omitted variable bias in our multivariate estimates.

Implications for research, practice, and policy

These results suggest the need for greater empirical attention to the social dimensions of public-private human service contracting. Future research might approach this topic in two ways. First, studies might seek to further distinguish the social and interpersonal elements that comprise embedded contractual relationships. Research might examine the contexts in which social interactions between public and private organizations occur, focusing in particular on the evolution of cross-sector interpersonal partnerships at critical stages of contracting (e.g., during the early stages of contract implementation and service delivery) and/or in different institutional settings (e.g., amidst performance-based contracting, or where private organizations depend greatly vs. comparatively less upon a particular service contract). Such work might suggest alternative models for conceptualizing and operationalizing the nature of embeddedness between public and private human service organizations. Second, research is needed to explore the perspectives of public human service managers on their private managerial contract counterparts, as well as their contributions to contract-based service partnerships with private providers (Kramer, 1994). Methodologically, dyadic studies of public and private human service organizations linked by specific contracts are needed to explore these substantive topics further.

In addition, historical as well as prospective research on the development and evolution of embedded relationships and their influence on organizational functioning is warranted. Van Slyke (2007) notes that public-private relationships often begin as a contract, and grow increasingly embedded within social relationships over time as partners demonstrate performance, and build trust. Thus, relationships between private organizations and public agencies may grow increasingly embedded over time; considering how we found limited evidence for the relationship between fiscal embeddedness and agency functioning, early relationships based only on arms-length relationship may not yield substantial benefits for private organizations. Rather, it may take time and continued partnership to yield benefits for private organizations.

Such research can elucidate the social dimensions of human service contracting processes. From a theoretical perspective, the dominant approaches to human service contracting have tended to focus on institutional explanations of private organizational behavior. In particular, institutional theory and agency theory (including stewardship theory) have tended to concentrate upon the social and economic forces enabling or constraining organizational behavior (Van Slyke, 2007). Yet recent empirical studies reflecting a relational contracting perspective have emphasized the importance of managers—including managerial expectations, past experiences with contract-based counterparts, and behaviors—in shaping cross-sector contract partnerships and interorganizational collaboration more generally (Gazley, 2016). These studies highlight the need for middle range theorizing that links institutional studies of contracting with research exploring how public and private human service managers engage in joint problem solving to address service delivery issues and promote beneficial agency outcomes. Empirical studies are also needed that test the downstream consequences of these contracting approaches, and strong public-private relationships for children and their families.

The current study also has implications for private human service managers. Our results confirm the importance of social exchange processes, interorganizational relational development, and interpersonal relationships for human service contracting (Collins-Camargo, McBeath, & Ensign, 2011). The current findings suggest greater attention to the precursors of effective interorganizational partnerships [e.g., reflecting the Wilder Collaboration Factors Inventory, (Mattessich, Murray-Close, & Monsey, 2001)] (Chuang, McBeath, Collins-Camargo, & Armstrong, 2014). In brief, our results suggest that if contractual processes indeed give rise to and are facilitated by relational processes, then private human service managers should attend to the maintenance and sustainment of strong, positive relationships with their public manager contract counterparts. These social relationships may strengthen public-private child welfare partnerships, promote stability among contractors, reduce transactions costs, and create efficiencies at the organizational and system levels.

It should be acknowledged that strong, reciprocal, and trust-based relationships between public and private managers do not necessarily translate to high performing systems. The evolution of social norms, patterns, and habits by managers over the years, and the consequent effects on levels of embeddedness at the dyadic level, may also generate inertia making it difficult to transform or dissolve partnerships (Kim, Oh, & Swaminathan, 2006). For example, managers in private child welfare organizations may have difficulty developing, implementing, or adjusting innovative service programs unless sanctioned by their public child welfare partner. Public managers may be constrained by such long-standing social relationships, which may limit their ability to evaluate contractors' performance rigorously and discontinue contracts with poor performers. Together, these challenges for public and private organizations may have cascading consequences for developing performance-oriented child welfare systems in which provider outcomes are determined by the ability to improve children's safety, permanence, and wellbeing (rather than their institutional relationships as indicated by length of time providing a particular service).

In relation to this logic, our results suggest greater attention to how public child welfare agency managers leverage the strong social context for these contractual relationships to improve performance and outcomes. Public agency managers may seek to promote a culture of innovation and performance among their private partners by using inclusive planning and monitoring strategies such as cross-sector strategic planning, collaborative contract development, joint identification of meaningful performance metrics, and regular review of performance data (Chuang et al., 2014; Collins-Camargo, Armstrong, McBeath, & Chuang, 2013; Collins-Camargo et al., 2011; Garstka, Collins-Camargo, Hall, Neal, & Ensign, 2012). By coupling these collaborative approaches with formal contracting tools, including sanctions for poor performance (Girth, 2014), public agency managers may be able to hold private organizations accountable for their performance, and help push for a more data-driven, outcome-oriented system.

These considerations highlight an important distinction between embedded relationships characterized by (a) unilateral decision making vs. (b) partnership-focused planning (in which each partner is aware and considerate of potential repercussions for the other organization) when public and private human service managers engage in dialogue concerning strategic initiatives and commonly shared goals. Embedded relationships need not involve the latter, although we would argue that client and systemic outcomes are enhanced when such considerations are taken into account. Public child welfare managers may want to be cautious when imposing sanctions heavy-handedly, especially in areas where private child welfare organizations take on substantial financial or programming risks.

For instance, public child welfare agencies may ask their private partners to experiment with innovative programs that require new infrastructure and training (e.g., a new, untested program that addresses parental opioid dependence). A private organization may feel pressure to do so—despite the financial risk it may be forced to accept—in order to retain its social ties to the public funder.

However, should the public agency later decide not to contract for the new program, or discontinue the contract prematurely because of implementation challenges (which are to be expected) or poor outcomes, the private partner assumes a loss. An embeddedness perspective centered upon mutual planning might suggest that the private and public agencies negotiate and work through informal social channels to secure alternative contracting terms of benefit to each organization. These "push and pull" relational dynamics may be expected within embedded public-private relationships, and may be expected to inform the development of any specific policy or governance initiatives proposed by public agencies.

It is important that public and private agency leaders acknowledge the economic and social dimensions of their relationships. Understanding how embedded interagency relationships may influence the perceived functioning of private sector organizations is a useful step in the direction of examining the extent to which they impact actual functioning and outcome achievement. Keeping the potential downside in mind, managers in both sectors can benefit——from understanding how these embedded relationships can be leveraged to promote overall system improvement for children and families they serve.

Acknowledgments

This research was conducted under the Quality Improvement Center on Privatization of Child Welfare Services funded by the U.S. Department of Health and Human Services, Administration for Youth and Families, Children's Bureau.

Funding

This work was supported by U.S. Children's Bureau [Quality Improvement Center on Privatization of Child Welfare Services].

ORCID

Alicia C. Bunger ⓘ http://orcid.org/0000-0002-6407-5111

References

Akingbola, K. (2004). Staffing, retention, and government funding: A case study. *Nonprofit Management and Leadership*, *14*(4), 453–465. doi:10.1002/nml.46

Alexander, J. (2000). Adaptive strategies of nonprofit human service organizations in an era of devolution and new public management. *Nonprofit Management and Leadership*, *10*(3), 287–303. doi:10.1002/nml.10305

Amirkhanyan, A. A., Kim, H. J., & Lambright, K. T. (2012). Closer than "arms length": Understanding the factors associated with collaborative contracting. *The American Review of Public Administration*, *42*(3), 341–366. doi:10.1177/0275074011402319

Austin, M. J. (2003). The changing relationship between nonprofit organizations and public social service agencies in the era of welfare reform. *Nonprofit and Voluntary Sector Quarterly*, *32*(1), 97–114. doi:10.1177/0899764002250008

Baum, J. A. C., & Oliver, C. (1992). Institutional embeddedness and the dynamics of organizational populations. *American Sociological Review*, *57*(4), 540–559.

Behn, R. D., & Kant, P. A. (1999). Strategies for avoiding the pitfalls of performance contracting. *Public Productivity & Management Review*, *22*(4), 470–489. doi:10.2307/3380931

Bertelli, A. M., & Smith, C. R. (2010). Relational contracting and network management. *Journal of Public Administration Research and Theory*, *20*(Supplement 1), i21–i40. doi:10.1093/jopart/mup033

Boris, E. T., De Leon, E., Roeger, K. L., & Niklova, M. (2010). Human Service Nonprofits and Government Collaboration: Findings from the 2010 National Survey of Nonprofit Government Contracting and Grants. Retrieved from http://www.urban.org

Bowman, W. (2011). Financial capacity and sustainability of ordinary nonprofits. *Nonprofit Management and Leadership*, *22*(1), 37–51. doi:10.1002/nml.20039

Brown, T. L., Potoski, M., & Van Slyke, D. M. (2010). Contracting for complex products. *Journal of Public Administration Research and Theory*, *20*(Supplement 1), i41–i58. doi:10.1093/jopart/muv004

Brown, T. L., Potoski, M., & Van, S. D. (2016). Managing complex contracts: A theoretical approach. *Journal of Public Administration Research and Theory, 26*(2), 294–308. doi:10.1093/jopart/mup034

Bunger, A. C., Cao, Y., Girth, A. M., Hoffman, J., & Robertson, H. A. (2016). Constraints and Benefits of Child Welfare Contracts with Behavioral Health Providers: Conditions that Shape Service Access. Administration and Policy in Mental Health and Mental Health Services Research, 43(5), 728–739. https://doi.org/10.1007/s10488-015-0686-1

Burns, B. J., Phillips, S., Wagner, H. R., Barth, R. P., Kolko, D. J., Campbell, Y., & Landsverk, J. (2004). Mental health need and access to mental health services by youths involved with child welfare: A national survey. *Journal of the American Academy of Child & Adolescent Psychiatry, 43*(8), 960–970.

Calabrese, T. D. (2012). The accumulation of nonprofit profits: A dynamic analysis. *Nonprofit and Voluntary Sector Quarterly, 41*(2), 300–324. doi:10.1177/0899764011404080

Carroll, D. A., & Stater, K. J. (2009). Revenue diversification in nonprofit organizations: Does it lead to financial stability? *Journal of Public Administration Research and Theory, 19*(4), 947–966. doi:10.1093/jopart/mun025

Chuang, E., McBeath, B., Collins-Camargo, C., & Armstrong, M. I. (2014). Strengthening public-private partnerships in state child welfare systems: Results of a multi-state strategic planning process. *Journal of Public Child Welfare, 8*(1), 1–24. doi:10.1080/15548732.2013.852152

Chuang, E., & Wells, R. (2010). The role of inter-agency collaboration in facilitating receipt of behavioral health services for youth involved with child welfare and juvenile justice. *Children and Youth Services Review, 32*, 1814–1822. doi:10.1016/j.childyouth.2010.08.002

Collins-Camargo, C., Armstrong, M. I., McBeath, B., & Chuang, E. (2013). Promoting cross-sector partnerships in child welfare: Qualitative results from a five-state strategic planning process. *Child Welfare, 92*(1), 33–63. Retrieved from http://europepmc.org/abstract/MED/23984485/reload=0

Collins-Camargo, C., McBeath, B., & Ensign, K. (2011). Privatization and performance-based contracting in child welfare: Recent trends and implications for social service administrators. *Administration in Social Work, 35*(5), 494–516. doi:10.1080/03643107.2011.614531

Dacin, M. T., Ventresca, M. J., & Beal, B. D. (1999). The embeddedness of organizations: Dialogue and directions. *Journal of Management, 25*(3), 317–356.

Damanpour, F. (1992). Organizational Size and Innovation. *Organization Studies, 13*(3), 375–402. doi:10.1177/017084069201300304

Dicke, L. A. (2002). Ensuring accountability in human services contracting: can stewardship theory fill the bill? *The American Review of Public Administration, 32*(4), 455–470. doi:10.1177/027507402237870

DiMaggio, P. J., & Powell, W. W. (1983). The iron cage revisited: Institutional isomorphism and collective rationality in organizational fields. *American Sociological Review, 48*(2), 147–160.

Fernandez, S. (2007). What works best when contracting for services? An analysis of contracting performance at the local level in the us. *Public Administration, 85*(4), 1119–1141. doi:10.1111/j.1467-9299.2007.00688.x

Flaherty, C., Collins-Camargo, C., & Lee, E. (2008). Privatization of child welfare services: Lessons learned from experienced states regarding site readiness assessment and planning. *Children and Youth Services Review, 30*(7), 809–820. doi:10.1016/j.childyouth.2007.12.009

Garstka, T. A., Collins-Camargo, C., Hall, J. G., Neal, M., & Ensign, K. (2012). Implementing performance-based contracts and quality assurance systems in child welfare services: Results from a national cross-site evaluation. *Journal of Public Child Welfare, 6*(1), 12–41. doi:10.1080/15548732.2012.644200

Gazley, B. (2016). The current state of interorganizational collaboration: Lessons for human service research and management. *Human Service Organizations: Management, Leadership & Governance*, 1–5. doi:10.1080/23303131.2015.1095582

Girth, A. M. (2014). A closer look at contract accountability: Exploring the determinants of sanctions for unsatisfactory contract performance. *Journal of Public Administration Research & Theory, 24*(2), 317–348. doi:10.1093/jopart/mus033

Graaf, G., Hengeveld-Bidmon, E., Carnochan, S., Radu, P., & Austin, M. J. (2016). The impact of the great recession on county human-service organizations: A cross-case analysis. *Human Service Organizations: Management, Leadership & Governance, 40*(2), 152–169. doi:10.1080/23303131.2015.1124820

Granovetter, M. (1985). Economic action and social structure: The problem of embeddedness. *American Journal of Sociology, 91*(3), 481–510. doi:10.1086/228311

Granovetter, M. (1992). Economic institutions as social constructions: A framework for analysis. *Acta Sociologica, 35*(1), 3–11. doi:10.1177/000169939203500101

Grønbjerg, K. (1993). *Understanding nonprofit funding : Managing revenues in social services and community development organizations*. San Francisco, CA, USA: Jossey-Bass.

Gronbjerg, K. A. (1993). *Understanding nonprofit funding: Managing revenues in social services and community development organizations*. San Francisco, CA: Jossey-Bass Inc.

Guo, C., & Acar, M. (2005). Understanding collaboration among nonprofit organizations: Combining resource dependency, institutional, and network perspectives. *Nonprofit and Voluntary Sector Quarterly, 34*(3), 340–361. doi:10.1177/0899764005275411

Hasenfeld, Y. (2015). What exactly is human services management? *Human Service Organizations Management, Leadership & Governance, 39*(1), 1–5. doi:10.1080/23303131.2015.1007773

Hasenfeld, Y., & Garrow, E. E. (2012). Nonprofit human-service organizations, social rights, and advocacy in a neoliberal welfare state. *Social Service Review, 86*(2), 295–322. doi:10.1086/666391

Holloway, S. S., & Parmigiani, A. (2016). Friends and profits don't mix: The performance implications of repeated partnerships. *Academy of Management Journal, 59*(2), 460–478. doi:10.0.21.89/amj.2013.0581

Horwitz, S. M., Hurlburt, M. S., Goldhaber-Fiebert, J. D., Heneghan, A. M., Zhang, J., Rolls-Reutz, J., … Stein, R. E. K. (2012). Mental health services use by children investigated by child welfare agencies. *Pediatrics, 130*(5), 861–869. doi:10.1542/peds.2012-1330

Hurlburt, M. S., Leslie, L. K., Landsverk, J., Barth, R. P., Burns, B. J., Gibbons, R. D., … Zhang, J. (2004). Contextual predictors of mental health service use among children open to child welfare. *Archives of General Psychiatry, 61*(12), 1217–1224.

Johnston, J. M., & Romzek, B. S. (2008). Social welfare contracts as networks: The impact of network stability on management and performance. *Administration & Society, 40*(2), 115–146. doi:10.1177/0095399707312826

Kapucu, N. (2006). Public-nonprofit partnerships for collective action in dynamic contexts of emergencies. *Public Administration, 84*(1), 205–220. doi:10.1111/j.0033-3298.2006.00500.x

Kim, M. (2016). The relationship of nonprofits financial health to program outcomes: Empirical evidence from nonprofit arts organizations. *Nonprofit and Voluntary Sector Quarterly*, 899764016662914. doi:10.1177/0899764016662914

Kim, T.-Y., Oh, H., & Swaminathan, A. (2006). Framing interorganizational network change: A network inertia perspective. *Academy of Management Review, 31*(3), 704–720.

Kramer, R. M. (1994). Voluntary agencies and the contract culture: "Dream or nightmare?". *Social Service Review, 68*(1), 33–60. doi:10.1086/604032

Lamothe, S. (2014). How competitive is "competitive" procurement in the social services? *The American Review of Public Administration*, 0275074013520563. doi:10.1177/0275074013520563

Marwell, N. P., & Calabrese, T. (2015). A deficit model of collaborative governance: Government–nonprofit fiscal relations in the provision of child welfare services. *Journal of Public Administration Research and Theory, 25*(4), 1031–1058. doi:10.1093/jopart/muu047

Mattessich, P. W., Murray-Close, M., & Monsey, B. R. (2001). *Wilder collaboration factors inventory*. St. Paul, MN: Wilder Research.

McBeath, B., Collins-Camargo, C., & Chuang, E. (2012). The role of the private sector in child welfare: Historical reflections and a contemporary snapshot based on the National Survey of Private Child and Family Serving Agencies. *Journal of Public Child Welfare, 6*(4), 459–481. https://doi.org/10.1080/15548732.2012.701839

McBeath, B., & Meezan, W. (2010). Governance in motion: Service provision and child welfare outcomes in a performance-based, managed care contracting environment. *Journal of Public Administration Research and Theory, 20*(Supplement 1), i101–i123. doi:10.1093/jopart/mup037

Meyers, P. W., Sivakumar, K., & Nakata, C. (1999). Implementation of industrial process innovations: Factors, effects, and marketing implications. *Journal of Product Innovation Management, 16*(3), 295–311. doi:10.1111/1540-5885.1630295

Moran, P. (2005). Structural vs. relational embeddedness: Social capital and managerial performance. *Strategic Management Journal, 26*(12), 1129–1151. doi:10.1002/smj.486

Murphy, H., & Waters Robichau, R. (2016). Open access governmental influences on organizational capacity: The case of child welfare nonprofits. *Nonprofit Policy Forum, 7*(3), 339–367. doi:10.1515/npf-2015-0040

Nahapiet, J., & Ghoshal, S. (1998). Social capital, intellectual capital, and the organizational advantage. *The Academy of Management Review, 23*(2), 242. doi:10.2307/259373

O'Connell, A. A. (2006). *Logistic regression models for ordinal response variables*. Thousand Oaks, CA, USA: SAGE Publications.

Radu, P. T., Carnochan, S., & Austin, M. J. (2015). Obstacles to social service collaboration in response to the great recession: The case of the Contra Costa County safety net initiative. *Journal of Community Practice, 23*(3–4), 323–347. doi:10.1080/10705422.2015.1091803

Romzek, B. S., LeRoux, K., & Blackmar, J. M. (2012). A preliminary theory of informal accountability among network organizational actors. *Public Administration Review, 72*(3), 442–453. doi:10.1111/j.1540-6210.2011.02547.x

Rosenthal, M. G. (2000). Public or private children's services? Privatization in retrospect. *Social Service Review, 74*(2), 281–305. doi:10.1086/514480

Salamon, L. M. (1987). Of market failure, voluntary failure, and third-party government: Toward a theory of government-nonprofit relations in the modern welfare state. *Nonprofit and Voluntary Sector Quarterly, 16*(1–2), 29–49. doi:10.1177/089976408701600104

Savas, E. S. (2002). Competition and choice in New York City. Social services. *Public Administration Review, 62*(1), 82–91. doi:10.1111/1540-6210.00157

Smith, S., & Lipsky, M. (1993). *Nonprofits for hire: The welfare state in the age of contracting*. Cambridge, MA: Harvard University Press.

Smith, S. R. (2016). Chapter twenty: Managing the challenges of government contracts. In: D. O. Renz (Ed.), *The Jossey-Bass handbook of nonprofit leadership and management* (4th ed., pp. 536–563). Hoboken, NJ: John Wiley & Sons.

StataCorp. (2015). *Stata statistical software: Release 14*. College Station, TX: Author.

Stone, M. M., Hager, M. A., & Griffin, J. J. (2001). Organizational characteristics and funding environments: A Study of a population of united way-affiliated nonprofits. *Public Administration Review, 61*(3), 276–289. doi:10.1111/0033-3352.00030

Swedberg, R. (1991). Major traditions of economic sociology. *Annual Review of Sociology, 17*, 251–276.

Swedberg, R. (1997). New economic sociology: What has been accomplished, what is ahead? *Acta Sociologica, 40*(2), 161–182.

Tuckman, H. P., & Chang, C. F. (1991). A methodology for measuring the financial vulnerability of charitable nonprofit organizations. *Nonprofit and Voluntary Sector Quarterly, 20*(4), 445–460. doi:10.1177/089976409102000407

United States Government Accountability Office [GAO]. (2003). *HHS could play a greater role in helping child welfare agencies recruit and retain staff*. Retrieved from http://www.gao.gov/new.items/d03357.pdf

Uzzi, B. (1996). The sources and consequences of embeddedness for the economic performance of organizations: The network effect. *American Sociological Review, 61*(4), 674–698.

Uzzi, B. (1997). Social structure and competition in interfirm networks: The paradox of embeddedness. *Administrative Science Quarterly, 42*(1), 35–67. doi:10.2307/2393808

Van Slyke, D. M. (2007). Agents or stewards: Using theory to understand the government-nonprofit social service contracting relationship. *Journal of Public Administration Research and Theory, 17*(2), 157–187. doi:10.1093/jopart/mul012

Wells, R., Jolles, M. P., Chuang, E., McBeath, B., & Collins-Camargo, C. (2014). Trends in local public child welfare agencies 1999–2009. *Children and Youth Services Review, 38*, 93–100. doi:10.1016/j.childyouth.2014.01.015

Willging, C. E., Aarons, G. A., Trott, E. M., Green, A. E., Finn, N., Ehrhart, M. G., & Hecht, D. B. (2016). Contracting and procurement for evidence-based interventions in public-sector human services: A case study. *Administration and Policy in Mental Health and Mental Health Services Research, 43*(5), 675–692. doi:10.1007/s10488-015-0681-6

Williams, R. (2006). Generalized ordered logit/partial proportional odds models for ordinal dependent variables. *The Stata Journal, 6*(1), 58–82.

Williams, R. (2016). Understanding and interpreting generalized ordered logit models. *The Journal of Mathematical Sociology, 40*(1), 7–20. doi:10.1080/0022250X.2015.1112384

Wulczyn, F., Chen, L., & Orlebeke, B. (2009). Evaluating contract agency performance in achieving reunification. *Children and Youth Services Review, 31*(5), 506–512. doi:10.1016/j.childyouth.2008.10.006

Zukin, S., & DiMaggio, P. (1990). *Structures of capital: The social organization of the economy - google books*. New York, NY, USA: Cambridge University Press. Retrieved from https://books.google.com/books?hl=en&id=LsE6AAAAIAAJ&oi=fnd&pg=PR7&dq=zukin+dimaggio+embeddedness+1990&ots=OOFO7Rth28&sig=bPKUjFMZNk6G2g0xNp9lZ1cM2uI#v=onepage&q=zukin dimaggio embeddedness 1990&f=false

Index